Building Bridges,
Doing Justice

D1616896

Building Bridges, Doing Justice

Constructing a Latino/a Ecumenical Theology

Orlando O. Espín
Editor

ORBIS BOOKS

Maryknoll, New York 10545

Founded in 1970, Orbis Books endeavors to publish works that enlighten the mind, nourish the spirit, and challenge the conscience. The publishing arm of the Maryknoll Fathers and Brothers, Orbis seeks to explore the global dimensions of the Christian faith and mission, to invite dialogue with diverse cultures and religious traditions, and to serve the cause of reconciliation and peace. The books published reflect the views of their authors and do not represent the official position of the Maryknoll Society. To learn more about Maryknoll and Orbis Books, please visit our website at www.maryknollsociety.org.

Manufactured in the United States of America.

Manuscript editing and typesetting by Joan Weber Laflamme.

Library of Congress Cataloguing-in-Publication Data

Building bridges, doing justice : constructing a Latino/a ecumenical theology / Orlando O. Espín, editor.
    p. cm.
  Includes bibliographical references and index.
  ISBN 978–1–57075–825–6 (pbk.)
  1. Hispanic Americans—Religion. 2. Theology. 3. Theology, Doctrinal. I. Espín, Orlando O.
  BR563.H57B85 2009
  230.089'68073—dc22

2008041152

Para Ricardo, compañero y amigo. Cada vez más.
Para Justo González, maestro y amigo, con el agradecimiento de la Iglesia.
Y
Para todos/as los/as que, desde la cátedra, el púlpito o la calle,
nos recuerdan a diario con sus vidas
que Dios *realmente* ama a *todos/as*
sin límites, sin excepciones, sin condiciones, siempre;
y especialmente a los/as más despreciados/as.
Esto es infinitamente más importante para el ecumenismo
que todo lo demás.

The new theology being done by those who are aware of their traditional voicelessness is acutely aware of the manner in which the dominant is confused with the universal. North American male theology is taken to be basic, normative, universal theology, to which then women, other minorities, and people from the younger churches may add their footnotes. What is said in Manila is very relevant for the Philippines. What is said in Tübingen, Oxford, or Yale is relevant for the entire church. White theologians do general theology; black theologians do black theology. Male theologians do general theology; female theologians do theology determined by their sex. Such a notion of "universality" based on the present unjust distribution of power is unacceptable to the new theology.

—Justo L. González

Contents

PART III
GRACE AND JUSTIFICATION
Soteriology and Theological Anthropology Shaped
a la latina

PART IV
ECCESIOLOGY *A LO MESTIZO/A Y MULATO/A*
What Happens to "Church" When We Move *Latinamente*
beyond Inherited Ecclesiologies?

PART V
TOWARD THE NEXT STEP

Contributors

Efraín Agosto. Professor of New Testament, and Academic Dean. Hartford Seminary (Hartford, Connecticut).

Neomi De Anda. Lecturer on Latino/a Catholicism. DePaul University (Chicago, Illinois).

Miguel H. Díaz. Professor of Systematic Theology. St. John's University (Collegeville, Minnesota).

Orlando O. Espín. Professor of Systematic Theology. University of San Diego (San Diego, California).

Roberto S. Goizueta. Professor of Systematic Theology. Boston College (Chestnut Hill, MA).

Juan Francisco Martínez. Associate Professor of Hispanic Studies and Pastoral Leadership. Fuller Theological Seminary (Pasadena, California).

Néstor Medina. Instructor on Faith and Culture. University of Toronto (Toronto, Ontario).

Carmen M. Nanko-Fernández. Assistant Professor of Pastoral Ministry and Director of Field Education. Catholic Theological Union (Chicago, Illinois).

Mayra Rivera. Assistant Professor of Systematic Theology. Pacific School of Religion (Berkeley, California).

José D. Rodríguez. Professor of Systematic Theology. Lutheran School of Theology (Chicago, Illinois).

Jean-Pierre Ruiz. Associate Professor of Biblical Studies. St. John's University (New York, New York).

Introduction

Constructing a Conversation

Culture, Ecumenical Dialogue, and a Renewed Pneumatology

Orlando O. Espín

Ecumenical dialogues are built over time on shared prayer and shared service, on mutual trust, and through serious conversations. Personal relationships and friendships, pastoral realities, and good theology all need to come together in order to move ecumenical conversations significantly forward. The present volume is but one moment in an ongoing conversation among Latino/a Protestant and Catholic theologians.[1]

In 2008 the Academy of Catholic Hispanic Theologians of the United States (ACHTUS)[2] celebrated its twentieth anniversary. Over these last twenty years its annual colloquia have discussed many topics of importance for U.S. Latino/a theology and for the U.S. churches. One such important topic was the focus of the ACHTUS 2007 colloquium in Los Angeles. Its general theme was "Building a Latino/a Ecumenical Theology."

Approximately fifty Latino/a theologians (Catholics and Protestants) participated in this ground-breaking conversation. These scholars dedicated many hours—before, during, and after the Los Angeles colloquium—to this ecumenical adventure. Although none claims to speak officially for the churches, as Latino/a theologians they have very important questions, issues, proposals and perspectives to contribute to ecumenical dialogue among Christians. Latino/a scholars cannot remain an afterthought in ecumenical conversations that purport to represent our churches; the cultural and demographic transformation of our churches, as well as the ever-increasing importance of Latinos/as in ministry and theology, can be no longer ignored by any serious ecumenical dialogue. The present volume is another step, taken by Latino/a initiative, to move forward an ecumenical movement oftentimes imprisoned and controlled by the provincial agendas of the dominant.

This essay is a modified version of my presidential address presented at the ACHTUS 2007 colloquium in Los Angeles. The original version of the presidential address appeared in the *eJournal of Hispanic/Latino Theology*. See www.latinotheology.org.

Participants were asked to present and discuss what (in their views) would need to be said and elaborated on various important theological topics in order to achieve a *Latina/o* ecumenical theology. Participants were also asked to be creative and courageous while being realistic and honest in the way they addressed their respective ecclesial traditions' (doctrinal, theological) positions and expectations on the road to an ecumenical theology. Therefore, the 2007 ACHTUS colloquium was really not interested in already known denominational doctrinal/theological positions. Moving beyond mere restatements, those gathered wanted to elaborate their respective theological positions honestly *and* in ways that would (given further reflection and dialogue) lead to breakthroughs that yield an *ecumenical* theology constructed *latinamente*.

Of course, this task is more easily stated (and wished for) than accomplished, but I think that after the Los Angeles colloquium we have moved forward, we have jointly "pushed the envelope," and we have come to a better understanding of each other, of our respective denominational perspectives and of the road ahead.

AN ECUMENICAL CONVERSATION, *LATINAMENTE*

As Latinos/as, our shared cultural heritage crosses denominational boundaries and allows us to recognize in one another much that is still missing in other ecumenical conversations. No ecumenical relation or dialogue today in the United States can be truly reflective of our respective churches unless Latinos/as (and their faith and their lives) are acknowledged as indispensable and equal conversation partners. We are not the "minorities"[3] that denominational leaders regard as mainly objects of their pastoral charity but whom they clearly disregard when substantive theological and ecclesial issues are at stake. We are, have been, and will be the church of Jesus Christ as much as anyone else in our country. We *are* the church—and our respective denominations need to get used to that fact. We cannot be dismissed except at the risk of dismissing the most foundational of all Christian ecclesiological positions: that the church *is* the people of God.

Others will need to reflect on the power relations implied in and assumed by their continued disregard of Latinos/as as their equals, as church, and as theologians. The academy and the church are being impoverished because some cling to power as if it were their birthright. And in a parallel manner, the claims or perspectives of a group do not become universally legitimate, valid, or true just because of the asymmetrical exercise of power.

It is within this growing sentiment among Latinos/as throughout the country, and also within the theological academy, that we have to understand ecumenical dialogue among Latino/a Christians. This is not merely a conversation about doctrines or about interpretations of the Bible, although God knows we continue to discuss them because we must.

Ecumenical conversations among Latinos/as are also, and indispensably, the building of trust, of alliances, of mutual support, *because* most of us (regardless of denominational contexts) are facing many of the same biases, the same stereotyping, the same injustices, the same difficulties within society, within our churches, and within the theological academy. Ecumenical dialogue among Latinos/as, therefore, *necessarily* includes awareness of and reflection on cultural and social justice issues, as well as a commitment to equality for all. Ecumenism among Latinos/as is about building doctrinal bridges as much as it is about doing justice.

Latino/a ecumenical conversations certainly and evidently include doctrinal and biblical issues, but they do not and cannot remain there—because Bible and doctrines don't believe in themselves. Doctrines and Bible have meaning or importance because real people believe in them, because real people are affected by them, and because real women and men guide their real lives by what they believe to be expressed in them—otherwise, Bible and doctrines would be nothing more than archaeologically interesting literary texts or sterile theoretical propositions to be discussed or played with by the idle or the irrelevant.

Whatever real differences can be found among our denominations, these have inescapably to do with the real lives of our people—with the lives of our Latino/a people. And so, belief must be understood among us not as if it were merely a cerebral exercise but rather as a life-engaging adventure ultimately guided by God. The consequence of this for ecumenical conversations is evident: these important dialogues cannot and must not focus *exclusively* on doctrines and on interpretations of biblical passages—as if these were detached from real life or real people.

Ecumenical conversations, although necessarily discussing doctrines and Bible, must *also* and emphatically acknowledge the believers, and the cultural contexts, and power asymmetries in which believers find themselves—cultural contexts and power asymmetries that very much affect and mold (and have historically affected and molded) the very doctrines and biblical interpretations that ecumenical dialogue must now contend with.

Most important, ecumenical dialogue must be broader than the doctrinal, the scriptural, or the canonical because it is a dialogue among Christians. And because it is a dialogue among Christians, it is a dialogue among *humans* who have committed their lives to (and claim to pattern their lives after) a God who self-defines as limitless, compassionate love. The ethical, therefore, is an indispensable dimension and ground of all ecumenical dialogues.[4]

But, I ask, Is all of this so evident? Where, theologically, might we discover a first common task for Latino/a theologians that—without falsifying or dismissing our real denominational differences—will allow us to build together and walk together as we engage in further ecumenical dialogue?

Let me answer the first question by theologically grounding the reasons for my asking it, and then I'll answer the second question by suggesting an avenue for our shared ecumenical adventure. Required brevity will not allow me to delve into detailed arguments or elaborations.

GROUNDING THE QUESTION

All Christians believe in God, but not in *any* God. The Christian God is not philosophically generic. We believe in God as proclaimed and revealed to us *in* the person, message, life, death, and resurrection of Jesus the Christ.

And yet, Jesus was a first-century Palestinian Jew, and we all know that it is simply impossible to understand him or his God, and thus simply impossible to understand the Christian gospel, without understanding the Jewishness of Jesus and his (and the early church's) roots in and relationship with Second-Temple Judaism. Or, put another way, *culture*—the culture of Jesus and of the earliest disciples—is an unavoidable prism through which we must pass in order to understand Christ and the early church. And after the first Christian generations, culture remains an indispensable interpretive tool without which we run the risk of misinterpreting Christian origins, Christian history, all Christian doctrines, and ultimately the very gospel. This is why we cannot dispense with real people and with their real cultures when attempting to engage in ecumenical dialogue—indeed, without the contexts and prism of culture, Christians cannot even speak of God's grace.

Culture is a necessary prism through which we perceive God's grace and through which we respond to it. Therefore, to be Latino/a, for example, is not a superficial accident of birth, but rather *the very condition within and through which we can hear the gospel and respond to it in faith*. Those of us who are Christian are not just Christians who happen to be Latino/a—we are Christian in a Latino/a way, and we cannot be Christian in any other way. Our Latino/a cultures make us experience the grace of God in specific ways not available to us were we not Latino/a.

But we may ask (because sooner or later it must be asked), has humanity—this humanness created in the image of God—ever existed *as human* without culture?

No human society and no human individual can even dream of the possibility of existing without culture. That dream itself would be a cultural exercise, made possible precisely by the culture of the dreamer. We are in culture and nothing human (as well as no human being) can ever be truly human if a-cultural, because (among other important reasons) cultures provide us with meaning and with the tools for constructing meaning—and without meaning no creature (and no society) could conceive of itself as truly *human*.

In the very long history of culture, individuals and communities have never explained or viewed themselves except through the tools of understanding granted them by culture. The Christian church is no exception to this rule of culture. Formed by individuals and communities of the most diverse cultural backgrounds, it would be nonsense to pretend that the cultures of its members have not affected the ways in which the church has understood the gospel, lived it, and reflected upon it throughout the centuries.

All Christians have lived in historical, geographical, and cultural contexts. All Christian preaching and sacramental celebrations, all Christian witnessing and living, all Christian readings and interpretations of the Bible, all Christian theologizing and doctrinal statements, and all shapes of the church throughout history, have occurred within specific cultural contexts that have, of necessity and inevitably, acted as occasions, prisms, assumptions, molds, and tools for all that Christians do, live, preach, and believe.

Nothing human in Christianity is a-cultural. Nothing! That which is unlimited by culture in the church is only that which we also find unlimited by Christ's humanness: the God of love, and the love of God. This is why the Christian message, which is ultimately the message of God, can be preached, believed, and lived in *any* human culture, because being God's, it transcends *all* cultures. However, the ones who preach, receive, understand, believe, and live the gospel are human beings, and though the source of the gospel is not limited by culture, Christian human beings are. Therefore, their understanding and reception of revelation and of the gospel will inevitably be cultural.

This implies many things, but for our purposes here, this inevitable centrality of culture means that, for Christianity, the way a people or a person experientially perceives the love and grace of God, the way a people or a person responds to God, will always be cultural. In other words, there is no a-cultural Christianity, just as there is no a-cultural option for God, love, faith, or salvation. Doctrines and biblical interpretations, therefore, are *never* a-cultural.

If to be human is to be an image of God, then *this* is also a cultural reality, because no one can be truly human outside of culture. But just as humans can dehumanize themselves, so can cultures bear the sinful imprint of the humans that create them. Cultures, all cultures, are also dehumanized and dehumanizing, and in need of the liberating love of God. All cultures need salvation. Which leads me to say that, as a consequence, no culture can ever claim to be—of itself, or in comparison with other cultures—better suited to incarnate the Christian message, or better at expressing Christian doctrines, or a better context for ecumenical dialogue.

The Trinity is certainly beyond all time and limit. Not so the human creature. God is eternally transcending history and culture, but that same God would be utterly meaningless and beyond our perception unless God's revelation and grace entered our creaturely world, worked through and within our history and our cultures, and fashioned the manners of revelation and grace within the possibilities of our cultural understanding, enabling us to "see and touch" the "gracious" actions of the God-who-is-for-us. This, after all, is the most fundamental reason for the incarnation.

But, given the historical, changing character of our cultures, these actions of God for us must in turn be changing, adapting, and molding themselves to our diversity. Thus, what can truthfully be called a "graced" moment, action or understanding in one place or at one time or for one group in human history might not be truthfully "graced" at or for another. Perhaps it could even be perceived as "disgrace" in another context.

To trample on or dismiss the culture of a human group, therefore, cannot be justified in the name of the Christian God, because it would imply a denial of the incarnation of grace. Furthermore, to do so would be to reject the very possibility that the trampled-on or dismissed human group might have of perceiving and responding to the love of the God-for-them without the evils of colonization.

It can be reasonably stated that the experience of grace possible to U.S. Latinos/as, to be authentically an experience of the God-for-us, must be culturally Latino/a. *Deculturization,* in the name of Christianity would be dehumanizing and sinful. To trample on or dismiss Latino/a culture while pretending to evangelize it is to impede the very experience of the God-that-saves, because the experience of grace can only be had in and through one's culture.

A COMMON TASK FOR OUR ECUMENICAL ADVENTURE

Now you see why I asked earlier if it was evident for us that ecumenical dialogue among Christians is inescapably a dialogue among "cultured" humans.

Ecumenical conversations on doctrines, biblical interpretations, and so on, are not and cannot be *just* about doctrines or biblical interpretations, and even less about ecclesial polities. Ecumenical conversations *also* have to be about real people, real lives, and, most emphatically, about the cultural (and other) contexts that make real people human, that allow them to hear and respond to the gospel, and that mold and influence every doctrine, every biblical interpretation, every ethical claim, and every faith experience.

However, cultures are ultimately insufficient common ground for ecumenical dialogue among Christians—because the real goal of the ecumenical adventure is not an improvement in relations or even better mutual understanding. The ultimate goal of all ecumenical dialogue is the unity of the church of Christ. And with this goal in mind, the absolutely inevitable and necessary acknowledgment of the crucial roles of culture will nevertheless not suffice as common ground. The unity of Christians will not be ultimately *just* the work of Christians—it will also be, and emphatically so, the work of the Spirit of God.

As Christians we need to acknowledge jointly, therefore, that the ultimate common ground for our ecumenical adventure is the action of the Spirit of God within and among us—further acknowledging that the Spirit of God is never under our guidance or control, and thus is always free from the constrictions of our denominational understandings or of our cultures.

But then, how can we practically (as Latino/a theologians, with all this implies) move the ecumenical adventure forward on this common ground? Maybe we need first to think about pneumatology. Always remembering that just as cultures make meaning and understanding possible, and just as they are the means through which we hear the gospel and respond to it in faith, cultures can *also* blind or adulterate faith and gospel among Christians. Consequently, the action of the Spirit of God among humans and in human cultures could go unidentified, misread, and misinterpreted by Christians because of their cultures. There can never be an innocent theology and, thus, there can never be an innocent pneumatology, devoid of all falsifications.

The long history of the Christian church amply demonstrates that Christians of all denominations are quite capable of falsifying, adulterating, blindfolding, or "negotiating" their own faith and gospel, and of misreading the actions of the Holy Spirit (even when, for those historically involved, what they were doing seemed nothing of the sort). The long history of the Christian church is full of examples of theologies and theologians who, knowingly or not, lent themselves to the task of explaining and justifying the falsifications, adulterations, and the "negotiations"—all in the name of gospel, faith, and truth.

I remind you of the long history of black slavery as one blatant example of how very many otherwise well-meaning Christians (and well-meaning theologians) falsified, blindfolded, adulterated and "negotiated" the gospel and their own faith, and woefully misread the actions of the Holy Spirit. In support of slavery, doctrines were developed, supposedly "evident" biblical interpretations were worked through and proclaimed, and ethical claims were made that perhaps sincerely but blatantly denied and adulterated the most fundamental of Christian commandments and myriad Christian doctrines. I think we can argue that today we may be witnessing other very different but yet very similar situations among many Christians—in the name of gospel and faith we too are quite capable of spitting on the face of other human beings and other human groups while persecuting them and denying them their most basic rights.

In the name of gospel and faith we Christians have often assumed that our culturally possible and therefore inescapably limited understandings of God's revelation are correct, complete, and undeniable. But if all mutually contradictory Christian claims were so evident, then we would need to explain how the Holy Spirit can contradict the Holy Spirit, given that the contradicting claims are said to be all guided and prompted by the same Holy Spirit.

The Spirit of God, who is the Spirit of Love, Faith, Hope, and Truth, is telling us that there is nothing wrong or contradictory with the Spirit but with our inclination to self-idolatry. Christians are inclined to see and condemn the sins or shortcomings of others while all too often being blind to their own self-idolatry. We see the doctrinal, biblical, and/or sacramental insufficiencies of others while being blind to our own (or, worse, justifying our own). Perhaps what the Spirit is suggesting to all of us is that we should listen not just to biblical interpretations or to doctrinal statements but to real lives, to real hearts, to human dreams, and to human suffering as we arrive at discussions on doctrines, biblical texts, or ethical claims.

Given the immense and inescapable role of culture in the molding of all that is human—included faith and ecumenical dialogues—perhaps we might want to remember that prayer and contemplation, self-honesty and conversion, personal authenticity and love of neighbor (with a long *etcetera*) *must* accompany any ecumenical conversation that expects to be more than a cerebral, theoretical exercise destined to fruitless irrelevance.

Latino/a theologians, who as humans need to walk their own paths of cultural humanness, might want to think if one of the most crucial and still missing components in our ecumenical dialogue is a renewed pneumatology—a pneumatology that methodologically combines rigorous, systematic theological reflection with prayerful thanksgiving, effectively compassionate service of neighbor (especially of those in greatest need), and real reflection on the real cultural, contextual lives of real Christians.

A renewed or possibly new pneumatology, so crafted by us, might be that one common theological ground on which to build an ecumenical adventure that can help us investigate gospel and faith, doctrines and biblical interpretations, ethics, worship, and polities, with full awareness of the "cultural-ness" of it all, *latinamente*.

This ecumenical adventure, although not new, still has a long way to go.

A NOTE ON THE ACHTUS ANNUAL COLLOQUIA, TO CONTEXTUALIZE THE PRESENT VOLUME

The present volume includes the papers presented at the 2007 ACHTUS colloquium, held at Mount St. Mary's College in Los Angeles. The reader should be aware that the ACHTUS annual colloquia do not include the "reading" of scholarly papers by presenters, as do other professional conventions. Rather, our yearly gatherings are designed as conversations (hence, *colloquia*) around specific aspects of a general theme. Two scholars are invited as partners *to start the conversation* at each of the four three-hour sessions. Before the annual colloquium begins, however, formal papers are sent by the designated partners to all who will participate in the colloquium, thereby promoting reflection and the start of conversations on the various topics well before the meeting actually begins. Once the annual colloquium starts (and because the respective papers have already been read beforehand by all participants), the sessions are dedicated to an open discussion of the sessions' topics (aided by the papers and the partners).[5]

The papers included in the present volume reflect and variously incorporate the conversations that preceded and followed the 2007 Los Angeles colloquium, as well as the discussions that occurred therein. Consequently, this volume is *not* a mere anthology of practically disconnected scholarly texts; rather, this book is the result of an ongoing conversation among those who authored these papers, further engaged by the other Protestant and Catholic theologians who also participated in the ACHTUS meeting in Los Angeles.

It might be useful for the reader to follow the order and the coupling of papers, indicated in the Contents, because the texts herein were intentionally written in conversation with partners.

During the colloquium Professor Leticia Guardiola-Sáenz was Professor Jean-Pierre Ruiz's conversation partner. However, Guardiola-Sáenz was not able (for reasons beyond her control) to submit the revised version of her original paper for publication herein. We are very grateful that Professor Efraín Agosto then joined this conversation as Ruiz's conversation partner in fact and print.

The Los Angeles meeting was a truly remarkable ecumenical event. It is our collective hope that the reader will find this volume challenging, ecumenically enlightening and, especially, useful for the promotion of deeper relations and discussions among Christians—Latinos/as or not. I certainly hope the publication of these papers helps us all build bridges and do justice.

Finally, my special thanks to Dr. Carmen M. Nanko-Fernández, without whose help the 2007 colloquium could not have taken place. Equal thanks to the editor-in-chief and staff of Orbis Books for their unwavering support to Latino/a theology and theologians.

NOTES

[1] It is hard to say historically, when ecumenical conversations began among U.S. Latinas/os. However, momentum was created with the establishment (in the late 1980s and early 1990s) of very successful joint programs such as the Hispanic Summer Program (HSP) and the Hispanic Theological Initiative (HTI), both founded by Justo González, the renowned United Methodist historian and theologian. The present conversation, it can be claimed, is one consequence of the ecumenical bridges built at HSP and HTI over the years.

[2] For information on ACHTUS, please visit its website at www.achtus.org. ACHTUS publishes the *eJournal of Hispanic/Latino Theology*. The contents of the present volume first appeared there, in a somewhat different version, and are used here with permission.

[3] *Minoritized,* historically and socially, is a more accurate term. We owe this particular term to Dr. Carmen M. Nanko-Fernández.

[4] Is this a significant difference between Latino/a ecumenism and the ecumenism of our European and European American colleagues? Have they left the ethical to what is individual and theoretical? Are the real-life ethical behavior and commitments of our Christian communities/denominations not immensely more important?

[5] In order to protect and enhance the conversational character of its meetings, ACHTUS restricts participation at its colloquia to its members and invited guests. Most annual colloquia provide opportunities for participants also to meet and interact with local academic, pastoral, and community leaders. Every year the colloquium is held at a different U.S. city.

PART I

POWER RELATIONS AND SOCIAL ISSUES

Do/Should These Shape and Critique
Latina/o (Christian) Understandings of God?

1

From *Pájaro* to Paraclete

Retrieving the Spirit of God in the Company of Mary

Carmen M. Nanko-Fernández

I recently had an opportunity to attend a meeting on the grounds of the Trappist Abbey of Gethsemani, Kentucky.[1] For anyone aware of my hyperactive disposition, the thought of me staying more than five minutes—let alone three days—at a monastery noted for "prayer, labor, and silence" was the source of amusement. The experience resonated con mi alma hispana,[2] as this was a place and a community where the sacredness of the daily was presumed and the ordinary rhythms of time were marked as tolling bells called our attention to that which was already assumed, a religious world view that has created what Eldin Villafañe has called *homo religiosus*. For *homo religiosus* "there is no area of life, no matter how trivial, that is not 'transmuted' by the religious sentiment."[3] Quite simply, "the Hispanic American community is a theological community,"[4] a community where distinction between sacred and secular can be blurred or even nonexistent. Even the recent study by the Pew Hispanic Center admitted "For the great majority of Latinos, regardless of their religious tradition, God is an active force in daily life."[5]

The privileging of lo cotidiano in theologizing latinamente is reflected as well in the "dailiness" of both Catholic and Protestant popular religious expressions. The words of Elizabeth Conde-Frazier describing the role of daily devotions in Hispanic Protestant spiritually could just as easily apply to popular Catholicism: "A distinctive emphasis of Protestant Hispanic spirituality is that it belongs to the people, or the laity, as opposed to the ordained or professional clergy. It is not leisurely contemplation, but rather, the tools of survival and struggle for those who are part of the busy rhythms of work and life."[6] As Orlando Espín affirms, it is popular Christianity within lo cotidiano, at the intersection of public and private, that serves not as "a parenthesis to real life or a side show to so-called mainstream Christianity. It is part, mirror, and hermeneut of daily life and of Christianity . . . and is one of the key bearers . . . of cultural identity."[7]

13

GRASSROOTS ECUMENICAL DIALOGUE

It is this daily reminder of the sacred amid the ordinary that one finds beneath the overpass of Chicago's Kennedy Expressway, tucked between the entrance and exit ramps. If you look carefully as you travel on Fullerton Avenue, you will see evidence of what appears to be a makeshift shrine that is tended on a regular basis. Flickering candles, prayer graffiti, plastic saints, and artificial roses, images of Guadalupe and assorted vírgenes, all mark this unusual space as holy ground—an accident investigation site on a heavily trafficked Chicago thoroughfare. Cleaning products resting discreetly to the side point to the regular care this shrine receives. The source of this ongoing devotional popular[8] attention is a controversial appearance in April 2005 of an apparition or a stain, depending on your perspective.[9]

The timing of the appearance, as well as the communities of the faithful, and of the skeptical and the curious that gathered, invited unusual media attention. Among the first credited with spreading the word was Obdulia Delgado. On April 10, consumed by her daily worries, she prayed to Mary with a particular need—to pass a culinary school final exam. She spotted the image on her commute: "Monday through Friday I go to school and Saturday and Sunday I work, so since I haven't been able to go to church, I asked her, 'Please help me with school because I'm having my finals,' but I felt like she was like, 'If you can come to me, I'm going to go to you.'"[10]

The shrine that grew up around the apparition revealed a range of luchas cotidianas that preoccupied the faithful and the hopeful on the personal, local, and global levels. Prayers and pilgrims begged for los milagros: healing for a child with muscular dystrophy, sight for a blind family dog, and so on. Polish and Vatican flags attested to the profound sense of loss experienced within the Polish community at the death of John Paul II as well as the anxiety within the Catholic community over who would replace him. Interpretations varied, but a Marian one prevailed—though which one of las vírgenes had appeared was a matter of contention as multiple and competing images, statues, and holy cards continued to be reverently placed at the shrine.

At this crossroads of daily living, grassroots ecumenical dialogue began when a bike-riding Latino Protestant painted across the apparition the words "Big lie!" Victor González was arrested for criminal defacement of public property, an irony not lost on some when one considered the growing prayer graffiti added amid the usual street script, vulgarities, and wistful support for the Cubs. In a three-part video documentary posted on YouTube,[11] González is interviewed and articulates the reasons for his actions. In his explanation González cites concerns that the image is "in my neighborhood" and wonders why people spend their money on candles. While he is respectful of the posters of the recently deceased pope, he is troubled that the Fullerton pilgrims have tried to compare a stain to the mother of God and, in doing so, have broken the second commandment: "You shall not make for yourself a graven image, or any likeness of anything that is in heaven above, or that is in the earth beneath, or that is in the water under the earth; you shall not bow down to them or serve them" (Ex 20:4–5).[12] The lie, in effect, is the creation of a graven image given legitimacy by priests coming by to bless it "with holy water and olive oil."

At the direction of the Chicago police, employees of the Illinois Department of Transportation painted over both the image and the offending (or prophetic, depending on one's perspective) indictment. In response, the ecumenical dialogue continued the next day as two Catholic employees from the neighboring Express Car Wash, Rosa Díaz and Anna Reczek, armed with the industrial-strength cleaning products of their daily labor, did what they could to restore the image.[13]

This grassroots dialogue underscored a shared sacral world view that many Latin@ theologians and scholars of religion have long held to be typical of latinidad. However, while acceptance of divine intervention in the daily was implicit, two distinct interpretations of the divine presence in lo cotidiano were also operative: one that perceives the divine in terms of accompaniment in ordinary time with what some have described as a sacramental imagination; and the other driven by a rapture theology that comprehends divine intervention in terms of rupturing the daily.[14] Either way, the very real presence of the divine in the daily and the local was presupposed. Both are popular, in the sense of being of the people, and are surely not the only hermeneutical lenses through which Hispan@ Christians read the daily.

But at the root of this grassroots dialogue is a fundamental theological discourse about God and divine representation, fueled by centuries of mutual miscommunication, misunderstanding, and, sadly, even abuse, at levels popular as well as official. Among the misunderstandings illustrated in the Fullerton dialogue is the charge of idolatrous worship. It is important to note that Catholic tradition numbers the commandments differently than Protestant traditions. What Victor González understood as the second commandment is seen by Catholics as part of the first commandment; the second concerns respect for the holiness of God's name. Furthermore as the *Catechism of the Catholic Church* explains:

> Basing itself on the mystery of the incarnate Word, the seventh ecumenical council at Nicaea (787) justified against the iconoclasts the veneration of icons—of Christ, but also of the Mother of God, the angels, and all the saints. By becoming incarnate, the Son of God introduced a new "economy" of images. [2131] The Christian veneration of images is not contrary to the first commandment which proscribes idols. . . .The honor paid to sacred images is a "respectful veneration," not the adoration due to God alone [2132].

Sacred images ultimately point to God. To know, revere, and relate to the one to whom the image directs our attention is to relate with God en conjunto with the company God keeps. However the distinction between veneration and adoration at the grassroots level is not always evident, according to some Protestants. Enrique González, pastor of El Mesías United Methodist Church in Elgin, Illinois, who also served as a minister in his native Mexico, writes:

> Doctrinal statements in Roman Catholicism talk clearly about the veneration (doulia) of Mary, not the worship (or adoration, latreia) of Mary. In any kind of academic theological arena, Catholic theologians will emphasize the word "veneration" rather than "adoration." Yet the practical theology in the life of Catholicism in Latin America promotes the adoration of Mary. It promotes not only adoration of her as a person but the adoration of the doctrines of Mary (for example, that of the Immaculate Conception of Mary, which is enforced by devotion to la Virgen de la Inmaculada Concepción in Mexico), even to the point of claiming the supremacy of Mary over Jesus Christ. For example, "la Virgen de Guadalupe" is spoken of as the Holy Mother and Patron of Mexico and Latin America. For these reasons Methodists and other mainstream denominations in Latin America tend to restrict the veneration of Mary. We recognize her as the special instrument that God chose to bring his Son among us, we recognize her as the mother of Jesus—but not as the mother of God. . . . Our policy against icons is a way of resisting the Catholicism that seems to want to placate people with bread and circuses.[15]

Meanwhile, at El Amor de Dios Methodist Church on Chicago's South Side, Rev. José Landaverde credits the boost in his church's enrollment to the addition of familiar Marian elements that he considers primarily cultural. "Flanking the altar are two Mary statues with fresh roses at their feet, and hanging from the hands of the baby Jesus is a Rosary. The altar cover presents the church's most stunning image: Mary again, this time totally surrounded by a multicolored halo, in the traditional iconography of the Our Lady of Guadalupe."[16]

The curious absence of Mary on the formal programs of two ACHTUS colloquia centered on ecumenical dialogue may indicate an un-reflected upon avoidance of a neuralgic topic. Our inattention to Mary when we are ecumenically en conjunto may result in the perpetuation of mutual false impressions within our communities of accountability as well as deprive us of a potentially fruitful direction for theological dialogue. If, as Roberto Goizueta maintains, "community is indeed constitutive of the person, then to know Mary, the mother of Jesus, is (at least partially) to know Jesus. Conversely, one cannot know Jesus without also knowing Mary."[17] I would add that to come to an appreciation of Mary as one filled with the Holy Spirit will refocus our attention on the Trinity. In that sense, to speak of Mary is to speak of God.

HAIL MARY, FULL OF GRACE

The connection of Mary to the evangelization of Hispania by means of a pre-assumption apparition to the apostle James, while undoubtedly questionable as reality or historical fact, is undeniable in the popular imagination of what became Spain. While there is reference in Romans to Paul's intent to visit—"I hope to see you in passing as I go to Spain" (Rom 15:24; see also 15:28), "there is no evidence that any Christian community in Hispania attributed its foundation to Paul or James, the apostle venerated today as the evangelizer of Iberia. In the case of James, attributions are made to him beginning in the seventh century in scholarly circles. . . . Popular devotion to him begins only in the eleventh century."[18] However, Nuestra Señora del Pilar remains the patron of Spain, and Marian patronage—besides apparitions and miraculously recovered religious articles—abounds across Iberian-influenced tierras from the Americas to the Philippines with a phenomenal cross-cultural appeal that still needs to be explored in greater critical depth.

Scholarly speculations suggest a range of possibilities, from Mary's effectiveness as a tool of evangelization to an intersecting familiarity or even syncretism with indigenous and African female divine dimensions. Whatever the appeal, the result of the Iberian colonizing project and the subsequent 'encounters' with different peoples is the development of an enduring and complex relationship with the mother of God under a variety of titles in multiple contexts. The endearing diminutives—Lupita, Cachita, la Morenita, La Chinita—suggest an intimacy one would hope is possible with God, and at the same time reflect a profound devotional loyalty. Just consider the outrage triggered in Brazil in 1995 when, on October 12, televangelist Sergio von Helde (from the Pentecostal movement Igreja Universal do Reino de Deus) kicked a statue of the Virgin of Aparecida (the patron of Brazil) on Brazilian television. His "point about the emptiness of icons" was lost as he fled the country after offending the nation's Catholics by proclaiming, "This is no saint. . . . Can God really be compared to this ugly thing?"[19]

Deficient theologies, especially as they pertain to the first and third Persons of the Trinity, in some ways are responsible for Mary filling roles that appear to equate her as either the feminine face of God or as the Holy Spirit. Christian overdependence on androcentric, patriarchal, feudal, imperial, and colonizing language, imagery, and metaphor to articulate the mystery of God opens human imaginations to entertain other less limiting possibilities. I suspect that the collective groan that arises from Latin@ theologians at the prospect of this being yet another "Guadalupe paper" conceals our struggle to navigate and mine a rich, ambiguous, and multivalent symbol in response to lacunae in our theologies and pneumatologies. But is there a way to appreciate Mary, "full of grace," as a sacrament of God? As the Spirit-filled one who gives concrete expression to animation by the Holy Spirit? Is there wisdom in popular Marian devotion for which our theologizing has not provided a sufficient vocabulary?

DIME CON QUIÉN ANDAS Y TE DIRÉ QUIÉN ERES

Miguel Díaz's theological reflections on la Virgen de la Caridad del Cobre illuminate aspects of the divine that are accessible by way of los cuentos of an embodied relationship between Cachita and the copper-mining community of the marginalized she accompanied. Díaz observes, "Were we to agree that in Jesus Christ God embodies a specific marginalized cultural reality, namely that of a Galilean Jew, we could perhaps embrace the symbolic accompaniment of Our Lady of Charity as an ongoing expression of how the Christian God identifies with marginalized persons and assumes their marginalized cultural reality."[20] This accompaniment is marked by its mutuality as demonstrated by what Díaz calls "sacramental interactions" and is revelatory of God's solidarity with the forgotten and oppressed:

> While these interactions suggest affirming relationships—persons care for her, abide with her, converse with her, and even disagree with some of her actions (for example, her unexplained disappearances)—the story also witnesses less affirming relationships. The vanquishment of the members of this copper-mining community and the pillaging of the land they abide in reveal the kind of oppressive relationships challenged by the *Virgen de la Caridad.*[21]

For Díaz, Caridad is not the feminine face of God; rather, she "offers a praxis for imaging who God is." This accompaniment carries ethical import as Díaz closes, appropriately from the Magnificat (Lk 1:46–55), with the ensuing obligations of those who have been accompanied: "we lift the lowly, depose the mighty, and feed the hungry—thereby fulfilling the promises God made to all our ancestors now and forever."[22]

ORTHODOX POPULAR PNEUMATOLOGY

How the divine is perceived to be present in the daily is also a pneumatological question. Theologically what remains systematically under-pursued is an observation initially made by Orlando Espín over a decade ago. "Why can't we understand the 'Mary' categories of Latino Catholicism as *orthodox popular pneumatology*?"[23] The ease with which Marian apparitions are assumed, defended, dismissed, problematized, or mocked keeps the focus from underlying questions that deserve a more penetrating analysis: Within Latin@ Catholic sacramental world views are some Marian manifestations "theophanies"? Are the attributions to Mary of divine interventions, revelations, and miracles pointing toward a functional pneumatology?

With Guadalupe particularly in mind, Espín queries whether it is possible that what ecclesial authorities interpreted as an inculturated mariology was instead an inculturated pneumatology. He does not posit Mary of Nazareth as the feminine or maternal face of God, nor does he claim that Mary or any of las vírgenes are the third Person of the Trinity; he does question whether Guadalupe has any connection to Mary, the mother of Jesus. Espín wonders, "If colonial Mexico (and Tridentine Spain) were not really free to choose a pneumatological language truly adequate to proper evangelization about the Spirit . . . [might not] the Mexican population . . . have borrowed culturally meaningful Marian language (symbols, imagery, etc.), readily available in and through Catholic speech and practice, thereby allowing orthodox pneumatology to *understandably* speak with and to them."[24] Espín speculates on the possible role of a pneumatological reading of Guadalupe as a bridge in "intra-Latino/a ecumenical conversation."[25] Would ecumenical agreement on Guadalupe as "an authentic cultural way of doctrinally expressing and existentially experiencing the Holy Spirit" yield new ecumenical perspectives?[26]

Whether one subscribes to a mariological or pneumatological interpretation of the Guadalupe experience (as with Díaz's interpretation of la Virgen de la Caridad del Cobre), what emerges is the need to understand the divine in terms of being in an embodied relationship, accompanied by the God who keeps company, especially with the vulnerable and marginalized, in the very concrete reality of daily and local existence. Díaz summarizes Latin@ Catholic theological stances on Mary, in her many permutations:

> Whether understood as the female face of God (Rodríguez, Elizondo), a symbol of the Holy Spirit (Espín), the poetry of the Trinitarian God (García), or the *mestizo* face of the divine (Goizueta), it is clear that U.S. Hispanic theologians understand Marian symbols as mediators of the life of grace, especially to and within the experience of the poor and marginalized.[27]

RE-IMAGINING MARY

Together with Justo González, I am not so naive as to suspect that las vírgenes of popular Catholicism offer a fruitful starting point for ecumenical dialogue on God "lest we misjudge the depth of the conflicts bequeathed to us by our theological and ecclesiastical ancestors."[28] While I am attracted to Espín's pneumatological interpretation of Guadalupe, I have reservations about its ability to serve as common ground. It is precisely her necessary "inculturatedness" that may prove a stumbling block in a cross-cultural intra-Latin@ ecumenical understanding of God. Nora Lozano-Díaz's assessment of

Guadalupe critiques overly liberative Catholic interpretations.[29] She finds no liberating options for Protestant Mexican and Mexican American women in appealing to the Virgin as a religious symbol too closely associated with life lived in the shadows of men. While approaching Guadalupe as a cultural symbol may have more impact in Protestant circles, Lozano-Díaz turns to the Bible as a resource "to challenge the traditional image of the Lady of Guadalupe."[30] Here she finds a Mary whose song celebrates God's justice in favor of the poor and oppressed, a Mary who is neither passive nor submissive but rather is a disciple.

With these cautions in mind, I am proposing that Catholic theologian Elizabeth Johnson's retrieval of the Mary of scripture as one filled with the Holy Spirit, situated within the communion of the saints, offers possibilities for engaging latinamente and ecumenically in conversation with the insights of our Hispan@ theologies that by intention are grounded in nuestras vidas cotidianas.[31] Such a mutual conversation can serve to re-imagine Mary, especially within Protestant contexts; re-imagine the third Person of the Trinity, especially within Catholic contexts; and enrich Johnson's theology with perspectives that both concretize and open up the communion of saints in light of accompaniment.

BUSCANDO A MARÍA

The past decade has been marked in Protestant circles by a renewed interest in Mary of Nazareth as accessible through the scriptures.[32] Ironically among the many reasons for this growing interest is the increasing presence of Latin@s in Protestant churches. Reclaiming a more positive view of Mary held by the reformers, Daniel Migliore observes, "If Protestants find reason for complaint in the excesses of Catholic mariology, Catholics in turn can complain of Protestant neglect of Mary and the unrelieved masculinity of Protestant faith with its exclusively male symbols, its all-male liturgical language, and its all-male models of Christian life."[33] Migliore goes on to ask, "What would a new picture of Mary look like from a Reformed faith perspective?"[34] Among the elements drawn from scripture that he includes as significant are three that relate directly to our discussion: Mary's consent to her election by God, whereby she is a "witness to the sovereign grace of God"; Mary's solidarity with the poor, especially as expressed in the Magnificat and its affirmation of God's justice; and Mary's participation in the company of those prayerfully awaiting the Spirit.[35]

FILLED WITH THE SPIRIT

At the heart of Elizabeth Johnson's pneumatological retrieval of Mary is the hope "that interpreting Mary in relation to the Spirit as a graced, concrete historical person amid the company of saints in heaven and on earth crafts a theology capable of promoting action on behalf of global justice and liberation, particularly empowering to the flourishing of women, coherent with elements of biblical, classical, and conciliar teaching, and productive of religious sense for our times."[36] Johnson begins with the contention that God is encountered in history and with the understanding that even the thin biblical record is diverse in its presentations of Mary, a difference that bears ecumenical significance. Drawing on the work of Georg Kretschmar and René Laurentin, she observes that "Protestants traditionally follow Mark's rather negative assessment of Jesus' mother; Catholics take from Luke a positive, personalistic view of her as full of grace and favor from God, a women who cooperated with the divine adventure of bringing the Redeemer into human flesh; while Orthodox approach Mary in the iconic, symbolic manner of John."[37] Undoubtedly the scant record of Mary in the New Testament enables her flexible appropriation across generations and contexts.

Johnson does not perceive Mary as the female face of God; she prefers God to "have her own maternal face." However, she acknowledges that there are times and places where Marian devotion mediates divine presence for individuals and communities. She grounds her proposal to situate Mary within the communion of saints in the third article of the Apostles' Creed: "We believe in the Holy Spirit, the holy catholic church, the communion of saints, the forgiveness of sins, the resurrection of the body and life everlasting." The dual benefits of this grounding are that Mary is connected across time and space to all men and women who have lived their lives in response to the Spirit; and "it allows female imagery of God, traditionally associated with the Spirit, to play a guiding role in interpretation."[38]

Appropriately, Johnson closes her systematic exploration of Mary as woman of the Spirit, mother of Jesus, our sister, and friend of God and prophet, with the Magnificat, Mary's own "gospel prayer" in response to the gracious action of God's Spirit. This canticle is the longest passage from the mouth of a woman in the New Testament and places Mary in a long Jewish tradition of women "who also sang dangerous songs of salvation." With this revolutionary prayer on her lips, Johnson "situates Mary in the whole cloud of witnesses who accompany the church on its following of Jesus."[39]

BEYOND THE PIGEON PARADIGM: INTERSECTING AGENDAS

The directive to the conjunto conversation partners, by convener Orlando Espín, was a bit paradoxical—namely, think outside the box but be realistic and, I suppose, practical. Navigation of these Marian waters muddied by abuses on all sides calls us to negotiate the extremes in all of our traditions while maintaining our respective confessional integrities. This ecumenical conversation becomes increasingly necessary because nuestra comunidad Latina is expanding exponentially in the United States and in our churches, and, some would claim, transforming both. As discussed earlier, the discourse around Mary is taking place already on grassroots levels: in the pews and in the barrios, in families and, as Fullerton demonstrates, in the streets.

Inspiration for our navigational chart may be found in one medieval artistic representation of the annunciation. Produced in the workshop of artist Juan de Carrión, in either Burgos or Segovia, this particular annunciation is a manuscript illustration in *The Little Office of the Blessed Virgin Mary,* an abbreviated version of the monastic Liturgy of the Hours designed for the laity who could afford such books, in this case for the Infante Don Alfonso of Castile. Like its monastic cousin, this book was intended for focused daily prayer of the psalms throughout the course of a day. The image faces the opening page of the Office, which contains the invitatory for morning prayer, "Lord open my lips . . . ," drawn from Psalm 51:15. The figures contained in the miniature are the angel Gabriel, Mary of Nazareth, and a dove representing the Holy Spirit.[40] The context of the illustration reflects the artist's and patron's contemporary experience more so than that of first-century, Roman-occupied Palestine. The words forming the border around the image are from the Gospel of Luke (1:26), as are the words in the scroll held by Gabriel (Lk 1:28).

With the annunciation as a starting point, as the image reminds us, an ecumenical conversation can begin grounded in the Gospels, at a point where the Spirit of God is clearly the animating force. This encounter occurs within the context of our daily living; we are interpreters before texts that speak to us anew in our own time, keenly aware of our non-innocent histories of interpretation and translation. As with the artists and patrons, we as theologians are to some degree also among the elite, in the sense that our education brings a privilege that many in our communities cannot afford, which is precisely why our teologías de conjunto cannot ignore the equally integral pastoral de conjunto of our accountable theologizing. The words of Psalm 51:15 remind us that all is in praise of God, something the Lucan Mary proclaims in Luke 1:46–55.

Again in the presence of the Spirit and in the company of her pregnant cousin, Elizabeth, Mary proclaims the revolutionary power of the saving God who stirs her soul and overturns the status quo. This song of the lowly ones raised up by a merciful God has ethical implications for those who are filled by the Spirit. It is the same Spirit that finds Mary in the company of the disciples gathered in the upper room (Acts 1:14), also illustrated in the *Hours of Infante Don Alfonso of Castile.*[41]

The retrieval of Mary as one filled with the Spirit of God perhaps makes Mary more accessible to some Protestant sensibilities; at the same time, it also makes the Holy Spirit accessible to Catholics in a church that has not warmly embraced Spirit-led movements. In many ways the Spirit is the most difficult Person of the Trinity to comprehend, especially for sacramental imaginations. When it comes to depicting the Spirit in image or metaphor, Catholics in particular experience a colossal failure of the artistic imagination or profound humility in the presence of true mystery. How does one depict an animating force, the renewer of the face of the earth, the advocate, sanctifier, consoler, counselor, wisdom, builder, nurturer and sustainer of community—as a humble pigeon? Is it possible to *see* the Spirit?

Pentecostal theologian Samuel Solicán approaches this question from what he calls the depersonalization of the Holy Spirit. For Solicán, references to the Spirit as a force or energy or influence reduce the sense of the Spirit's "Person" within the Trinity. He claims the personalization of the Spirit is important to the development of Latin@ pneumatologies because "the relationship of the Spirit to persons . . . who daily experience treatment as nonpersons, can provide a transformative model of personhood and self-esteem. . . . The depersonalization of the Holy Spirit serves the interest of those who would employ a divine image to further their own desires for control, those who seek to domesticate the divine, the ultimate expression of idolatry."[42] Calling for a correction of what he terms "pneumatological docetism," Solicán reminds us that it is "the person of the Holy Spirit given to the church and present in believers who make possible and necessary the cultural, ethnic, and linguistic diversity of the body of Christ."[43]

The Spirit is made visible, embodied, so to speak, in the communities and individuals within whom the Spirit dwells and whom the Spirit animates— in those who respond to the gracious invitation of God by living and acting justly. It is here that Johnson's placement of Mary firmly in the communion of saints intersects with contributions of Latin@ theologies and daily lived experience. The creation of communities through networks of kinship and mutual accountability that transcend time and space is a familiar part of lo cotidiano. Through compadrazgo/comadrazgo, webs of relationships tie families to one another, to pueblos, and beyond. In some ways, for the sacramental imagination, the communion of saints is the eschatological compadrazgo/comadrazgo with expectations on all sides, and in many ways, for some Catholics, lived through popular religion on a daily basis. The Spirit is made known in the company the Spirit keeps. Therefore, to know Mary is to know, in some way, the Spirit of God—the Spirit that accompanies, animates, renews, sustains, advocates, consoles, and counsels. ¡Dime con quién andas y te diré quién eres!

RELIGIOUS PROFILING UNMASKED

For theologians and scholars of religion committed to ecumenical dialogue latinamente, the caution of Eldin Villafañe deserves heed: "The depth of Hispanic religiosity cannot be fathomed by mere statistical qualification of church attendance . . . statistical surveys or religious profiles."[44] The recently released study from the Pew Hispanic Center entitled *Changing Faiths: Latinos and the Transformation of American Religion,* while rich in unprecedented information about the religious practices of a significant sampling of nuestra comunidad Latina, leaps to a conclusion about Hispanic Catholicism based on insufficient data. The study reports that "according to the survey, even Latino Catholics who do not describe themselves as charismatic or pentecostal are more likely than non-Latino Catholics to report having experienced or witnessed supernatural practices such as divine healings or revelations from God."[45] The study concludes that the presence of such elements in Hispanic Catholicism must indeed be due to renewalist practices that "seem to have been incorporated into Hispanic Catholicism without displacing Catholic identity." This quick and uncritical move from belief in miracles and divine revelation to the assumption of renewalist influence is troublesome. Over five hundred years of popular Catholic impulse and religious practice, rooted in the intersection of Amerindian, African, and Iberian daily encounters, is ignored. For our purposes such a facile conclusion not only does not recognize that belief in miracles and divine revelations are a part of popular Catholicism, but it conveys an exaggerated sense of the Spirit among Catholics. There is an assumption that Catholics connect such activities with the work of the Spirit rather than with Mary and the saints. Since the necessary follow-up questions were not asked, this conclusion remains unfounded, yet it is this Pentecostal/Charismatic renewalism that the study implies is transforming the Catholic Church. Curiously, the study never pursued the growing influence of Mary in the Protestant churches.

DANOS HOY . . .

It is no surprise to me that over three years later the Fullerton Avenue shrine beneath the Kennedy Expressway in Chicago is still tended and visited. The prayer graffiti provides some clue as to what is on the minds of pilgrims as messages about Mexico coincide with the growing violent disruptions of daily life perpetuated in the name of homeland security by Immigration and Customs Enforcement (appropriately identified by the acronym ICE) and other federal agencies. In fact, as some of us were traveling to Los Angeles this Saturday for ACHTUS, immigrants gathered on the Mall in Washington DC to call attention to the real-life consequences of pending immigration legislation. As tensions mount and the rhythms and geographies of the day no longer provide stability; as work, school, and even shopping are now sources of fear and anxiety, especially for those of us who are alternately documented; a sign of divine accompaniment at the crossroads of vida cotidiana may indeed be consoling. Perhaps what is occurring is not superstition or false worship but recognition of the Spirit among us, connecting us with the one whom the Spanish Carmelites have called "mother and teacher in the Spirit," one who accompanies the community as a faithful sister, ever pointing toward a liberating God.[46]

It is the recognition of the Spirit that prompts the song of Mary and reminds us all that these are not privatized revelations; they bear communal responsibility. The presence of the divine in lo cotidiano reminds us of our obligations to one another in the company of those across time and space who are animated by the Spirit and move in solidarity, especially with those who are like us, vulnerable and struggling on the margins. To retrieve Mary as someone, in companionship, within whom the Spirit dwells is to free our imaginations to allow God to be God.

NOTES

[1] Thanks to my CTU colleague Steve Bevans and to project coordinator Wil Steinbacher for the invitation to participate in the Glenmary Seminar, a project to create resources for parish ministry in the United States. The meeting was held in April 2007 at Gethsemane.

[2] Unless they appear as such in a cited quotation, words and expressions in Spanish in this paper are not italicized. This reflects the dynamic interaction between Spanish and English in the daily lived experience of U.S. Latin@s. Instead of using the umbrella terms *Hispanic* and *Latino/a,* unless they appear as such in a cited quotation, I employ @, the "at" symbol with an accent mark, as a suffix. I use Latin@ or Hispan@ to deal with the issue of grammatically gendered endings in Spanish. I use these terms so as not to suggest false correspondences between grammatically and socially constructed gender. In other words, I will not use *Latino* to refer collectively to males and females, as I would not use *man* to refer collectively to males and females. My use of @ is intentional: it conveniently combines the o and a into one symbol; as the symbol for "at" it intensifies the significance of social location for theologizing latinamente; its relationship to electronic communication marks it as both contemporary and as a means of highlighting networks of connection, two aspects constitutive of the Latin@ presence in the U.S.; and the accent mark is a reminder of the fluidity of languages. I identify as Hispan@ out of respect for my maternal grandparents, who emigrated from Spain to Cuba to New York in the early part of the twentieth century. My preference for the term is rooted in the observation by Agustín Laó-Montes in the book *Mambo Montage,* "the denomination *hispano* in early- twentieth-century New York City was widely used as a sign of solidarity among working-class immigrants of Hispanic Caribbean and Spanish descent" (5). For me the term underscores my family's immigrant roots, my first language of Spanish, and my U.S. context.

[3] Eldin Villafañe, *The Liberating Spirit: Toward an Hispanic Pentecostal Social Ethic* (Grand Rapids, MI: Eerdmans, 1993), 41. Cited in José David Rodríguez and Loida Martell-Otero, eds., *Teología en Conjunto: A Collaborative Hispanic Protestant Theology* (Louisville, KY: Westminster John Knox Press, 1997), 3.

[4] José David Rodriguez and Loida Martell-Otero, "Introduction," in Rodríguez and Martell-Otero, *Teología en Conjunto,* 3.

[5] Pew Hispanic Center, *Changing Faiths: Latinos and the Transformation of American Religion* (Washington DC: Pew Hispanic Center, 2007), 17. Available online.

[6] Elizabeth Conde-Frazier, "Hispanic Protestant Spirituality," in Rodriguez and Martell-Otero, *Teología en Conjunto,* 131.

[7] Orlando O. Espín, "Traditioning: Culture, Daily Life and Popular Religion, and Their Impact on Christian Tradition," in *Futuring Our Past: Explorations in the Theology*

of Tradition, ed. Orlando O. Espín and Gary Macy (Maryknoll, NY: Orbis Books, 2006), 7.

[8] I use *popular* here in the sense of arising from and belonging to the people.

[9] See Maureen O'Donnell, "We Believe It's a Miracle," *Chicago Sun-Times,* April 19, 2005; Jennifer Lebovich, "Faithful See Mary on Underpass Wall," *Chicago Tribune,* April 19, 2005; Brandon S. Honig and Randi Belisomo, "Believers See Virgin Mary under Kennedy Expressway As New Pope Is Announced," Medill News Service, April 19, 2005.

[10] "Faithful Call Image on Underpass Wall 'Beautiful,'" April 18, 2005, WMAQ Chicago NBC 5. Available online.

[11] Frank Tamas, *Emergency Exit Ramp,* 3 parts. Available on the youtube.com website. For another film on the Fullerton "appearance," see Scott Sonnenberg, *The Virge.* Available on the youtube.com website.

[12] Adapted RSV/NRSV translation used in English-language version of the *Catechism of the Catholic Church.* Available online.

[13] Rummana Hussain, "Mary Returns after Graffiti Attack," *Chicago Sun-Times,* May 7, 2005.

[14] In the documentary, González affirms his belief in and explains in detail his understanding of the rapture.

[15] Enrique González, "The Problem with Mary (A Latin American View)," *The Christian Century* (December 14, 2004). Available online.

[16] José Landaverde, quoted in David Van Biema, "Hail, Mary," *Time* (March 13, 2005). Available online.

[17] Roberto S. Goizueta, *Caminemos con Jesús: Toward a Hispanic/Latino Theology of Accompaniment* (Maryknoll, NY: Orbis Books, 1995), 66.

[18] Raúl Gómez-Ruiz, *Mozarabs, Hispanics, and the Cross* (Maryknoll, NY: Orbis Books, 2007), 14. Chapter 2 contains a helpful and concise history of Iberian Christianity.

[19] See "Holy Wars: Brazil (Religious Icon Sparks Furor between Catholics and Protestants),"*The Economist (US)* (November 1995); Marina Mirabella , "Evangelicals Challenge Catholics in Brazil" *CNN World News* (December 22, 1995); Jack Epstein, "Kicking of Icon Outrages Brazil Catholics," *The Dallas Morning News* (November 24, 1995); John L. Allen, Jr., "A Look Ahead to Benedict in Brazil," *All Things Catholic, National Catholic Reporter Conversation Café* (May 3, 2007). All available online.

[20] Miguel H. Díaz, "*Dime con quíen andas y te diré quíen eres:* We Walk with Our Lady of Charity," in *From the Heart of Our People: Latino/a Explorations in Catholic Systematic Theology*, ed. Orlando O. Espín and Miguel H. Díaz (Maryknoll, NY: Orbis Books, 1999), 160.

[21] Ibid., 158.

[22] Ibid., 165, 166.

[23] Orlando O. Espín, *The Faith of the People: Theological Reflections on Popular Catholicism* (Maryknoll, NY: Orbis Books, 1997), 9.

[24] Ibid.

[25] Orlando O. Espín, "An Exploration into the Theology of Grace and Sin," in Espín and Díaz, *From the Heart of Our People,* 149–150n36.

[26] Espín, *The Faith of the People,* 9–10.

[27] Miguel Díaz, *On Being Human: U.S. Hispanic and Rahnerian Perspectives* (Maryknoll, NY: Orbis Books, 2001), 125. Also cited in Elizabeth A. Johnson, *Truly Our Sister: A Theology of Mary in the Communion of Saints* (New York: Continuum, 2003), 85.

[28] Justo L. González, "Reinventing Dogmatics," in Espín and Díaz, *From the Heart of Our People*, 224.

[29] Nora O. Lozano-Díaz, "Ignored Virgin or Unaware Women: A Mexican-American Protestant Reflection on the Virgin of Guadalupe," in *A Reader in Latina Feminist Theology: Religion and Justice*, ed. María Pilar Aquino et al. (Austin: University of Texas Press, 2002), 210–211. It should be noted that others, including Catholic Latinas, have critiqued the patriarchal use of Mary and Guadalupe to oppress women in both church and society by upholding submission as a value. See, for example, Nancy Pineda-Madrid, "Notes toward a Chicana/Feminist Epistemology (and Why It Is Important for Latina Feminists)," in Aquino et al., *A Reader in Latina Feminist Theology*, 253–260.

[30] Lozano-Díaz, "Ignored Virgin or Unaware Women," 213.

[31] In her theological work Elizabeth Johnson makes a concerted effort to engage theological perspectives often ignored in the academy. Latin@ theologians as well as Latin American theologians are frequently visible as conversation partners, sources, and resources in her publications and courses. Johnson's work also employs feminist critiques of the Christian tradition.

[32] For example, see Beverly Roberts Gaventa and Cynthia L. Rigby, eds., *Blessed One: Protestant Perspectives on Mary* (Louisville, KY: Westminster John Knox Press, 2002); *Christian History and Biography* (July 1, 2004), the entire issue is titled "Mary"; Protestant Mary," *Religion and Ethics News Weekly* 816 (December 17, 2004); David Van Biema, "Hail, Mary," *Time* (March 13, 2005). Articles are available online. Mary's presence in the New Testament is thin; for a list, see "Mary in the Imagination of the Church," *Christian History and Biography* (July 1, 2004): "Gabriel announces her election as mother of the Messiah (Luke 1:26–38); she visits Elizabeth (Luke 1:39–56); she travels to Bethlehem and gives birth to Jesus (Luke 2:1–20); she presents Jesus at the Temple to Simeon and Anna (Luke 2:21–39); she discovers Jesus discoursing in the Temple with the elders (Luke 2:40–52); she asks Jesus to help the wine stewards at the Cana wedding (John 2:1–11); she visits Jesus with his brothers (Matt. 12:46; Mark 3:31–35; Luke 8:19–21); at the foot of the cross, she hears her son's last words to her (John 19:26–27); she experiences Pentecost with the apostles (Acts 1:14)." What is notable are the references to her in relation to the Spirit (see the annunciation, the visitation to Elizabeth, the presentation in the Temple, and Pentecost). Available online.

[33] Daniel L. Migliore, "Mary: A Reformed Theological Perspective," *Theology Today* (October 1999), available online; also reprinted in Gaventa and Rigby, *Blessed One*.

[34] Ibid.

[35] Ibid.

[36] Johnson, *Truly Our Sister*, 113.

[37] Ibid., 3.

[38] See ibid., 92, 102.

[39] Ibid., 262–263. Johnson treats the Magnificat in detail on 258–274, 322–325.

[40] "Virgin Mary: Annunciation," folio, in *Hours of Infante Don Alfonso of Castile* (1465–1480), MS M.854 fol. 53v. Available at the utu.morganlibrary.org website.

[41] "Pentecost," folio, in *Hours of Infante Don Alfonso of Castile* (1465–1480), MS M.0854, fol. 209v. Available at the corsair.morganlibrary.org website.

[42] Samuel Solivan, "The Holy Spirit: A Pentecostal Hispanic Perspective," in Rodríguez and Martell-Otero, *Teología en Conjunto*, 53.

[43] Ibid., 55.

[44] Villafañe, *The Liberating Spirit,* 41. Cited in Rodríguez and Martell-Otero, *Teología en Conjunto,* 3.

[45] Pew Hispanic Center, *Changing Faiths*, 30. In reading this report, it is important to look at the section "Topline Research," which contains all the survey questions and responses, with more complete statistical data.

[46] See excerpts from the introductory commentary to the Mass, "Collection of Masses of the Blessed Virgin Mary," vol. 1, *Sacramentary* (Totowa, NJ: Catholic Book Publishing Co., 1992), 229.

2

God and Difference

Mayra Rivera

A hundred years ago a Protestant missionary arrived in Puerto Rico as part of an effort to spread the Good News in the newly acquired territory. To his fellow missionaries, he offered the following advice: "To *know the mind of God* is the first requisite of the missionary, but next to that he must come to *knowledge of the mind of the people* over whom he shall be placed by the Holy Spirit."[1] In the colonial context in which this statement was uttered, "knowledge" hardly disguises its links to the aims of power and control. Knowledge here is an attempt to grasp, to comprehend, to gain control over people. But this is what makes this statement especially interesting for me: it makes surprisingly clear that there is a close relationship between objectifying and controlling other people and objectifying God. The claim "to know the mind of God" is considered the foundation of the claim to know (and rule over) the subjected other. A lot has changed since 1898, and Protestantism has become an important part of the Puerto Rican landscape. But the idea of possessing a certain kind knowledge of God that leads us to assert control over other peoples has all but disappeared—both in its well-intentioned and its plainly malicious versions. My reflections here are motivated by a concern for respecting human difference and divine otherness—which I consider to be deeply interrelated.

What do power relations have to do with God? Should mundane issues such as the organization of societies and the influences of culture shape God-talk? I have been asked to address these questions that have occupied theology at least since Ludwig Feuerbach—issues with which every constructive theologian has to wrestle. In the context of this conversation among Catholic and Protestant Latina/o theologians, I welcome these questions as an invitation to reflect explicitly and collectively on the potential contributions of Latina/o theologies to a doctrine of God, as well as on the meaning of God-talk, as it relates to power relations. This is a relatively unexplored territory, for while Latina/o theologies have offered important contributions to Christology and theological anthropology, there have been surprisingly fewer attempts to engage critically and constructively with the doctrine of God.[2]

29

As a small contribution to this important conversation, this essay focuses on the possible connections between the epistemological claims of Latina/o theologies, their theological anthropology, and cosmology. In other words, I am attempting to tease out the implications of our arguments about the contextual nature of knowledge and the relationality of identity for describing the relationship between God and creation. These are, of course, only initial thoughts offered in the hopes of luring others into further conversation on the subject. An additional disclaimer is in order. My engagement with texts in Latina/o theologies is only intended to provide examples rather than to survey the rich contributions of these theologies to the subject. A more in-depth analysis of those subjects would certainly enrich the conversation, but for the purposes of this essay I can only hint at some broad but, in my view, crucial theological connections.

THE PARTICULARITIES OF GOD-TALK

According to Benjamin Valentin, the distinctiveness of Hispanic theologies resides in their upholding of culture as a resource for theological discourse, their attention to issues of cultural and social identity, and their emphasis on the collaborative nature of theological work.[3] The assumption underlying these general traits is that theology cannot be dissociated from the concrete historical, cultural, and sociopolitical milieu in which it is enunciated, indeed, that theology is enmeshed in the relationships that constitute the fabric of society and the collective imaginary. Concepts are closely linked to concrete practices as their product and shaping force.

Like Latin American liberation theology, Latina/o theology affirms that God-talk has direct implications for sociopolitical realities and seeks not merely to describe those realities, but also to transform them. This principle, which calls into question the strict boundaries between intellectual production and the material realities, implies not only the necessity to assess and represent the Latina/o religious and social contexts, but also a commitment to a critical engagement with theology.

In his introductory notes to the theology section of a 1998 bibliography of Protestant Hispanic Christianity, Justo L. González describes the relationship between Latino/a theologies and "traditional" theology as follows:

> They tend to be radical in their insistence in claiming their own culture and experience as the place from which they must do their theology. . . . But on the other hand they will then do this on the basis of Scriptural authority, or in the name of orthodox Christian doctrine and faith— which will seem quite conservative from the perspective of the same people who consider them radical in other matters.[4]

Surely not all Latina/o theologies conform to this description, but the idea of the possibility of separating sociopolitical stance from theological critique is indeed quite common. It is thus worth observing that as radical as an insistence on a particular locus of enunciation may be, an a priori decision to stay within the boundaries of predominant Christian dogma is not without consequences. To foreground the truth-value of the knowledge that emerges from marginalized contexts consistently and to challenge ideologies that present themselves as universal, we need to grapple with the profound implications of the contextual character of all knowledge, including scripture and what we call traditional theology. The images of "orthodox" Christian doctrine are as "contextual" as those offered by "constructive" or "contextual" theologies. Indeed, as Orlando Espín puts it, "nothing human is acultural."[5] Thus the radical questioning of prevalent structures of oppression should lead to a questioning of their supporting principles, whether they are theological or not.

On the opposite end of the theological spectrum, Latina/o theologies also struggle with their well-founded but potentially limiting suspicion of "systematic" theology. Although I share the misgivings about the pretensions of completeness that the term *systematic* often conveys, and I do not claim it as a descriptor of my work, this is by no means a refusal to engage doctrinal language critically and constructively, assessing its continuity with other concepts in our collective imaginary. Thus, an awareness of the close relationships among power, sociopolitical relations, and our understanding of God should not lead us to distance ourselves from doctrinal discussions, but rather to engage them differently, for unless dominant formulations of Christian doctrines and theological language are challenged and/or rearticulated, they will be assumed as given and continue to guide silently the ways in which we think about God and power.

I would like to suggest that Latina/o theologies spring out of two contrasting impulses: the need to challenge theological symbols for their collusion with hegemonic systems, on the one hand, and the affirmation of experience as a vital source not only for challenging dominant systems, but also for shaping Christian life, on the other. The first of these is, in its own particular way, in evident continuity with liberation theologies in Latin America and the United States, which profoundly challenged the role of dominant theological symbols. For example, in *Mañana* Justo González challenged the ideas of divine omnipotence, impassibility, and changelessness, arguing that these attributes were developed by elites and thus tend to privilege the values that benefited their class. González extends his analysis to draw parallels between the ideals then proclaimed about God and the characteristics on which contemporary economic powers build. "If the essential attributes of God," González explains, "are omnipresence, omnipotence, and omniscience, it follows that the most 'godlike' institutions of our time are the transnational corporations, for they more than any other approach the ideals of omnipotence, omnipresence, and omniscience."[6] These general observations illustrate the deconstructive aspect of theological work, which scrutinizes the contexts from which theological arguments emerge and traces the continuity between theological images and ideological constructs in their ancient and/or contemporary settings.[7]

The second stream of theological production—which cannot be separated from the first—nourishes Latina/o theologies' *constructive* commitments. Latina/o theologies have proposed new understandings of religion and theology using concepts and images that arise from and are believed to contribute to the empowerment of Latina/os. This constructive endeavor is grounded, explicitly or implicitly, on the trust that human experience is deeply related to the divine and that the particularity of the struggles and experiences of Latina/os are sites of divine revelation. For instance, Orlando Espín's observation that in popular religiosity "God is not the powerful, conquering divinity of the victorious and successful, but a paternal (maternal!), familial, communal God whose providence is encouragement and support,"[8] is not just a statement about the beliefs of a community, but an affirmation of broader theological implications; it is a positive statement about who God is.

The emphasis that Catholic Latina/o theologies have placed on popular religiosity is grounded in an affirmation of the significance of the finite, embodied existence as a source of understanding of divine reality. In a call to embrace the theopoetic power of Latina/o popular Catholicism, Roberto Goizueta argues that "to stifle that theopoetic power by trying to 'make sense' of it theologically, or trying to 'make sense' of it ethically, *before* one has actually *participated in it* would be to stifle the voice of God."[9] Affirming the collective participation in theopoetic power challenges the subordination of the aesthetic to the ethical/critical dimensions of theology. Such challenge does not entail, however, a dismissal of the need for critical vigilance and political analysis. Quite to the contrary, it is an invitation to a more complex understanding of the relationship between deconstructive critique and constructive theology. "This fundamental unity and rootedness in praxis preclude the possibility of a theopoetics immune to theological and ethical critique." Refusing the assumed dichotomy between intellectual and political, on the one hand, and the affects, on the other, Goizueta relates their fundamental unity to the body. "There can be no apolitical or atheological affect any more than there can be an apolitical or affectless theology," he observes; "the most sterile logic cannot be completely devoid of affect any more than a mind can exist without a body."[10] This feminist theologian is indeed delighted with a Latino's theopoetical embrace of bodily wisdom.

The constructive endeavor is grounded in the conviction not only that the *ideas* about God influence human action, but also that human realities offer us insight into the divine reality—a reality that is ultimately beyond every construct. God-talk is enmeshed in and affects the sociopolitical realm, but this does not reduce God to an incidental product of the collective imagination. Furthermore, the collective imagination is never purely apolitical or atheological.

As Espín observes, "Popular Christianity does not refer solely to those relationships or contents that might be typically labeled religious in contemporary European-American culture; it refers to *all* human relationships."[11]

Thus, Latina/o understandings of the significance of God-talk must maintain the balance between its deconstructive and constructive aspects in order to avoid either isolating theology from the positive powers of divine/human relation or failing to explore the complexities and ambiguities of experience by neglecting the epistemological critique. To seek theological insight in the lives and experiences of Latina/os further implies that those theologies are significant not merely for Latina/os but that they are relevant for all God-talk, inasmuch as they offer a unique glimpse of the divine. But the realm of human experience is not protected from the force fields of ideological productions, and what is experienced as true and immediate reality by dominant or marginalized communities is also affected by dominant ideologies.

Latina/o theologies' affirmation of the intricate and complex relationship among personal, sociopolitical, and theological aspects of reality rests on a cosmological vision that is frequently only implicit in Latina/o theologies.[12] I have argued elsewhere that a relational image of God and creation reflects the metaphysical values implicit in Latina/o theologies.[13] However, the close connection between the interhuman values and metaphysical structures is not always admitted. Theology often sets up a clear contrast between the values espoused for interhuman relations and those attributed to God, which tends to undermine the significance of lived experience as a source for theology. Because affirming such metaphysical disjuncture would undercut the very basis for Latina/o constructive theology, I here trace its appearance in a foundational Latino theological text. My goal in foregrounding this example is to call attention to the importance of developing cosmological accounts that can ground not only Latina/o theologies' assertions about God, but also their epistemological and ethical claims.

GOD AND EMBODIED MULTIPLICITY

The absolute simplicity, unchangeability, and unaffected independence from the world associated with dominant images of God are mirrored by, and legitimize models of subjectivity that value—indeed, produce the ideal and illusion of—purity, permanent self-identity, and individual autonomy. Latina/o theologies challenge this ideal by raising their complex understandings of identity not merely as *descriptions* of Latina/o identities (conceived as exceptions to the dominant rule), but as theoretical contributions toward the development of alternative ideals of identity-in-relation that may promote more equitable social relations.

It is hard to overestimate the impact of Virgilio Elizondo's *Galilean Journey* for Latina/o theologies' discussions of identity, which commonly address the significance of the terms *mestizaje* and *mulatez*.[14] Ada María Isasi-Díaz's assertion that "the locus theologicus, the place from which we do mujerista theology, is our mestizaje and mulatez" seems to be confirmed by every survey of Latina/o theologies. Taking as its point of departure a concept that highlights impurity and fluidity, Latina/o theologies could contribute to a profound subversion of social values of purity and sameness, rereading a founding meta-narrative of Western theology (and philosophy) to reinscribe in it "denied knowledges" and foreclosed otherness.[15] *Mestizaje* foregrounds the emergence of subjects from relationships through continuous processes that cannot be reduced to internal sameness or definable characteristics. It places relations at the heart of the self. But I must emphasize this is a potential contribution, because at some points Latina/o theologies have tended to reduce *mestizaje* to another identity label, thus falling prey to the tendencies of the dominant traditions to privilege unity and commonality in ways that can easily reify self-enclosed identity and reproduce exclusivist paradigms.[16]

Elizondo views the word *mestizo* as a defining paradigm of Mexican American experience. Describing the first *mestizaje*, he depicts the internal texture of the colonizing mindset that created, on the one hand, the idea of a universal humankind and Christianity as "the only and absolute way to God," and, on the other hand, separated humanity in "a multiplicity of races." The effect of the colonial encounter, he explains, was a destruction of the world views of the conquered peoples. However, from this encounter a new race was born and, in Our Lady of Guadalupe, "the cultural clash of sixteenth-century Spain and Mexico was resolved and reconciled."[17] In contrast with the first one, in the second *mestizaje*—the one with the Anglo culture—the clash is far from resolved. Like the hybrid in Homi Bhabha's theorizing of colonial rule, this second *mestizo* represents for Elizondo an unfinished identity, which continues to evolve in its multiple and conflicting relations.

However, although he historicizes its roots and argues that Hispanic identity does not fit American categories, he also affirms an essential sameness when he claims that "we have a common soul" and asserts that colonization, with all its vices, created a new "race." This "new race" becomes a new category in which to fit "Mexican Americans" and eventually "Hispanics." In this move, otherness becomes assimilated into the structures that organize U.S. society. The value of heterogeneity and fluidity are undermined when they are interpreted as moving toward a homogenizing telos. Whether it is based on an assumed biological inheritance or on cultural legacy, essentialism threatens to undermine the distinctive relationality affirmed by Latina/o theorizations of identity.[18]

This tension between the critique of dominant models of identity and the incorporation into a new internally variegated but stable (and potentially exclusive) paradigm intensifies as Elizondo embraces dominant theological ideas of God as preeminently One and Absolute. Rather than an image of what is revealed in the complex and multiple relationality of life, God—as the one who is absolved from relations—is depicted as the exception that relativizes such values as merely human. Elizondo writes, "In this intimacy with God, Jesus also reveals a new anthropology: dignity, confidence, security, *docility*, and self-respect based on freely chosen dependence on the *one*

Absolute: God. This *unquestioned dependence* on and confidence in the *one Absolute* in turn frees his followers from all other humanly made absolutes or dependencies" (italics added).[19] The new egalitarian order is to be established by dependence on the one God who is itself freed from the affects of relations.

This is, to be sure, a common theological structure, where the divine relativizes human structures. My purpose in highlighting it is only to foreground the creator/creature dichotomy on which it rests and to invite a questioning of its potential effects. What does it mean for our theologies to assert that ultimately there is just one absolute? As a sign of irreducible complexity and relationality, *mestizaje* can be used to subvert the self-legitimating constructions purity, homogeneity, autonomy, and separation of the dominant value systems. But, can we subvert the privilege given to pure origin, absolute (but knowable) differences, oneness, and so forth, while claiming these to be the characteristics that define God? Doesn't anything that we claim about God immediately become our greatest value and, if so, wouldn't that reinscribe *mestizaje* as a fallen state rather than as the basic principle of reality?

Latina/o theologies' assertion of the inextricability of the sociopolitical from the theological, the personal from the communal, and the spiritual from the material realities of life implies, I think, a critique not only of ideologies that dismiss the reality of the divine, but also of those that compartmentalize realms of existence, envisioning the cosmos as the precarious juncture of purely sacred and profane realms. Theologies that depict God and creation as two extrinsic realities simplify God and reduce creation to something that can be fully grasped by human constructs or reduced to categories within social systems. Furthermore, in these models the complexity of the relational transformations that occur in the world tends to be overwhelmed by appeals to a separate divinity—absolute, independent, unconstrained—that renders the worldly processes ultimately insignificant. The externality of that God also directs the attention of theology to a realm imagined as unconditioned by the world, assumed as the source of otherworldly principles and absolute novelty. The imaginary space of exteriority that is thus opened elicits desire for the external realm of God that such space represents: a longing for unmediated access to a pure outside and for a future that does not depend on the arduous and endless work entailed by all worldly relational transformations.

In contrast, when Latina/o theologies' constructive project embraces images of a world infused by God and always open to that which is beyond (but not outside) itself, they may reclaim the complexity and dynamism subordinated by dominant depictions of the world. Indeed a relational theological anthropology—one that is embodied, relational, and unfinished—calls for a thoroughly incarnate theological vision that does not shy away from its irreducible multiplicity, where the divine embraces the particularity of bodies.

OTHERNESS IN INTER-HUMAN RELATIONS

Latin American liberation theology has long affirmed the inextricability between the sacred and social relations, particularly the relations to the poor and marginalized. This interest in foregrounding the ethical and religious imperative of responding to the needs of the other requires challenging the dominant privilege of sameness, defending instead the value of difference. Such vision led liberation thinkers to focus on the idea of divine otherness. While resisting the strict division between the sacred and the profane, liberation theologies emphasized —especially in their early formulations—the idea of divine transcendence. Divine transcendence and interhuman difference are joined analytically, as examples of relationship with otherness, and ontologically; models of God and theological anthropology are interdependent. Latina/o theological anthropology's attention to otherness and relationality offers rich resources for rethinking divine transcendence with, and in some aspects beyond, the early models offered by Latin American liberation thinkers. In this section I highlight some of the insights of Latina/o theological anthropology for rethinking interhuman otherness while the next section engages a model of creature/divine relationality.

In his early work Enrique Dussel describes the relation to the human other using Emmanuel Levinas's concept of exteriority. Dussel describes the otherness of the excluded person as his or her exteriority in relation to "the system," which he likens to God's transcendence also imagined as God's exteriority in relation to creation. Those who are excluded from the system are, like God, exterior. This establishes a special relationship between God and the excluded person, which implies that God's revelation takes place in that which is "other than the system, the poor." The excluded person "is the 'locus' of God's epiphany in those who are non-system."[20]

Divine transcendence is thus a central category for those trying to challenge the totalitarian tendencies to eliminate or undermine differences. As Roberto Goizueta states: "In an era dominated . . . by capitalist economic monopolies . . . the defense of human *and* divine transcendence is no longer a mere option; it is the principal and most urgent imperative. And that global defense can be articulated theologically only in the form of . . . theologies which proclaim the irreducibility of both God and the person to any system."[21] Divine *and* human transcendence, the irreducibility of both God *and* the person—respect for God's otherness becomes inextricable from our respect for other creatures.

Dussel's conceptualization of transcendence as externality, however, tends to evoke images of absolute difference and undermine the intricate relationality from which differences emerge.[22] Latina/o theologies' relational, complex, and open constructions of identity and subjectivity fruitfully problematize this model and suggest possibilities for developing alternate models that attend to otherness in relation. Latina/o theologies are, by definition, theologies of the others *within* the territory of hegemonic power, of the others *within* the same. It is not surprising, then, that in Latina/o theologies otherness is not described through metaphors of spatial exteriority that have informed important contributions of Latin American liberation theology. Latina/o theologies' theorization of the encounter between a dominant system and its other relies on an understanding of the other as other, not absolutely other.

As I mentioned before, Latina/o theologies thus take as their point of departure a complex and ambiguous concept: *mestizaje/mulatez* deployed catachrestically to embrace the constant intermixing as a principle that defines their identity. That is, *mestizaje/mulatez* in contemporary Latina/o discourses can be used not only to embrace the complex and ambiguous product of a colonial past, but also as a hermeneutical tool for rethinking identity in/as mixture.[23] Choosing *mestizaje/mulatez* as privileged metaphors for the articulation of identity implies that the singularity of an individual person becomes unthinkable outside a network of relations—sociopolitical as much as familial—that extends spatially through continents and temporally through generations.[24] *Mestizaje/mulatez* suggests a model of subjectivity formed by relationships that are nevertheless marked by the ambiguities of human history.[25] Interhuman otherness is not static exteriority, but difference that evolves through history.

In addition to attending to the historical dimension of subjectivity, Latina/o theologies emphasize the relational nature of subjects, a trait that leads to an anthropology turned to the outside, to others. Goizueta grounds this assertion of the "more" of interhuman existence: "The assertion that personal identity is intrinsically relational [is] the corollary of a sacramental worldview which asserts that the identity of every concrete, particular entity is relational."[26] In this world view, the cosmos is "an intrinsically relational reality" where "each member is necessarily related to every other member."[27]

Each subject mirrors the cosmos by being also an "intrinsically relational reality": the human person is a subject-in-community. Community pre-exists and is constitutive of the individual, regardless of choice.[28] Therefore, Goizueta explains, a relational anthropology implies that "the option for the poor" is not simply an act of will. It is "*an active recognition of that which we already are through no choice of our own.*"[29] The encounter of the other reveals to the subject the priority of the other. In opting for the poor, the subject realizes itself as always already in relation to others.

God-talk should reflect the relational cosmic structure assumed by these depictions of interhuman relationality, where the divine is revealed not only in the engagement with explicitly religious symbols, but also in the ethical encounter with the other. Through these complex relations with interhuman otherness, the otherness of God is revealed. Rather than reducing God to an unrelated simplicity, God-talk shall thus be faithful to and reflect the interhuman relationality from which it arises, respecting the heterogeneity and irreducibility of the divine and the human. Our proclamation of the otherness of God shall not undermine the irreducibility of human others, but that irreducibility need not be conceived as absolute separation.

INTRACOSMIC TRANSCENDENCE

Given the problems that dominant Western cultures have had relating positively with otherness, it is perhaps not surprising that divine transcendence has been depicted in terms that highlight distance and separation. Indeed, transcendence is commonly equated to God's absolute separation from creation. Theologies that challenge such images of the God-world relation—like feminist and liberation theologies—are often accused of compromising divine transcendence. Those accusations rest on ideas of absolute difference that Latina/o theologies have challenged. Latina/o theological understandings of the relationality of the cosmos and the reconfiguration of the boundary between the sacred and the profane inform not only for Latina/o cosmology but also its liberationist stance. For, as Ignacio Ellacuría argued, as long as we continue to think of God as extrinsic to creation, we will not be able to realize the profound implications of liberation theologies' key assertion: that salvation is historical. Ignacio Ellacuría, who developed one of the most explicit descriptions of a liberationist interpretation of divine transcendence in relation to the cosmological vision that grounds it, attributes to "pernicious philosophical influences" the fact that transcendence has been identified with *separateness*.[30] The root of this misleading identification of transcendence with separation is a world view that opposes rationality to the senses, and spirituality to physicality, leading to depictions of the cosmos and God as realities extrinsic to each other and closed around themselves.[31]

In Latina/o theologies, discussions of the God/creation relationship occur most often as part of expositions on the character of popular Catholicism. As Latina/o theologians interpret it, the sacramental understanding of creation that undergirds popular Catholicism represents an affirmation of the "real divine presence in material realities" and of the "intrinsic value of the concrete and particular."[32] While these theologies focus on explicitly religious symbols, I have tried to envision the cosmology that they assume and contribute to: a broad cosmic sacramentality that embraces the interhuman encounters and the nonhuman world. Moving against reductionist understandings of creation, these affirmations of the sacramentality of creation can ground understandings of the doctrine of God that are, as Justo González suggests, also based on the notion of incarnation.[33]

Ellacuría's work offers invaluable resources to develop such a theology of God in creation. In order to overcome reductionist views of creation, Ellacuría draws from the work of the Basque philosopher Xavier Zubiri to develop a model of history that takes physicality as its unavoidable ground.[34] As I have said, such understanding is at the heart of Latina/o theologies' views of identity, where differences are seen as emerging from and subtending relationships. Ellacuría's cosmology takes as its starting point the unity and the intrinsically dynamic character of reality. Reality is a "single physical unity that is complex and differentiated, in such a way that the unity does not nullify differences and the differences do not nullify the unity."[35] Rather than being isolated entities, we are all open to one another. It is not simply that things necessarily relate to one another, but that they only are what they are, or better, they only *become* in relation to others. The unity of the universe is more than a conceptual abstraction; it is a principle of reality: everything is intrinsically and constitutively connected to all other things.

The emergence of new things from within the cosmos and the dynamic unity of reality are signs that divine transcendence subtends all reality. Transcendence is thus not imagined in terms of distance, exteriority, or otherworldliness. Instead, transcendence "calls attention to a contextual structural difference without implying a duality."[36] In a cosmological vision that affirms "the dual unity of God in humanity and humanity in God," transcendence "enables us to speak of an intrinsic unity without implying a strict identity."[37]

Rather than the static images of spatial gap between God and creation, this notion of transcendence is a dynamic one that alludes to the transformative power that infuses creation. Because transformation always presupposes the historical, material, and biological developments that make new things possible, transcendence is seen in its relation to all these aspects of reality. It is possible "to see transcendence as something that transcends *in* and not as something that transcends *away* from; as something that physically impels to more but not by taking out of; as something that *pushes* forward, but at the same time *retains*" (italics added), Ellacuría submits.[38] In this model of intracosmic transcendence—where transcendence pushes forward and retains—the future emerges from within the matrices of relations that characterize created life, which include sociopolitical relations as well as the organic energies that sustain life and evolution in the cosmos. As in the case of cultural traditions, the old does not predetermine the new, but supports it. The future emerges not simply by unfolding spontaneously from culturally or genetically inherited potentiality, but it is never independent from, or external to, the organic processes. Transcendence in history implies that new things emerge that are not predetermined by biological legacies, but they come in and through the physical, vital reality that we call nature: a reality that is grounded in the divine.

This description of intracosmic transcendence is never a denial of divine involvement, but quite to the contrary, the affirmation of the internal relations between God and creation. Divine causality is internal rather than external to creatures. Within creation, God sustains and directs creation. Even the end *(telos)* toward which creation moves, which is represented by the vision of the reign of God, emerges and is constantly reconstituted within history. In contrast with the classical ideas that place teleological ends in the realm of the unchanging, intracosmic transcendence and the concept of the reign of God suggest an interpretation of final causes that are not eternal, external, or predetermined, but rather spring from the complex and dynamic fabric of reality.

Against theological descriptions of creatures that emphasize that their value derives from their dependence on a transcendent (external) source, liberation theologies should insist upon a certain innate worth, even divinity, in their finitude. All creation is grounded in and linked to God, who is its source. However, that relation is not something external or superadded to reality, but something inherent to reality. Thus, the value of human life does not reside outside of it, in something to which one may or may not relate or respond; this vision places the value of human life *in* human life. Ellacuría asserts that God's creation is the "grafting *ad extra* of Trinitarian life itself," and thus "each thing, within its own limits, is a limited way of being God. This limited way is precisely the *nature* of each thing" (italics added).[39] It is not "simply that God is in all things, as essence, presence, and potential," but that the trinitarian life is "*intrinsic* to all things" (italics added).[40] Things are inherently linked to the divine.

In this model human beings are essentially open to other things and to one another; human beings become in relation to others. That openness may lead to the actualization of possibilities that result in greater creative possibilities as well as to the foreclosure of those possibilities. In the very openness to other things and to others, human beings are indeed in contact with the divine fountain. However, God and reality are not the same thing: God transcends in reality. To open oneself to "God's more" entails an awareness of divine transcendence in all beings. An awareness of intracosmic transcendence leads humans toward the rest of creation, not away from it. Opening to God's more not only prevents each human person from closing around himself or herself, from absolutizing her or his own particularity, but also calls that person to turn toward creation and toward the human other.

EMBODIED MYSTERIES

I suggested above that recovering a relational notion of divine transcendence affects not only our ideas about God, but should also help us reconceive human beings as transcendent creatures: irreducible to social and representational systems, as always unfinished, in the process of becoming in relation to their ever-evolving contexts, and embraced by the mystery of their sacramental relationship to the divine.

To say that a person is irreducible to social systems (dominant or marginalized) is to affirm that although the system puts us into categories and those categories do affect who we might become, we are not reducible to them. No name or category can possibly describe all a person is. Not because we are absolutely separate from the system or from one another, but because persons exceed all systems. Their transcendence is neither abstract nor otherworldly, but openness at the heart of relation.

Even those communal aspects that most influence the becoming of subjectivity are inherently dynamic, and so are our relationships with them. Identity is thus never completed. Each aspect of a person's identity develops in relation to realities that transcend that person's particularity, but which he or she also transcends—community, country of origin, sexual identity. For instance, the realities of my own community—its past history, its language, the geography in which I feel most at home—all embrace me, not only as a *past* reality, but as something which I continue to relate to, to be transformed by, and to transform. And yet I never grasp it, just as it never completely defines me. *I* am always in process, always unfinished.

If we recognize this transcendence in our bodies, and even in the bodies of those who have been marginalized, without losing sight of our embodied historicity, we can also re-envision divine transcendence. Marcella Althaus-Reid finds the seeds for that image of God in her reading of the God of liberation theology. She writes: "Latin American liberation theology, which is based on the search for the materiality of transcendence, knows how God is to be found in the presence of the untouchables. . . . [Transcendence] is God touching its own limits in the untouchables."[41] A theology that grounds the ethical relations between creatures should not reinforce the image creation as *one* self-enclosed thing in relation to an external God, for this may lead us to lose sight of the transcendence of the created other. Instead, we should remember that "through [our] relation to the Other [we] are in touch with God," as Levinas asserts.[42] If God is to be found in the Other, in the "presence of the untouchables," if God links us to the other and embraces the very otherness of the other, ethics becomes a central concern for theology.

NOTES

[1] Robert McLean, *Old Spain in New America* (New York: Association Press, 1916), 134.

[2] Orlando Espín's *The Faith of the People* is a notable exception. Indeed, some of the challenges raised in that book have not yet been addressed constructively. See Orlando O. Espín, *The Faith of the People: Theological Reflections on Popular Catholicism* (Maryknoll, NY: Orbis Books, 1997).

[3] Anthony B. Pinn and Benjamin Valentin, *The Ties That Bind: African American and Hispanic American/Latino/a Theologies in Dialogue* (New York: Continuum, 2001).

[4] Justo L. González, "Characteristics of Latino Protestant Theology," in *Hispanic Christianity within Mainline Protestant Traditions*, ed. Paul Barton and David Maldonado (Decatur, GA: Asociación para la Educación Teológica Hispana, 1998), 13.

[5] Espín, *The Faith of the People,* 4.

[6] González, "Characteristics of Latino Protestant Theology," 99.

[7] Orlando Espín's interrogation of the "conquering God" is another example of deconstructive engagement with this doctrine (Espín, *The Faith of the People*, 36–37).

⁸ Ibid., 26.

⁹ Roberto Goizueta, "U.S. Hispanic Popular Catholicism as Theopoetics," in *Hispanic/Latino Theology*, ed. Ada María Isasi-Díaz and Fernando F. Segovia (Minneapolis: Fortress Press, 1996), 287. I confess being a bit puzzled as I try to imagine what that "before" might be, and this is perhaps an irreducible perplexity that theology shall never lose sight of: the very statement of the priority of participation in theopoetic power is a way of "making sense" of our experience.

¹⁰ Ibid., 264.

¹¹ Espín, *The Faith of the People*, 7. In this view, for instance, "Popular Christian religion . . . embodies and epistemologically organizes these daily relationships and symbolically expresses their connections to/with the broader social networks—including the 'sacred' networks—through rites, beliefs, objects, and experiences of people's religion" (6).

¹² I suspect that Protestant theologies tend to be more affected by this lack of explicit discussions of the God-world relationship, for the emphasis of Catholic theologies on sacramentality lends itself to such cosmological discussion.

¹³ My work has focused on the relationship between theological understandings of the otherness of God (divine transcendence) and constructions of interhuman difference and engaged the ethical critiques and reconstruction of models of interhuman difference to offer a theological model of relational transcendence. The project assents to the feminist and liberationist critiques of images of God as absolute simplicity, unchangeability, and unaffected independence from the world, which, they argue, mirror and legitimize models of subjectivity that value purity, permanent self-identity, and autonomy against multiplicity, embodiment, and relationality. But the project also affirms the value of difference that the concept of divine transcendence implies, and thus it seeks to reconceive transcendence in relation, rather than to abandon the notion. The insights of Latin American liberation theologies and Latina/o theologies are indispensable for such reconstruction. I will here highlight two aspects of that theological proposal: the contours of an intra-cosmic understanding of transcendence, and the view of otherness in relation that it entails. See Mayra Rivera, *The Touch of Transcendence: A Postcolonial Theology of God* (Louisville, KY: Westminster John Knox, 2007).

¹⁴ Virgilio Elizondo, *Galilean Journey: The Mexican-American Promise* (Maryknoll, N.Y. Orbis Books, 1993).

¹⁵ Homi K. Bhabha, *The Location of Culture* (London: Routledge, 1994).

¹⁶ There are also significant critiques against the use of the category, both in Latina/o theologies and in ethnic studies. These critiques foreground, on the one hand, the origins of the category as a derogative term against so-called mixed races (Robert J. C. Young, *Colonial Desire: Hybridity in Theory, Culture and Race* [London: Routledge, 1995]), and, on the other hand, the ways in which *mestizaje* has been used to exclude Africans or indigenous communities from nationalist definitions of identity.

¹⁷ Elizondo, *Galilean Journey*, 8, 9, 12.

¹⁸ Ibid., 2. Elizondo's use of *mestizaje* could be strengthened by an elucidation of how dominant views—social, philosophical, and theological—conceal and repress certain aspects of reality. Hybridity is not originally created in a colonial encounter; it is always already there. The Spaniards and the Anglos were hybrids. Furthermore, Spaniard and Anglo as group identities are—no less than *mestizo*—impure, and created as a product of the encounter with what they label other. Colonial powers have

hidden their dependence—economic and conceptual—on subordinated peoples behind ideas of pure origin, self-purity, and absolute (knowable) difference. When used as a distinctive trait of Latina/o communities, *mestizaje* denotes more accurately an attitude toward otherness than a unique biological feature.

[19] Ibid., 58.

[20] Enrique Dussel, *Ethics and the Theology of Liberation* (Maryknoll, NY: Orbis Books, 1978), 139.

[21] Roberto S. Goizueta, *Liberation, Method, and Dialogue: Enrique Dussel and North American Theological Discourse,* ed. Susan Thistlethwaite, American Academy of Religion Academy Series (Atlanta: Scholars Press, 1988), 166.

[22] For an analysis of the problematic implications of the idea of exteriority, see Rivera, *The Touch of Transcendence.*

[23] I am not claiming that the image of the *mestizo* should replace the other in our theological discussions as the locus of revelations, but rather that conceptualizations of difference shall be complexified based on the insights gained from discussions of hybridity.

[24] Roberto Goizueta explains that identity, as inextricable from community, extends "not only spatially but also temporally: that community includes my ancestors as well as my progeny and their progeny" (Roberto S. Goizueta, *Caminemos con Jesús: Toward a Hispanic/Latino Theology of Accompaniment* [Maryknoll, NY: Orbis Books, 1995], 52).

[25] Jorge Aquino identifies what he calls an "ambivalent identity" as a shortcoming of Roberto Goizueta's *Caminemos con Jesús* (see Jorge A. Aquino, "The Prophetic Horizon of Latino Theology," in *Rethinking Latino(a) Religion and Identity*, ed. Miguel A. de la Torre and Gastón Espinosa [Cleveland: Pilgrim Press, 2006], 101–125). In my view, however, the irresolvable identity that marks Latina/o identity is not its shortcoming, but a crucial insight that informs (or should inform) our epistemology. Chicana scholars have deeply explored and fruitfully employed this ambivalence to critique dominant modernist epistemologies. (See, for instance, Chela Sandoval, *Methodology of the Oppressed* [Minneapolis: University of Minnesota Press, 2000]). Latina/o theologies might still explore this ambivalence with greater self-critical subtlety.

[26] Goizueta, *Caminemos con Jesús*, 50.

[27] Ibid.

[28] Ibid., 64.

[29] Ibid., 179.

[30] Ignacio Ellacuría, "The Historicity of Christian Salvation," in *Mysterium Liberationis: Fundamental Concepts of Liberation Theology,* ed. Ignacio Ellacuría and Jon Sobrino (Maryknoll, NY: Orbis Books, 1993), 254.

[31] Ignacio Ellacuría, "Historia de la salvación y salvación en la historia," in *Escritos Teológicos* (San Salvador: UCA Editores, 2000), 528.

[32] Goizueta, *Caminemos con Jesús*, 49.

[33] Justo L. González, *Mañana: Christian Theology from a Hispanic Perspective* (Nashville, TN: Abingdon Press, 1990).

[34] For a detailed analysis of the relation between Ellacuría and Zubiri, focusing on its impact on Ellacuría's notion of transcendence, see Michael E. Lee, "Liberation Theology's Transcendent Moment: The Work of Xavier Zubiri and Ignacio Ellacuría as Noncontrastive Discourse," *Journal of Religion* 83, no. 2 (2003).

[35] Ignacio Ellacuría, *Filosofía de la realidad histórica* (San Salvador: UCA Editores, 1990), 31.

[36] Ellacuría, "The Historicity of Christian Salvation," 254.

[37] Ibid., 263–264, 254.

[38] Ibid., 254.

[39] Ibid., 276. See also Xavier Zubiri, *El hombre y Dios*, 7th ed. (Madrid: Fundación Xavier Zubiri and Alianza Editorial, 2003), 307–324.

[40] Ellacuría, "Historicity of Christian Salvation," 277.

[41] Marcella Althaus-Reid, "El Todado (Le Toucher): Sexual Irregularities in the Translation of God," in *Derrida and Religion: Other Testaments*, ed. Y. Sherwood and K. Hart (New York: Routledge, 2004), 394.

[42] Emmanuel Levinas, *Difficult Freedom: Essays in Judaism* (Baltimore: Johns Hopkins University Press, 1990), 17.

PART II

RELATING BIBLE AND TRADITION
Can Latinas/os Do It Differently?

3

The Word Became Flesh and the Flesh Becomes Word

Notes toward a U.S. Latino/a Theology of Revelation

Jean-Pierre Ruiz

In the beginning was the Word; so it states on the first page of one of the most important books known to us. What is meant in that book is that the Word of God is the source of all creation. But surely the same could be said, figuratively speaking, of every human action? And indeed, words can be said to be the very source of our being, and in fact the very substance of the cosmic life form we call man. Spirit, the human soul, our self awareness, our ability to generalize and think in concepts, to perceive the world as the world (and not just as our locality), and lastly, our capacity for knowing that we will die—and living in spite of that knowledge: surely all these are mediated or actually created by words?

If the Word of God is the source of God's entire creation, then that part of God's creation which is the human race exists as such only thanks to another of God's miracles—the miracle of human speech. And if this miracle is the key to the history of mankind, then it is also the key to the history of society. Indeed, it might well be the former just because it is the latter. For the fact is that if they were not a means of communication between two or more human "I"s, then words would probably not exist at all.

—Václav Havel, "Words about Words"

I am grateful to the participants at the ACHTUS 2007 Colloquium for their comments and recommendations on an earlier version of this essay, which I presented for discussion in that setting.

For things above the earth we learn to pine,
Our spirits yearn for revelation,
Which nowhere burns with purer beauty blent,
Than here in the New Testament.
To ope the ancient text an impulse strong
Impels me, and its sacred lore,
With honest purpose to explore,
And render into my loved German tongue.
(He opens a volume, and applies himself to it.)
'Tis writ, "In the beginning was the Word!"
I pause, perplex'd! Who now will help afford?
I cannot the mere Word so highly prize;
I must translate it otherwise,
If by the spirit guided as I read.
"In the beginning was the Sense!" Take heed,
The import of this primal sentence weigh,
Lest thy too hasty pen be led astray!
Is force creative then of Sense the dower?
"In the beginning was the Power!"
Thus should it stand: yet, while the line I trace.
A something warns me, once more to efface.
The spirit aids! from anxious scruples freed,
I write, "In the beginning was the Deed!"

—JOHANN WOLFGANG VON GOETHE, *FAUST*

INTRODUCTION

It was not long after I accepted the invitation extended by Orlando Espín to enter into conversation at this colloquium with Leticia Guardiola-Sáenz and with all of you that I came to notice the strange friendship between U.S. Christian Latina/o biblical scholars and the Johannine literature. This is especially curious, given the fact that our numbers as teachers and scholars continue to be as disproportionately small in the academy as they are disproportionately large in the churches. To be sure, there are some of our number whose efforts have focused on the Pauline literature (Efraín Agosto, for example).[1] Others among us have paid attention to a variety of texts from the Hebrew Bible (Francisco García-Treto, for example).[2] Yet there does seem to be a particular relationship between U.S. Christian Latina/o biblical scholars and the Johannine literature, a relationship for which the metaphor of book as friend applies especially well.

Canadian Jewish New Testament scholar Adele Reinhartz successfully develops this metaphor in the second chapter of her book on the Fourth

Gospel, *Befriending the Beloved Disciple: A Jewish Reading of the Gospel of John*. Reinhartz notes that literary critic Wayne Booth, in formulating what he calls "ethical criticism," holds

> that our interactions with books parallel our interactions with friends in the "real" world, not only in the pleasures they bring but also in the ethical stances they foster. . . . Booth warns us not to take our literary friend for granted, not to drift along in easy, unquestioning companionship. He exhorts us, rather, to engage with books fully, honestly, and with commitment, to address rather than to bracket the ethical considerations with which our human relationships are fraught.[3]

Indeed the category of friendship seems especially appropriate to describe a reader's critical engagement with the Johannine literature, for Sharon Ringe has shown us clearly how wisdom and friendship are deeply intertwined and central categories in the Fourth Gospel.[4]

Among U.S. Latina/o biblical scholars, none has entered into a deeper friendship with the Johannine literature than Fernando F. Segovia. Beginning with his 1978 Notre Dame doctoral dissertation, directed by Elisabeth Schüssler Fiorenza (who was herself the student of a distinguished German scholar of the Johannine literature, Rudolf Schnackenburg), Segovia has established himself as a preeminent scholar of the Fourth Gospel and as a catalyst for the transformation of biblical scholarship as this discipline entered the twenty-first century.[5] At the end of *The Farewell of the Word: The Johannine Call to Abide*, his important literary and rhetorical critical study of the farewell discourse in John 13—16, Segovia modestly concludes that the project he set out to accomplish remains unfinished. It is unfinished not only because it defers consideration of John 17 ("the climax of the farewell speech, the farewell prayer of the departing Word of God") to a promised future project, but more important, because, as Segovia admits, "I have deliberately left out of consideration my own perspective as a reader." He goes on to explain:

> This perspective could be described in a number of different ways. It is sufficient to say in this context that this reader was born and raised in the Third World (in Latin America, to be exact) and now lives in the First World (in North America). The reader thus stands within a distinct and peculiar setting, that of the Hispanic-American, and as such belongs to a group that is bicultural and faced at all times and at a fundamental level with socioeconomic deprivation, sociopolitical and socioreligious exclusion, and sociocultural disdain and assimilation. For this reader, therefore, the call to abide and endure in a world of oppression represents much more than an ancient option: it continues to be a living dilemma with profound cultural and religious dimensions. For this reader, the similar call of the Fourth Gospel—its reach, strategy,

and applicability—is open to complete analysis and evaluation in terms of the context and praxis of his group, to a reading of and for liberation. However, such an analysis must remain outside the scope of the present volume. This study represents but a first and basic step toward such a reading. The next step must be what I call an exercise in intercultural dialogue from the perspective of liberation and with the aim of liberation, which is after all a fundamental goal of the Fourth Gospel (8:32).[6]

These words, brought to a close with a citation of John 8:32 ("you will know the truth, and the truth will make you free"), mark an important shift in the orientation of Segovia's work as an academic interpreter of the Bible, a shift that Segovia himself has charted with great candor and to which he has contributed significantly, from the dominance of historical criticism (with its deliberate suppression of the personal voice), to cultural studies (with the irruption of the personal voice), to postcolonial criticism.[7] Segovia explains, "At a fundamental level I have used my life story as a foundation for my work as a critic in biblical studies, as a theologian in theological studies, and as a critic in cultural studies."[8] Indeed, Segovia's forthrightness about the ways in which his own career as a biblical scholar, constructive theologian, and cultural critic has intersected with rapidly shifting currents in the academy and in the church over the last several decades has been important in how he has directly and indirectly mentored more junior scholars—both his own doctoral students at Vanderbilt and others who have had the benefit of his wry wit and sage advice about when and under what circumstances it is appropriate for the novice racial/ethnic minority academic to be either as crafty as a snake or as innocent as a pigeon (Mt 10:16).[9]

"OUR SPIRITS YEARN FOR REVELATION"

On a number of occasions I have had the privilege of engaging with Fernando Segovia in the uniquely rich and productive *teología de conjunto* that marks conversations during the ACHTUS colloquia in ways that make them both more provocative and more productive (and more animated) than the zero-sum, take-no-prisoners posturing and politicking that is typical fare at other gatherings of academics. To set the stage for the concerns of the present discussion, I would like to recall a couple of pertinent observations that were precipitated by that earlier conversation. At that time I noted:

Over the last twenty or so years, U.S. Hispanic theologies have just begun to reckon with the place of the Bible in U.S. Hispanic religious experience and in theological discourse that takes that rich and diverse experience as a point of departure. Something analogous to the interdisciplinary research project headed by Vincent L. Wimbush, *African*

Americans and the Bible, remains a real desideratum for U.S. Hispanic Christian theologians.[10]

Taking Segovia's proposal for intercultural criticism seriously (as a strategy for reading across, undergirded with a hermeneutics of otherness and engagement) and stretching it beyond limitation to the Christian biblical canon, I asked a question about which I continue to brood:

> What are we to make of the conflicting claims of Jews, Christians, and Muslims about the different texts that constitute *scripture* for each of the three so-called Abrahamic religious traditions? Strictly speaking, such a discussion of reading across canons moves us beyond the well-charted precincts of biblical studies and into what remains, at least for U.S. Hispanic theologians, the unfamiliar territory of interreligious dialogue.[11]

While I submit that the challenge of reading across canons remains an urgent issue for interreligious dialogue and understanding—and not only for Latinas/os—we U.S. Latino/a Christian biblical scholars and theologians have a bit of homework to do before we can arrive at the table of interreligious dialogue fully equipped to listen with open minds and to contribute with respectful voices. One such prerequisite task—an indispensable one—is the elaboration of an adequate Latino/a Christian theology of revelation. Surprisingly enough, while passing mention has been made here and there in U.S Latino/a Christian theology of what we assume we mean when we speak of revelation, there has been very little sustained exploration of this foundational notion. For example, in the opening chapter of *The Faith of the People,* Orlando Espín declares, "Jesus of Nazareth definitively reveals God to humankind—and not only reveals but *is* himself the revelation of God."[12] With this affirmation as his starting point, Espín goes on to argue that "in and through the human experience of Jesus of Nazareth, God may be sensed as reaching and touching humankind in a definitive way."[13] As for the Bible, in an article that appeared in the first issue of the *Journal of Hispanic/Latino Theology*, Sixto J. Garcia turned to scripture as one source (among others) of Hispanic theology and affirmed:

> We hold, as a foundational belief, that the Scriptures are the Word of God. To even attempt to engage ourselves in a discussion concerning the interpretation of this statement would be to open a can of hermeneutical worms quite peripheral to our discussion. It is legitimate to say, however, that regardless of the different theological contours that different people might draw concerning "Scriptures as Word of God," we hold in common the normative dimension of the Scriptures (the Scriptures are the soul of all theology) for theological reflection on God's self communication.[14]

It is high time for us to take a deep breath and open the can of worms. After all, during this colloquium the participants were invited to be

> creative and courageous [in their presentations] but to, nevertheless, be realistic and honest in the way they address their respective ecclesial tradition's (doctrinal, theological) positions and expectations on the road to an ecumenical theology. Therefore, this colloquium is not mainly for sharing already known denominational doctrinal/theological positions but, moving beyond this, to elaborate these positions honestly in ways that can (given further reflection and dialogue) lead to Latina/o breakthroughs that will yield an ecumenical theology.[15]

"I PAUSE, PERPLEX'D! WHO NOW WILL HELP AFFORD?"

As crafty academicians, we might feel tempted to sidestep the charge that we have been given to be "creative and courageous" by retreating behind a smokescreen of philological or hermeneutical jargon to what passes for scholarly disputation in venues like the annual meeting of the Society of Biblical Literature (SBL). Taken at face value, SBL sessions and panels are the very models of ecumenical and interreligious harmony at the very highest levels of academic discourse, for at the SBL it matters not at all whether one is male or female; Jew or Greek; Catholic, Presbyterian, Pentecostal, Unitarian, Adventist, or Wiccan. Side by side, believers, nonbelievers, and those who find themselves somewhere in between debate energetically over the sense and significance of texts and contexts that matter a great deal to all concerned. Truth be told, though, this is only possible because participants are expected to check their denominational affiliations at the door and to refrain from the sort of serious attention to confessional differences that might trouble the waters. How all of this may or may not be affected by the unilateral decision by the American Academy of Religion (AAR) to hold its annual meeting separately from the SBL remains to be seen, even though the rescinding of the decision by AAR leadership means this will only be a temporary state of affairs. On the other hand, the SBL has provided its Latina/o members with an unintended fringe benefit, inasmuch as our significant underrepresentation as academically credentialed Latinas/os in the "guild" of professional interpreters of the Bible has led us to seek one another out and to make common cause with African American and Asian American members of the SBL on the basis of our underrepresentation, without regard for what might divide us in terms of our different affiliations (or non-affiliations) with a variety of faith communities.

On top of that, our (sometimes multiply) hyphenated condition as Latinos/as in the United States has brought us together under the auspices of such deliberately interdenominational strategic coalitions as the HTI and the HSP, so that our differently inflected Spanish and English, our Spanglish and our Inglañol, our status as immigrants from Mexico or as refugees from Cuba or as colonial subjects from Puerto Rico, or as Tejanos, matter far less than our shared heritage as sons and daughters of the Iberian colonization of this hemisphere, our present experience as members of multiply marginalized communities, and our commitment to advance biblical, theological, and religious studies for the next generation of Latinos/as. In that respect, we U.S. Latino/a Christian biblical scholars are challenged to find a common idiom with theologians and scholars of religion who share our heritage and our condition, even if we are not fluent in the arcana of one another's disciplinary jargon.[16]

All that being said, I suggest that this colloquium provides us with a timely opportunity to take at least a tentative step or two in the direction of the articulation of a U.S. Latina/o Christian theology of revelation that is ecumenically forthright inasmuch as it acknowledges historical and confessional differences in how we have come to understand divine self-disclosure, and that speaks "from the heart of our people" in ways that reflect our respectful attention to the daily experience of those communities with which our own lives are intertwined. This is neither the time nor the place to revisit the sixteenth century and to parse with the benefit of centuries of hindsight the tension between scripture and tradition, as did Luther on the one hand and the fathers of the Council of Trent on the other.[17] This is not to say that history is without important lessons for us. Yet the circumstances that now precipitate a twenty-first-century discussion of what it might take to construct a Latina/o Christian theology of revelation have more to do with the pressing present realities of our people. Thus, for example, whatever one might think of the recently released study by the Pew Hispanic Center and the Pew Forum on Religion and Public Life entitled *Changing Faiths: Latinos and the Transformation of American Religion*, we Latino/a biblical scholars need to reckon with the study's claim that

> more than three quarters of Latino evangelicals say the Bible is the word of God and is to be taken literally, word for word. Among Latino Catholics and other Christians, by contrast, fewer than half hold that view. Although Hispanic Catholics are less likely than evangelicals to view the Bible as literally true, they still stand out compared with non-Latino Catholics. Among Latino Catholics, for example, 49% interpret the Bible as literally true, a much higher figure than among non-Hispanic Catholics, only 18% of whom share this view.[18]

While our academic reflexes might prompt us to dismiss this finding as a matter of the naive, unenlightened fundamentalism of the grassroots, our better judgment ought to keep such smug elitism in check, prompting us instead to think much more generously and more deeply about the friendships that our faith communities have formed with the texts that they revere as sacred scripture. After all, as Wilfred Cantwell Smith reminds us:

No plant is "objectively" a weed: the term designates any plant that grows uncultivated in a situation where it is unwanted by human beings. No person is a husband in and of himself; he is a husband in correlation with another person, in this case a wife. No one is a king except in relation to a certain society and form of government; no building is a temple except in relation to a given community of persons. Fundamental, we suggest, to a new understanding of scripture is the recognition that no text is a scripture in itself and as such. People— a given community—make a text into scripture, or keep it scripture: by treating it in a certain way. I suggest: *scripture is a human activity.* . . . The quality of being scripture is not an attribute of texts. It is a characteristic of the attitude of persons—of groups of persons—to what outsiders perceive as texts. It denotes a relationship between a people and a text.[19]

The place of the Bible in the life of our people, the friendship—as it were—between our people and the Bible, invites those of us who profess to theorize and theologize "from the heart of our people" to take that friendship seriously and to reflect carefully about what that friendship says about our communities and the texts they recognize and constitute as scripture.

At this juncture, I want to recall the especially close friendship between U.S. Christian Latina/o biblical scholars and the Johannine literature, present company included.[20] I do so in order to sharpen the focus of our discussion about what it might mean to construct a U.S. Latino/a Christian theology of revelation by focusing on one distinctive portion of the biblical canon on which our efforts as professional interpreters of the Bible have been focused. The fact that Leticia Guardiola-Sáenz and Francisco Lozada, Jr., have both devoted attention to the Fourth Gospel in their research has not a little to do with the academic version of apostolic succession whereby both were students of Fernando Segovia at Vanderbilt.[21] For her part, Sharon Ringe makes it clear how profoundly her own work on John's Gospel, *Wisdom's Friends,* was influenced by her experiences of teaching at the Universidad Bíblica Latinoamericana in Costa Rica, experiences through which she has come to a deep understanding of what *acompañamiento* means. That experience, she notes, was a key event in the biography of her book.[22] If there is any truth in the saying *Dime con quién andas y te diré quién eres*, we learn quite a lot about Sharon Ringe from the company she keeps with the HTI and (together with R. S. Sugirtharajah, Fernando Segovia, Kwok Pui-lan, Ralph Broadbent, and Marcella Althaus-Reid) as a member of the editorial board for the Sheffield Academic Press series entitled the Bible and Postcolonialism.[23] Francisco Lozada and I were privileged to be among the twelve participants in the project—under the auspices of the Center for the Study of Latino/a Catholicism at the University of San Diego—that resulted in *Futuring Our Past: Explorations in the Theology of Tradition.* Several summers ago Leticia Guardiola-Sáenz and I had the privilege of teaching in the HSP when it convened at

Fuller Theological Seminary in Pasadena. That summer she taught a course on the Fourth Gospel, while I taught a course on the book of Revelation, with both courses emphasizing and encouraging Latina/o readings of these biblical texts with our students. Not long after that, Leticia and I were among the participants in a project (directed by Randall Bailey, Tat-siong Benny Liew, and Fernando Segovia) that brought together a group of African American, Asian American, and U.S. Latina/o biblical scholars to read *as* African Americans, Asian Americans, and U.S. Latinos/as, and to read *with* one another in order to attend to the convergent and divergent reading strategies that we adopted.

With that sort of history of reading and writing *en conjunto*, we find ourselves on solid common ground to begin to consider—with our readings of the Fourth Gospel as a test case—at least some of the elements that might be involved in articulating a U.S. Latina/o Christian theology of revelation that reckons adequately with the place of the Bible among Latino/a Christians.

"TO OPEN THE ANCIENT TEXT AN IMPULSE STRONG IMPELS ME, AND ITS SACRED LORE, WITH HONEST PURPOSE TO EXPLORE"

Leticia readily acknowledges what happens, for better and for worse, when people read the Bible:

Historically, the biblical text has proven to be powerful. The Bible has gone beyond its temporal and spatial boundaries not just for good, but also for evil, including massive destruction. Because of some evil interpretations of the biblical text, many people have been erased from the face of the earth. Others have been subjugated and oppressed for not conforming to hegemonic, often biblically grounded ideologies. Evidently, there is more power in the way biblical texts are consumed by readers than we would like to acknowledge. The Bible, read by a variety of readers, has certainly proven to be not only redemptive but also destructive, and all the possibilities in between.[24]

She proceeds to substantiate this affirmation by analyzing John 7:53—8:11, the narrative of the woman accused of adultery who is brought before Jesus by the scribes and Pharisees: "Although interpretations of the story of the accused woman might seem harmless and might not have caused the physical extermination of a people, the fact is that they have been equally destructive since they reinforce the patriarchal double-standard morality that oppresses women."[25] For her, the problem lies not with the biblical text itself but with the deficient ways in which the narrative has been understood. With appropriately postmodern academic modesty, Guardiola-Sáenz offers a "cultural, regional reading of Jn 7.53—8.11 from the hybrid experience of a bicultural Mexican-American subject from the borderlands, living in the diaspora" and admits (as any responsible reader should) that the reading she proposes "represents only an alternative reading, which is by no means objective or universal."[26] According to the reading of John 7:53—8:11 that she proposes

> the Johannine Jesus seems to live between borders, in a hybrid space which is an experience similar to that of Hispanics/Latin Americans in the postcolonial and neo-colonial era. Jesus, *the border-crosser*, the traveler between cities and villages, between heaven and earth, between suffering and bliss, comes to redeem the border-crosser who refuses to conform to the limits and borders of a society that has ignored her voice, her body and the borders of her identity as the Other. . . . By confronting the Pharisees and addressing the accused woman, Jesus brings a past of oppressive traditions and a silent present of subversiveness into an in-between space that innovates and interrupts the performance of the present. The new identity of the accused woman announces the interstitial creativity of the future: freed from the oppressive borders of the system, she is sent as a border-crosser, a model for building the future of the hybrid Johannine community and a model for a better life. On his part, Jesus, the hybrid par excellence in John's Gospel, contests all contact zones. He removes the structures that have been adopted by those in power and acts in ways that respond to a reality different from the one in which he is located.[27]

As a reader of John 7:53—8:11, I am less than fully convinced that the proposed reading unveils an emancipatory energy in the text that the prior history of interpretation of this troublesome text may have concealed or obscured. As a compliant reader of John 7:53—8:11, Guardiola-Sáenz may be more inclined to give the Fourth Gospel the benefit of the doubt. Yet by postulating a correspondence between the experience of the first-century Jesus as border-crosser with the experiences of "Hispanics/Latin Americans in the postcolonial and neo-colonial era," and by locating the energy of this text in its emancipation of the accused woman "from the oppressive borders of the system," this reading itself quite unintentionally leaves open the possible risk of perpetuating oppressive attitudes and behaviors by twenty-first century Christians with regard to twenty-first-century Jews.[28]

In his more recent writing about the Fourth Gospel, it seems to me that Fernando Segovia is much less likely than Leticia Guardiola-Sáenz to concede the benefit of the doubt to John. Segovia's "Dialogue with John" in his essay "The Gospel at the Close of the Century" focuses on three positions that he regards as fundamental to the Fourth Gospel: "(1) its characterization of the world; (2) its ideology of chosenness; (3) its view of life in the world."[29] With respect to its characterization of the world, Segovia recognizes that the Fourth Gospel adopts an emphatically negative posture:

Prior to the coming of the Word, the world is said to be in darkness; despite its creation by the Word, the world is described as in the power of supra-human evil spirits; with the coming of the Word, hatred of God emerges as its overriding and distinguishing characteristic; before the departure of the Word, the world is altogether excluded from the prayer of petition and intercession on the part of the Word.[30]

Reading the Fourth Gospel's characterization of the world from the diaspora, that is, as someone born in Latin America and living in the United States (and thus inhabiting two spaces at one and the same time), leads Segovia to recognize, first of all, that "from the perspective of the diaspora, the world of everyday life emerges as deeply divided: overridingly hostile, but calling forth struggle and resistance; fateful and inescapable, yet constantly arousing hopes of and strategies for change; a world of ultimate resignation and endless defiance." Thus Segovia finds that "there is much in John that resonates with the reality and experience of the diaspora: the world as fundamentally evil and unjust." Yet Segovia parts company with the Fourth Gospel's character-ization of the world, a characterization that he finds wanting. For him, there is "something missing in John. From the diaspora, such a stark view of the world is counterbalanced throughout by a clear and irrepressible thirst for justice and wellbeing, a desire to make the world a more pleasant and righ-teous place in which to dwell. And this, I must confess, I do not find in the Gospel."[31]

A similar tension between engagement and otherness surfaces in Segovia's dialogue with John with respect to the Fourth Gospel's ideology of chosenness: the followers of the Word are God's chosen ones, set over against the Word-rejecting world. Thus, this Gospel "presents human beings in terms of bi-nary oppositions: world versus those not of the world; children of the evil one vis-à-vis children of the Father; those in darkness versus the enlightened ones."[32] For those who read the Fourth Gospel in the diaspora, there is "a perception of one's voice and face as not of the world, as somehow set apart and specially enlightened," and so "there is much from the Gospel that reso-nates: the utter otherness of the Word of God in the world." Yet through the lens of Segovia's hermeneutic of otherness and engagement, what one hand gives the other takes away.[33] Thus, "on the basis of hard experience," a diasporic engagement with the Fourth Gospel approaches the text with "a profound suspicion of all engulfing narratives, over/against hermeneutics, and totalizing ideologies: in the end, with any ideology of chosenness, one is never far from a *Herrenvolk* concept, a concept of imperial manifest des-tiny," for the other face of an ideology of chosenness is the ideology of exclu-sion, and so Segovia finds that "there is much in the Gospel that repels."[34]

Turning to consider the Fourth Gospel's view of life in the world, on the one hand Segovia is not surprised to conclude that on the basis of its charac-terization of the world as evil and unjust, and the concomitant ideology of chosenness that regards the followers of the Word as in the world but not of the world ("they do not belong to the world, just as I do not belong to the world" [Jn 17–16]), the Fourth Gospel provides "no basic charter for change in the world or transformation of the world." Instead, "the call in the end is for patient and strategic abiding and endurance in the face of oppression, for eyes to be fixed on the real home, the real world, of the chosen ones: the house of the Father," and "in the meantime, one continues, under the harshest of circumstances, to attempt to bring light to the world, to attract people to the circle of loved ones, and to engage in love for and service of one another."[35] Reading from the diaspora, Segovia finds much that is appealing in this outlook: "Given our position in the world, the call for patient and strategic abiding and enduring again finds resonance. It is, after all, a call for a face, a voice, a home—a call with which we can readily identify."[36] Yet the appeal of this outlook is not without cost. For Segovia, "there is much here that disappoints: it is not on an other-world that we want to fix our eyes but on this-world. We remain very much in this world; we know that it is not the way it is solely by the will of God; and we wish to change it, alter it, transform it, with wellbeing and justice in mind. We look for a worldly face, a worldly voice, and a worldly home as well."[37]

In the end, caught in the tension between attraction to the Fourth Gospel's characterization of the world and a simultaneous resistance to the strategy it proposes, Segovia admits:

> I find myself both nodding and shaking my head as I read the Gospel. Out of my own praxis, I find myself in great sympathy with the point of view of the implied author: how can one speak of the presence of God, of justice and wellbeing, in the world? Out of my own praxis, I also find myself in profound disagreement with such a point of view: speak one must, over and over again, against all odds, for change and transformation, for wellbeing and justice, and for a God who needs to be very much present everywhere. From my diaspora, then, the significance of the Gospel, in terms of its assessment of the problem, remains unquestionable; its relevance, in terms of its proposed solution, must, however, be radically questioned and actively resisted. At the turn of the century, I can only go so far with it.[38]

Read according to the taxonomy that Reinhartz proposes, Segovia's approach to the Fourth Gospel through the lens of what he describes as a hermeneutics of the diaspora yields what Reinhartz would describe as an engaged reading, where the reader understands the befriended text as other. An engaged reading with the text-as-friend, Reinhartz suggests, "involves probing directly some of our deepest convictions, and our most profound differences. Between real friends, an engaged encounter would have two characteristics: reciprocity and acceptance of one another's otherness."[39] Unlike Leticia Guardiola-Saénz, whose Mexican American feminist reading of John 7:53— 8:11 unlocks "redemptive power" that is ultimately located *in* the biblical text (a redemptive power that is redeemed, as it were, by being read from the borderlands), Segovia's reading turns *against* the biblical text to confront what he finds wanting in its vision of the world and in its prescription for how readers are to conduct themselves in the light of that vision.

For his part, Francisco Lozada introduces his intercultural reading of John 6 by affirming that his is an engaged reading. He explains: "I read John 6 not for the sake of prescriptive answers on how to live in the tension of universality and particularity, but rather to help me better understand how universality and particularity are manifested in the Johannine story world as well as how to help me better understand this globalized world as a Latino Christian."[40] Like Segovia (who was present when Lozada delivered the original version of this study as his 2002 ACHTUS presidential address in Washington DC), Lozada balances his appreciation of the ways in which the Fourth Gospel frames key questions with caution in his evaluation of the ways in which the Fourth Gospel resolves the very questions it raises. Thus, for example, John 6 unfolds "in such a way that it puts certain interlocutors (crowd, 'the Jews,' and the disciples) in the position to demonstrate and defend their particularity when confronted," by the Johannine Jesus, "with a universalizing viewpoint. In short, their particularity is portrayed negatively."[41] Within the tightly policed borders of Johannine dualism, to disagree with the Johannine Jesus is to become an outsider. Lozada rejects the rhetorical strategy deployed by this text on ethical grounds, and does so with explicit reference to his own specific situation as a reader: "From the point of view of a Latino Christian, I would argue that such a rhetorical dimension of biblical text (John 6) to universalize different beliefs, values, and traditions is inherently dangerous. This has already been witnessed with the colonizing and missionary endeavors to civilize the Other throughout history."[42] Lozada—like Segovia—engages in a genuine dialogue with the text, a give and take in which the text itself never receives the benefit of the doubt. While Lozada's friendship with the Fourth Gospel calls him to be a respectful listener, it also empowers him to stand up to the text to contest its universalizing rhetoric when that rhetoric advocates the suppression of difference and imposes its own particularity on others.

"I CANNOT THE MERE WORD SO HIGHLY PRIZE; I MUST TRANSLATE IT OTHERWISE, IF BY THE SPIRIT GUIDED AS I READ"

Moving well beyond Segovia's studied ambivalence toward the biblical text, in his contribution to *Futuring Our Past* Francisco Lozada contends that social location hermeneutics "has yet to challenge the authority of the biblical tradition." To be sure, "the social location approach has made the biblical tradition much more relevant for many minority groups as a way to recognize their identities within a guild [*of academic biblical interpreters*] that marginalizes these groups as well as their approach to the tradition." Yet, "in the attempt to use the biblical tradition to legitimate their participation within the Christian tradition, it is the biblical tradition that confirms their 'otherness.' Rather than challenging the authority of the biblical tradition, minority readers use the biblical tradition to harmonize their otherness with the otherness represented within the biblical tradition."[43] Thus, for example, Lozada notes that "it is not uncommon to find U.S. Latino/a readers harmonizing their otherness with the marginalized Galilean experience in the gospels . . . or feminist readers paralleling their legitimacy as leaders within today's *ekklesia* with women who held leadership roles within the biblical tradition."[44] Paradoxically, as Lozada observes, the invocation of biblical tradition on the part of individuals who belong to marginalized groups can have the unintended effect of reinforcing their marginalized status: "The biblical tradition is maintaining their otherness every time the tradition is used to challenge— in the name of liberation—an existing, troubling representation."[45]

In order to remedy this vicious circle of marginalization and self-marginalization of and by minoritized groups, Lozada argues that "the notion of authority associated with biblical tradition needs revamping or eradication. It is this notion of authority that contributes strongly to the continued marginalization of many within the present day *ekklesia* and society."[46] While, at first blush, Lozada's call for revamping or even eradicating the notion of the authority of the biblical tradition might seem rather extreme, even he may be somewhat surprised to realize that his proposal is in fact a very Roman Catholic response to the problematic implementation of the Reformation principle *sola scriptura,* according to which the Bible is understood as the *norma normans non normata* in ways that are used to silence other (at least potentially) inspired voices both within and outside the churches.[47] He accurately observes:

> In this period of globalization, when many religious traditions are retreating to their sacred scriptures as a way to identify themselves against homogenization by the world, these traditions are at the same time reinforcing their authority. Christianity is no exception, given the rise of fundamentalism throughout the West with regard to the biblical tradition and also its teachings and practices.[48]

Lozada is by no means advocating the eradication of the biblical tradition, and he is certainly not telling U.S. Latino/a Christians and other minoritized groups to refrain from reading the Bible. Yet he is in fact very emphatically recommending that it would be in the best interest of minoritized communities to develop "alternate stances that aim to de-center and de-authorize the biblical tradition."[49]

I would argue that what Lozada suggests by proposing the de-centering of biblical tradition both presupposes and requires an understanding of revelation (understood as divine self-disclosure) that focuses less on the letter of the biblical *traditum* and less on tradition understood in a passive sense as the *depositum fidei* than it does on a more dynamic notion of *traditio* that encompasses both content and process.[50] According to this suppler notion of *traditio*, divine self-disclosure is by no means limited to the pages of the texts that are constituted as scripture by their reception in the Christian churches. In the words of the Johannine Jesus, "the *pneuma* blows where it chooses, and you hear the sound of it, but you do not know where it comes from or where it goes" (Jn 3:8). Thus an adequate Latino/a Christian theology of revelation (and, for that matter, *any* adequate theology of revelation) must call us to look in the most unlikely places and to listen attentively to the most improbable voices to encounter the incarnate *Logos* and the indwelling spirit.

What might such a de-centering of the biblical tradition look like in conversation with the many millions of U.S. Latina/o Christians for whom the biblical tradition is key to their identity and self-understanding as Christians? I suggest that what is called for, *inter alia,* is something beyond a unilateral homiletics of correlation, whereby we are invited to read our stories, our lived daily experience, in the light of the biblical tradition. Indeed, because that biblical tradition itself affirms that the Word became flesh and dwelt among us, our own stories and our own lived daily experiences are themselves brimming with revelatory potential and power.[51] The biblical tradition must not be invoked in ways that displace or eclipse other stories, or in ways that keep people from entering into dialogue with the biblical tradition, and a deficient reading of *sola scriptura* cannot be allowed to set boundaries beyond which God's spirit cannot soar. Thus, as Leticia Guardiola-Sáenz suggests, the borderlands can be a locus of divine self-disclosure, and a space where God's redemptive power is proclaimed and celebrated against all odds.

"IN THE BEGINNING WAS THE DEED"

I began this essay with a quotation from Goethe's *Faust*. My choice of these lines from *Faust* as food for thought at the outset of these reflections was not merely (or even mainly) to provide the raw material for clever subheadings throughout this essay. In these lines the protagonist wrestles mightily with the translation of the first verse of the first chapter of John's Gospel, "In the beginning was the *logos*." "In the beginning was the Word" fails to satisfy. Likewise, "In the beginning was the Sense" (German *Sinn*, which can be rendered as "sense" or "meaning") falls short; so too "In the beginning was the Power." Finally, it is only "In the beginning was the Deed" that constitutes a satisfying rendering of the first verse of what amounts to a midrash on Genesis 1, where God *speaks* creation into being.[52] The words of John's Prologue are no *mere* words. In his essay "John 1:1–18 as Entrée into Johannine Reality," Fernando Segovia concludes: "I regard the Johannine vision of reality advanced in John 1:1–18 not as an abstract entity, undefined and vaporous, but rather as a concrete perception and expression of reality in all its various components—historical and political, social and cultural, economic and military, intellectual and religious."[53]

Fernando Segovia is in very good company in recognizing the "historical and political, social and cultural, economic and military, intellectual and religious" dimensions of the Prologue of the Fourth Gospel. So too does Václav Havel, an excerpt from whose "Words about Words" is cited at the very beginning of this essay. These remarks formed part of his acceptance speech when he was awarded the Peace Prize of the German Booksellers Association at the Frankfurt Book Fair on October 15, 1989.[54] Playwright, statesman, and Czech patriot, Havel was among the architects of the so-called Velvet Revolution that toppled the totalitarian regime in Czechoslovakia in 1989 without bloodshed. Havel himself was imprisoned three times for his views, spending some five years in prison. The Czechoslovak government, acutely aware of the power of Havel's words to spark change, prohibited the publication of his works. In the end, though, it was the repressive Czechoslovak regime that crumbled, and in December 1989 Havel became president of Czechoslovakia.

In his Peace Prize acceptance speech, Havel goes on to ask: "Is the human word truly powerful enough to change the world and influence history? And even if there were epochs when it did exert such a power, does it still do so today?" His answer is an energetic and unequivocal yes:

> Yes, I do inhabit a system in which words are capable of shaking the entire structure of government, where words can prove mightier than ten military divisions, where Solzhenitsyn's words of truth were regarded as something so dangerous that their author had to be bundled into an airplane and shipped out. Yes, in the part of the world I inhabit, the word "Solidarity" was capable of shaking an entire power bloc.[55]

For Havel, the dangerous power of words is not to be taken lightly:

> My friend František Stárek was sent to prison for two and a half years for producing the independent cultural journal *Voknonot* not on some private printing press but with a squeaky, antediluvian duplicator. Not long before, my friend Ivan Jirous was sentenced to sixteen months' imprisonment for berating, on a typewriter, something that is common knowledge: that our country has seen many judicial murders and that even now it is possible for a person unjustly convicted to die from ill-treatment in prison. My friend Petr Cibulka is in prison for distributing *samizdat* texts and recordings of nonconformist singers and bands.[56]

Those who speak the truth to power know that there is no such thing as a "mere" word, and over the course of history many have come to know the power of words in their own martyred flesh. Latin America has had its own share of martyrs, women and men who, in the words of the Apocalypse of John, "have come through the great ordeal; they have washed their robes and made them white in the blood of the Lamb" (Rv 7:14).[57]

Havel harbors no illusions about the dangerous power of words, of weaponized words as a deadly two-edged sword:

> In truth, the power of words is neither unambiguous nor clear-cut. It is not merely the liberating power of Walesa's words or the warning power of Sakharov's. It is not just the power of [Salman] Rushdie's clearly misconstrued book. The point is that alongside Rushdie's words, we have Khomeini's. Alongside words that electrify society with their freedom and truthfulness, we have words that mesmerize, deceive, inflame, madden, beguile, words that are harmful—lethal, even. The word as arrow.[58]

Like Segovia, Havel does not easily let the words of scripture off the hook:

> But I'd go further and ask an even more provocative question: What was the true nature of Christ's words? Were they the beginning of an era of salvation and among the most powerful cultural impulses in the history of the world—or were they the spiritual source of the crusades, inquisitions, the cultural extermination of the American Indians, and, later, the entire expansion of the white race that was fraught with so many contradictions and had so many tragic consequences, including the fact that most of the human world has been consigned to that wretched category known as the "Third World"? I still tend to think that His words belonged to the former category, but at the same time I cannot ignore the mountain of books which demonstrate that, even in its purest and earliest form, there was something unconsciously encoded in Christianity which, when combined with a thousand other circumstances, including the relative permanence of human nature, could in some way pave the way spiritually, even for the sort of horrors I mentioned.

As daughters and sons of a non-innocent history, U.S. Latina/o Catholics and Protestants are painfully aware of the words that have been used to keep us apart, and of the words we have spoken to and about each other that have led to mutual alienation, hostility, and suspicion. As we begin a conversation toward the elaboration of a Latino/a Christian theology of revelation, let us hope that our words will be well chosen and spirit filled, that they will be as caring as they are challenging, that they will bridge borders that divide us without erasing the differences that enrich us. Let us pray that the texts we have befriended—texts from the biblical tradition and from the textures of our lives—may nourish our friendships with one another.

NOTES

[1] Efraín Agosto, *Servant Leadership: Jesus and Paul* (St. Louis, MO: Chalice Press, 2005).

[2] For example, see Francisco García-Treto, "Hyphenating Joseph: A View of Genesis 39–41 from the Cuban Diaspora," in *Interpreting beyond Borders*, ed. Fernando F. Segovia, 135–145 (Sheffield: Sheffield Academic Press, 2000). Also see C. Gilbert Romero, *Hispanic Devotional Piety: Tracing the Biblical Roots* (Maryknoll, NY: Orbis Books, 1991); Jean-Pierre Ruiz, "Among the Exiles by the River Chebar: A U.S. Hispanic American Reading of Prophetic Cosmology in Ezekiel 1:1–3," *Journal of Hispanic/Latino Theology* 6, no. 2 (November 1998): 43–67.

[3] Adele Reinhartz, *Befriending the Beloved Disciple: A Jewish Reading of the Gospel of John* (New York: Continuum, 2001), 18. Reinhartz refers to Wayne Booth, *The Company We Keep: The Ethics of Fiction* (Los Angeles and Berkeley: University of California Press, 1988). In her study Reinhartz goes on to suggest four readings of the Fourth Gospel, involving four different relationships between reader and text: "The Beloved Disciple as Mentor: A Compliant Reading of the Fourth Gospel" (54–80); "The Beloved Disciple as Opponent: A Resistant Reading of the Fourth Gospel" (81–98); "The Beloved Disciple as Colleague: A Sympathetic Reading of the Fourth Gospel" (99–130); and "The Beloved Disciple as Other: An Engaged Reading of the Fourth Gospel" (131–159). See the assessment of Reinhartz by Francisco Lozada, Jr., "Social Location and Johannine Scholarship: Looking Ahead," in *New Currents through John: A Global Perspective*, ed. Francisco Lozada, Jr., and Tom Thatcher, 192–195 (Atlanta, GA: Society of Biblical Literature, 2006).

[4] Sharon Ringe, *Wisdom's Friends: Community and Christology in the Fourth Gospel* (Louisville, KY: Westminster John Knox Press, 1999).

[5] Fernando F. Segovia, *Love Relationships in the Johannine Tradition: Agape/Agapan in 1 John and the Fourth Gospel,* Society of Biblical Literature Dissertation Series 56 (Chico, CA: Scholars Press, 1982). Appropriately enough, Segovia was the editor of *Toward a New Heaven and a New Earth: Essays in Honor of Elisabeth Schüssler Fiorenza* (Maryknoll, NY: Orbis Books, 2003).

[6] Fernando F. Segovia, *The Farewell of the Word: The Johannine Call to Abide* (Minneapolis: Augsburg Fortress, 1991), 328. Segovia turns to John 17, the last chapter of the Johannine farewell discourse, in "Inclusion and Exclusion in John 17," in *"What Is John?"* vol. 2, *Literary and Social Readings of the Fourth Gospel,* ed. Fernando F. Segovia (Atlanta, GA: Scholars Press, 1998), 183–209.

[7] For those who have eyes to see, Segovia's perspective as a diasporic Antillean reader of John's Gospel irrupts subtly but tellingly on the dust jacket of *The Farewell of the Word*, which depicts a Puerto Rican *santo de palo*, *"Cristo de los Milagros,"* created in 1990 by the noted *tallador* Antonio Avilés.

[8] Fernando F. Segovia, "My Personal Voice: The Making of a Postcolonial Critic," in Fernando F. Segovia, *Decolonizing Biblical Studies: A View from the Margins* (Maryknoll, NY: Orbis Books, 2000), 155.

[9] See Fernando F. Segovia, "Theological Education and Scholarship as Struggle: The Life of Racial/Ethnic Minorities in the Profession," *Journal of Hispanic/Latino Theology* 2 (1994): 5–25.

[10] Jean-Pierre Ruiz, "Reading across Canons: U.S. Hispanic reflections on Globalization and the Senses of Scripture," *Journal of Hispanic/Latino Theology* 10, no. 4

(May 2003): 28. My reflections constituted a conversation with the practice of intercultural criticism outlined by Fernando Segovia in "Reading-Across: Intercultural Criticism and Textual Posture," in Segovia, *Interpreting beyond Borders*, 59–83.

[11] Ruiz, "Reading across Canons," 30.

[12] Orlando O. Espín, *The Faith of the People: Theological Reflections on Popular Catholicism* (Maryknoll, NY: Orbis Books, 1997), 11.

[13] Ibid., 27.

[14] Sixto J. Garcia, "Sources and Loci of Hispanic Theology," *Journal of Hispanic/Latino Theology* 1, no. 1 (November 1993): 22–43; reprinted in *Mestizo Christianity: Theology from the Latino Perspective*, ed. Arturo J. Bañuelas (Maryknoll, NY: Orbis Books, 1995).

[15] 2007 ACHTUS Colloquium Program, available on the achtus.org website.

[16] See Jean-Pierre Ruiz, "Good Fences and Good Neighbors? Biblical Scholars and Theologians," *Electronic Journal of Hispanic/Latino Theology* (May 5, 2007). Available on the latinotheology.org website.

[17] See Jean-Pierre Ruiz, "Reading between the Lines: Toward a Latino/a (Re)configuration of Scripture and Tradition," in *Futuring Our Past: Explorations in the Theology of Tradition*, ed. Orlando O. Espín and Gary Macy, 83–112 (Maryknoll, NY: Orbis Books, 2006). On scripture and tradition, see Miguel H. Díaz, "A Trinitarian Approach to the Community-Building Process of Tradition: Oneness as Diversity in Christian Traditioning," in Espín and Macy, *Futuring Our Past*, 157–179, esp. 157–158.

[18] Roberto Suro et al., *Changing Faiths: Latinos and the Transformation of American Religion* (Washington DC: Pew Hispanic Center and the Pew Forum on Religion and Public Life, 2007), 23. Available online.

[19] Wilfred Cantwell Smith, *What Is Scripture? A Comparative Approach* (Minneapolis: Fortress Press, 1993), 18.

[20] While quite a bit of my attention has been and continues to be focused on the revelation to John, at best an eccentric and distant relative of the Fourth Gospel and the Johannine epistles, I reflected at some length on John 4 and John 20 in my contribution to a book co-edited by Fernando F. Segovia and Mary Ann Tolbert. See Jean-Pierre Ruiz, "Four Faces of Theology: Four Johannine Conversations," in *Teaching the Bible: The Discourses and Politics of Biblical Pedagogy*, ed. Fernando F. Segovia and Mary Ann Tolbert (Maryknoll, NY: Orbis Books, 1998), 86–101.

[21] See, for example, Leticia Guardiola-Sáenz, "Border-crossing and Its Redemptive Power in John 7.53—8.11: A Cultural Reading of Jesus and the *Accused*," in *John and Postcolonialism: Travel, Space, and Power*, ed. Musa W. Dube and Jeffrey L. Staley, 129–152 (Sheffield: Sheffield Academic Press, 2002); idem, "Reading from Ourselves: Identity and Hermeneutics among Mexican-American Feminists," in *A Reader in Latina Feminist Theology*, ed. María Pilar Aquino, Daisy L. Machado, and Jeanette Rodriguez, 80–97 (Austin: University of Texas Press, 2002). Also see Francisco Lozada, Jr., "Contesting an Interpretation of John 5: Moving Beyond Colonial Evangelism," in Dube and Staley, *John and Postcolonialism*, 76–93. Lozada is on especially familiar ground when he deals with John 5, for that chapter was the focus of his 1996 Vanderbilt doctoral dissertation, which was published as *A Literary Reading of John 5: Text as Construction* (New York: Peter Lang, 2000). Also see Francisco Lozada, Jr., "Johannine Universalism and Particularism: Toward an Intercultural Reading of John 6," in *Journal of Hispanic/Latino Theology* 10, no. 4 (May 2003): 5–21; and idem, "Reinventing the Biblical Tradition: An Exploration of Social Location Hermeneutics," in Espín and Macy, *Futuring Our Past*, 113–140.

[22] Ringe, *Wisdom's Friends*, xi–xii. Through this, she arrives at a deep understanding of what it means to be Wisdom's friends in the lived experience of *lo cotidiano*. For Ringe, "attention to the Fourth Gospel and its call to form a community of Wisdom's friends draws us toward our most vulnerable neighbors as those around whom and with whom the community takes shape" (96).

[23] See Miguel H. Díaz, "'*Dime con quién andas y te dire quién eres*': We Walk-with Our Lady of Charity," in *From the Heart of Our People*, ed. Orlando O. Espín and Miguel H. Díaz, 153–171 (Maryknoll, NY: Orbis Books, 1999). Volume 7 in the Bible and Postcolonialism series is Dube and Staley, *John and Postcolonialism*.

[24] Guardiola-Sáenz, "Border-crossing and Its Redemptive Power in John 7.53—8.11," 139–140.

[25] Ibid., 140.

[26] Ibid., 131.

[27] Ibid., 151.

[28] Amy-Jill Levine, *The Misunderstood Jew: The Church and the Scandal of the Jewish Jesus* (San Francisco: Harper San Francisco, 2006). Also see Daniel Boyarin, *Border Lines: The Partition of Judaeo-Christianity* (Philadelphia: University of Pennsylvania Press, 2004). According to Reinhartz, "A compliant reading allows one to enter into the Beloved Disciple's Gospel in a way that brings its appeal and its transformative message alive. The Beloved Disciple defines 'good' as accepting the gift of eternal life and, through a rhetoric of binary opposition, labels as 'bad' all those who refuse the gift. A compliant reader, by the very fact of his or her compliance with the Beloved Disciple's perspective and acceptance of the gift, will take on this assessment as well. Within the narrative and discourse of the Gospel, those who are 'bad,' are also labeled 'Jews'" (Reinhartz, *Befriending the Beloved Disciple*, 79). Francisco Lozada cautions that intercultural criticism should not be construed as "another hermeneutics of suspicion in disguise" (Lozada, "Johannine Universalism and Particularism").

[29] Fernando F. Segovia, "The Gospel at the Close of the Century: Engagement from the Diaspora," in Segovia, *"What Is John?"* 214.

[30] Ibid.

[31] Ibid.

[32] Ibid., 215.

[33] See Fernando F. Segovia, "Toward a Hermeneutics of the Diaspora: A Hermeneutics of Otherness and Engagement," in *Reading from This Place*, vol. 1, *Social Location and Biblical Interpretation in the United States*, ed. Fernando F. Segovia and Mary Ann Tolbert, 57–73 (Minneapolis: Fortress Press, 1995).

[34] Segovia, "The Gospel at the Close of the Century," 215.

[35] Ibid.

[36] Ibid., 215–216.

[37] Ibid., 216.

[38] Ibid.

[39] Reinhartz, *Befriending the Beloved Disciple*, 157.

[40] Lozada, "Johannine Universalism and Particularism," 20.

[41] Ibid.

[42] Ibid.

[43] Lozada, "Reinventing the Biblical Tradition," 114.

[44] Ibid. For an analysis and critique of correspondence hermeneutics regarding the "Galilean Jesus," see Ruiz, "Good Fences and Good Neighbors?"

[45] Lozada, "Reinventing the Biblical Tradition," 115.

[46] Ibid.

[47] See José R. Irizarry, "The Politics of Tradition in the Protestant Educational Endeavor for Colonial Puerto Rico," in Espín and Macy, *Futuring Our Past*, 229. Also see Bernard Cooke, "Authority and/or Tradition," in Espín and Macy, *Futuring Our Past*, 23–42.

[48] Lozada, "Reinventing the Biblical Tradition," 115.

[49] Ibid.

[50] See Gary Riebe-Estrella, "Tradition as Conversation," in Espín and Macy, *Futuring Our Past*, 141–156.

[51] Under the rubric of a U.S. Latina/o theology of revelation, this opens a door to take another look at the *sensus fidelium*. See Espín, *The Faith of the People*, esp. 63–60 ("Tradition and Popular Religion: An Understanding of the *Sensus Fidelium*").

[52] See Boyarin, *Border Lines*, 89–111 ("The Intertextual Birth of the Logos: The Prologue of John as a Jewish Midrash"). Boyarin argues (very persuasively, for me) that "nothing in Logos theology as a doctrine of God indicates or even implies a particularly Christian as opposed to Jewish, including Christian, kerygma" (95). He goes on to maintain: "For John, as for that other most 'Jewish' of Gospels, Matthew—but in a very different manner—Jesus comes to fulfill the mission of Moses, not to displace it. The Torah simply needed a better exegete, the Logos Ensarkos, a fitting teacher for flesh and blood. Rather than supersession in the explicitly temporal sense within which Paul inscribes it, John's typology of Torah and Logos Incarnate is more easily read within the context of what Jacques Derrida has argued is a prevailing assumption of Western thought: that oral teaching is more authentic and transparent than written texts. God thus first tried the text [Torah], and then sent his voice, incarnated in the voice of Jesus. After the Prologue, which truly introduces the narrative of the Word's coming into the world, its prehistory and its necessity, the Gospel moves naturally into the main Gospel narration, with a Christology informed at all points by the prehistoric, cosmic myth of the Prologue" (104).

[53] Fernando F. Segovia, "John 1:1–18 as Entrée into Johannine Reality: Representation and Ramifications," in *Word, Theology, and Community in John*, ed. John Painter, R. Alan Culpepper, and Fernando F. Segovia (St. Louis, MO: Chalice Press, 2002), 59. That being said, Segovia also remains profoundly ambivalent about this text, with its vision that he regards as "profoundly conflicted." He writes: "On the one hand, the vision [of John 1:1–18] offers a radical agenda. . . . It is a vision of 'true light' in the midst of pervasive 'darkness.' All standing visions of reality are dismissed as 'darkness'; it alone is advanced as 'enlightenment.' Moreover, it is a vision open to all human beings. All that is necessary for becoming a 'child of God' is to believe in Jesus, the Word. In the process, all barriers and divisions of human existence collapse: The children of God go beyond the categories of gender, class, ethnicity, race, and so forth. This is, therefore, a vision of liberation for humanity, now free to know itself in the light of the one and true God and his unique revealer, the Word. On the other hand, the vision also embodies a most conservative agenda. In going beyond all divisions of human existence, the vision actually creates a new and overarching division. All those who do not believe in Jesus and fail thereby to become children of God remain mired in 'darkness'—removed from God and indeed, enemies of God. This vision, therefore, is also a vision of oppression for humanity, a classic example of 'othering,' whereby all those who disagree with the vision and opt for a different path are regarded as misguided and antagonistic" (59). Segovia concludes by asking, "How is one to respond in the face of such a vision, both as a human being and as a

Christian? For respond one must." Segovia's response? "What I have done here is to bring into the sharpest relief possible the fundamental convictions and interests of the gospel; what now remains is to engage such interests and convictions in the sharpest possible way. For me this is no more and no less to do unto the gospel what the gospel has not hesitated to do unto others" (60).

[54] Václav Havel, translated by A. G. Brain. Havel's acceptance speech was reprinted in *The New York Review of Books* 36: 21–22 (January 18, 1990), 5.

[55] Václav Havel, *A Word about Words* (New York: Cooper Union, 1992).

[56] Ibid.

[57] See Jon Sobrino, "Ignacio Ellacuría, the Human Being and the Christian: 'Taking the Crucified People Down from the Cross,'" in *Love that Produces Hope: The Thought of Ignacio Ellacuría*, ed. Kevin F. Burke and Robert Lassalle-Klein, 1–67 (Collegeville, MN: The Liturgical Press, 2006).

[58] Havel, *A Word about Words*. Here Havel refers to the Iranian writer Salman Rushdie's 1988 novel *The Satanic Verses*, which Ayatollah Ruhollah Khomeini regarded as so blasphemous that in 1989 he called for Rushdie's death. In July 1991 the Japanese language translator of *The Satanic Verses* was stabbed to death, and the Italian language translator was seriously injured in an attempt on his life.

4

Sola Scriptura and Latino/a Protestant Hermeneutics

An Exploration

Efraín Agosto

INTRODUCTION

What would it mean to have an ecumenical Catholic-Protestant Latino/a theology of revelation? It seems to me that the process needs to include an exploration of that fundamental Protestant Reformation tenet—*sola scriptura*. The doctrine, not clearly stated and nuanced, could be a stumbling block to our efforts, given the Roman Catholic emphasis on scripture, tradition, *and* experience in biblical interpretation, about which Jean-Pierre Ruiz has so skillfully reminded us in his chapter in this volume. Thus, in this essay I wish to explore the concept of *sola scriptura* from a Latino/a Protestant perspective, as a contribution to the larger question of the various contours of an ecumenical Latino/a theology.

At the outset of such an exploration, I should share some caveats. First, while Protestant, I am not a Reformed theologian, although I now belong to a denomination that, at least in part, has Reformed theology in its historical roots (the United Church of Christ). In fact, I still consider myself Pentecostal in some shape or form, because that was the tradition in which I was reared. That is to say, I am more Wesleyan than Reformed, and still quite cognizant of the important role of religious experience in the Pentecostal believer's self-understanding, sometimes over against his or her grounding in the Bible or doctrinal expressions of the Bible.

Second, as a biblical scholar I have been trained to be more interested in history than theology. I was trained in traditional historical-critical methodologies of biblical interpretation, initially at the seminary level with Evangelical scholars like Gordon Fee, and later in graduate school with scholars such as Howard Kee, who were expanding the definition of what should be included in the historical-critical apparatus. Kee, in particular, exposed his students in the 1980s to the burgeoning field of social-scientific biblical criticism. None-theless, soon after graduate school I became immersed in the scholarly dis-cussions that questioned whether historical critical exegesis, supposedly objective and devoid of personal perspectives and backgrounds, could ever really be so.

New Testament scholar Fernando Segovia and church historian Justo González led the charge from the Latino/a side in the 1990s. I was greatly influenced in my work by this passage in González's 1990 work of system-atic theology, *Mañana*:

> The new theology, being done by those who are aware of their tradi-tional voicelessness, is acutely aware of the manner in which the domi-nant is confused with the universal. North American male theology is taken to be basic, normative, universal theology, to which then wom-en, other minorities, and people from the younger churches may add their footnotes. What is said in Manila is very relevant for the Philip-pines. What is said in Tübingen, Oxford or Yale is relevant for the en-tire church. White theologians do general theology; black theologians do black theology. Male theologians do general theology; female theo-logians do theology determined by their sex. Such a notion of "univer-sality" based on the present unjust distribution of power is unaccept-able to the new theology.[1]

The question as to whether Euro-centric theology, including biblical criti-cism, is "real" theology and Latino/a theology is just commentary motivated me to pursue more generic questions about biblical hermeneutics, not just what happened in the scriptural records of the New Testament, but how do we get at what happens and what does it all mean for us today, especially in light of our social location. I have moved beyond history (without neglecting it) to more theological and hermeneutical questions. Thus Fernando Segovia's quest to rescue the impact of social context, theological perspective and justice issues—the "decolonizing of biblical studies"—from the grips of the fallacy of detached, objective historical analysis has captured my interest as well.[2]

What does moving to a more engaged theological study of the Bible that takes seriously the historical context of the original text, but also the social, theological, and hermeneutical contexts of the reader mean for a Latino/a ecumenical theology of revelation? It means that *sola scriptura* cannot be understood as "whatever scripture says, we do." Of course, we should ask if it ever meant that. In what follows, I want to review briefly some defini-tions of the Protestant principle of *sola scriptura*. Then I want to turn to what Latino/a Protestant, especially Pentecostal, theologians and bible scholars have done with that principle, albeit more indirectly than directly. Very few Latino/a scholars that I have studied discuss the concept overtly. Nonetheless, their work engages the principle of the authority of scripture at least implicitly, if not always explicitly.

UNDERSTANDING *SOLA SCRIPTURA*
AS A PENTECOSTAL BIBLICAL SCHOLAR

If my friends and colleagues affiliated with Pentecostal denominations will allow me to call myself a Latino/a Pentecostal theologian, I would argue that *we* have always had a high view of scripture, although we have not always practiced it quite like our Anglo Protestant, especially evangelical, cohorts have. Writing about Pentecostal hermeneutics, Eldin Villafañe affirms Pentecostal "subscription to the four basic principles of the Reformation: *Sola Gracia, Solo Cristo, Sola Escritura,* and *Sola Fe.*" However, Pentecostalism, Villafañe asserts, has its roots in the "left-wing of the Reformation," which has significant implications "because of its constituency— the poor and the oppressed."[3] More to the point, Latino/a Pentecostalism in particular subscribes to the Reformation teaching about the internal witness of the Holy Spirit. Thus "implicitly Hispanic Pentecostals subscribe to a view of revelation that is dynamic and continuous in nature," reading the Bible in an "existential-spiritual manner."[4]

Thus *sola scriptura,* while understood to be a guiding principle, has not always been the most hotly contested theological concept among Latino/a Pentecostals, and I daresay among Latino/a Protestants in general. In fact, in his review of the emergence of biblical Latino/a hermeneutics, Francisco García-Treto acknowledges the growing ecumenicity of Latino/a Protestant and Roman Catholic biblical scholarship that transcends a separation based on Reformation principles:

> Today, within the U.S. Hispano/Latino/a churches, and specifically at the academic-theological professional level, a new ecumenical openness to cooperation, dialogue, and mutual acceptance has developed between mainline and other Protestant and Roman Catholic biblical scholars, to the extent that a true interpretative community . . . may already be identified.[5]

Rather than doctrinal principles, the focus is on community and the cultural/social nature of that community. Thus, García-Treto concludes:

> Just as a transnational Hispanic/Latino/a consciousness of being a people is emerging and setting a sociocultural agenda in the United States, so a transdenominational consciousness of being an interpretive community reading the Bible from the social location of our people has arisen and is beginning to bear noticeable fruit.[6]

If an ecumenical Hispanic/Latino/a biblical interpretation is emerging from at least the academic circles of biblical and theological scholarship across the Catholic and Protestant "divide," what has happened to such Reformation principles as *sola scriptura* in the minds and hearts of U.S. Latino/a Protestant scholars and practitioners in particular?

In fact, it can be argued that the Reformation principle has been misunderstood almost from the beginning of its articulation. In *An Introductory Dictionary of Theology and Religious Studies,* we read the following:

> The Lutheran slogan *sola scriptura* (Latin for scripture alone) did not mean for Lutheranism itself what it came to mean in later, more radical forms of sixteenth century Protestantism: the complete rejection of all tradition outside of scripture, and of church tradition in scriptural interpretation in favor of private interpretation "from scratch."[7]

For Luther, tradition was to be used in the service of scripture, "that is, tradition that truly confesses teaches and celebrates the scriptural gospel."[8] Nonetheless, he did not deny its importance and impact. Accordingly, in recent Lutheran-Catholic dialogue, both the Lutheran notion that tradition hands down "God's revelation in Christ" as revealed in scripture and the Catholic notion that tradition is no longer seen as a separate source in Catholicism but rather "together with Scripture as the Word of God for the life of the Church" were deemed acceptable.[9]

Thus the assumed divide between the Reformation principle of *sola scriptura* and Roman Catholic emphasis on the importance of tradition and experience is not so wide. Even some evangelical scholars, many of whom argue from Reformed positions, believe we are no longer in debate with Roman Catholics about the role of tradition in scripture. Writing about the divide *in evangelicalism* between "modern inerrantists" and those evangelical scholars who advocate a more moderate view of Scripture, the editors of *Evangelicals and Scripture* argue that those holding to an inerrant view of Scripture have "moved away from the Reformers' confession of the what, who, and why of Scripture as an article of faith to the how of Scripture as the foundation of an entire systematic theological program." Such a shift resulted because "evangelicals were no longer addressing a Roman Catholic position on Scripture and tradition, but rather the rising influence of a secularized culture and liberal theology."[10] The principle of *sola scriptura* had to be defended against rising secularism that affected both the Roman Catholic and Protestant churches. Nonetheless, in that defense *sola scriptura* becomes the rallying cry for the use of the Bible as the foundation for building correct Christian doctrine, often in propositional forms, rather than as a source of "spiritual sustenance" and the primary "means for nurturing the soul."[11] However, this latter understanding—Scripture as a source for spiritual nurture—is not far from the concerns of Latino/a Pentecostalism, as well as Latino/a

Protestantism in general. Both retain a focus on experience, including community experience, in the interpretation and application of Scripture.

Therefore, I posit that in Latino/a theology, both Protestant and Catholic, we are not too far from a Latino/a ecumenical theology of biblical revelation. I agree with Jean-Pierre Ruiz's assessment in Chapter 3 in this volume that it was a particular, "problematic implementation of the Reformation principle *sola scriptura* . . . in ways that are used to silence other (at least potentially) inspired voices both within and outside the churches" that led to a chasm that we are now beginning to close. Further, Ruiz suggests that "an adequate Latino/a Christian theology of revelation . . . must call us to look in the most unlikely places and to listen attentively to the most improbable voices to encounter the incarnate *Logos* and the indwelling spirit." I believe that Latino/a Pentecostal and Protestant voices are beginning to be heard in this way, and in what follows in this essay I invoke some of those voices of Latino/a biblical and theological scholarship and their use of the Bible. In that way we assess how the Protestant principle of *sola scriptura* does or does not see its way through these various Latino/a voices of interpretation.

A COMMUNITY OF INTERPRETATION

One of the fundamental understandings of how Latino/as read the Bible is their engagement in a community of interpretation. Rather than being "lone rangers" in the task of interpretation, Hispanic/Latino/as read scripture in light of community. Francisco García-Treto explores the concept of "interpretative community" in literary studies and concludes that the "emerging emphasis on contextual or 'social location' readings of the Bible converge" with "the *teología de conjunto* being developed in U.S. Hispanic churches"; that is, theology as a function of community implies that "new hermeneutical strategies and standpoints are being put in place."[12] Let me discuss three such strategies, by two Latino/a Pentecostals and one mainline Latina Protestant, which fundamentally engage with the question of Latino/a community as a hermeneutical point of departure.

PENTECOSTAL SCHOLARSHIP ON THE ROLE OF SCRIPTURE

First, Pentecostal scholar Eldin Villafañe explores the leadership of the prophet Amos in the Hebrew scriptures.[13] In so doing he discusses the nature of biblical justice that Amos calls for from his fellow compatriots in Israel. Justice, according to Villafañe in his reading of Amos, is about commitment to one's community.

> The picture that Scripture paints is that of the human person created in and for communion—created to live in community. In the

Old Testament, above all, one sees the importance of living in relationship with God and with each other. Individuals were in relationship
with God through the covenant that existed between God and his
people.[14]

Relationships in human life must be guided by the search for justice, because justice lies at the heart of divine nature. Thus, whether among nations
outside Israel or inside Israel itself, the practice of justice, especially to the
poor and oppressed, is a mark of closeness to God. Amos denounces injustice everywhere and calls for Israel in particular to practice justice as the
people of God.

Moreover, Villafañe posits that these are fundamental teachings of the
Bible. Liberation and justice, in community, lie at the heart of the gospel
message. To practice otherwise, even while invoking Scripture, does not carry
with it the fundamental message of the Bible. Thus, later in his argument,
Villafañe decries the tendency in Protestant evangelical scholarship to divide
the personal aspects of the gospel from its social aspects: "If our nation—for
that matter, our world—is to hear the whole Word of God, we must do away
with those false dichotomies that would limit the Word of God and define
the gospel as either evangelism or social justice. . . . We must completely
reverse the reversal of the early twentieth-century American church, which
divided the church into two camps." Such a division between personal salvation and social justice divides the gospel in two, and therefore undermines
the biblical teaching of one gospel that promotes God's "passionate concern
for justice for all—especially the poor, the weak, and the oppressed members of society."[15] A dichotomized gospel limits the creation of community.

These values of justice and community, which Villafañe and other Pentecostal and Protestant scholars and religious leaders find in the Bible, give a
wider context to their notion of *sola scriptura*. Scripture promotes justice
and community. Biblical interpretation that undermines these values is not
scriptural. The doctrine of *sola scriptura* is not about building a correct body
of propositional truth based on what scripture says, but rather finding in
scripture the building blocks of a more just community and world.

Samuel Solivan is a second Pentecostal scholar who explores a theology
of scripture and revelation that recognizes the need for justice and community. His work *The Spirit, Pathos, and Liberation* explores a Latino/a theology
of suffering from the perspective of U.S. Hispanic Pentecostals. His theological construction of "orthopathos"—redemptive suffering—is "informed fundamentally but not exclusively by the Scriptures of the Hebrew Bible, the
New Testament and the person of Jesus Christ as Savior." Besides the
christological focus that must inform all scriptural revelation, Solivan argues
that "alongside these we must place tradition, reason and critical reflection
on our present situation." We must include "modern critical scholarship which
appropriates the text and the sociopolitical situation" from which one reads
the text. Such an eclectic approach "demonstrates a high regard for the

authority of Scripture, a keen insight into the sociopolitical issues of the day, a great sensitivity to the needs of lay people and a wise use of critical biblical scholarship."[16]

In this way Soliván expands the nature of *sola scriptura* because each paradigm—the person and work of Christ, tradition, reason, critical scholarship, and reflection on the present situation—stands next to the others and to scripture, "both informing the issues and the present task." Otherwise, without such juxtaposition of the variety of social and theological issues, "the critical historical method tends to divest the Scripture of its power to speak anew to us today" when it stands alone. Soliván asserts that we must "shift" from a reliance on a so-called "objective" historical process by itself "to the witness of the Spirit both in the tradition of the church and in the reflecting community." Thus, the community "retains the power of the Word."[17]

Latino/a Pentecostal readings of the Bible, in particular, Soliván argues, help engender the focus on justice and community. Soliván distinguishes between Latino/a Pentecostals and Anglo-American Pentecostals because the latter "are presently much closer in their appropriation of Scripture to the old Princeton theology approach," which Soliván calls "a scholastic Reformed Calvinism . . . understood more in propositional terms than in the more dynamic terms that Hispanic Pentecostals employ."[18] By *dynamic* Soliván means that Hispanic Pentecostals include several interactive components in their reading of the Bible. First, there is the question of authority. Rather than rest authority in the internal witness of Scripture itself, Latino/a Pentecostals tend to seek out order or direction from those in authority related to family and community, including their religious community. The "need for order, direction and harmony is expressed in the church through the matrix of biblical and spiritual authority in both ordained and lay leadership." To biblical and spiritual authority, Hispanic Pentecostals add "a common-sense realism approach to life in general and to the Scriptures in particular," which is often put in tension with reason. "Of the two, reason and common sense are the more questionable due to our anthropological assumptions about the Fall and sin and their effects on rational faculties."[19]

Yet in a footnote to this point, Soliván asserts that Latino/a biblical interpretation from the perspective of Latino/a Pentecostalism owes its roots to its "ancestor," Methodism and the "quadrilateral principle of Scripture, experience, reason and tradition." Moreover, "of these four, Scripture as illuminated by the Holy Spirit and experience as guided by the Holy Spirit, in practice possess the greatest weight in authority."[20] In this sense Latino/a Pentecostalism goes back to Calvin and his assertion that "what lends authority to the Scriptures is not its authors or preciseness of its claims but the internal witness of the Holy Spirit in our hearts and minds which bears fruit in our transformation."[21] Pentecostals in general, Soliván argues, got away from such a "pneumatological" understanding of scriptural authority and interpretation in its desire to move from the "side streets" to "main streets" in terms of acceptance among North American fundamentalists and evangelicals with their faith statements about the inerrancy of scripture. Latino/a Pentecostals, ironically enough, "followed the clue given by Calvin in recognizing the internal witness of the Spirit in the Word and its transforming power in one's life (*Institutes* 7.5)."[22]

Moreover, there is a socioeconomic dimension to such a view of biblical authority by Latino/a Pentecostals. Pentecostalism as a whole "was and continues to be rooted in the life of the poor" and thus "the literary medium," not always accessible to the poor, "was regarded with suspicion." They employed a "hermeneutic of suspicion." Books, such as law books, had often been employed to control the poor. Thus "the letter of the law" could not be the only means of authority in their lives. Soliván cites the reality of transformed lives as a criterion for determining scriptural authority:

> Transformation, both personal and collective, [was] the canon against which questions of authority were to be determined. The verification of Scripture's claims was not to be found in the internal claims made by Scriptures themselves, but in the external power of the Holy Spirit transforming people's lives in light of those claims.[23]

Experiencing God through healing and transformation made scripture come alive and gave it its authority.

Nonetheless, personal healing and transformation were not the only signposts for biblical authority, argues Soliván, but also liberation from destructive patterns that alienate neighbor from neighbor. These too "point to Scripture's authority."[24] Thus, once again, justice and community come to the fore as the critical aspects of authentic biblical interpretation as understood by Latino/a Pentecostals. Scriptural authority—*sola scriptura*—relates to the power of such scripture, as experienced through God's Spirit, to bring about transformation.

Such a position, Soliván asserts, rejects the notion of "Scripture as a collection of propositional statements about God, Jesus, the church and the world." This cannot be the singular understanding of the nature of scripture. Such an approach "lacks the dynamic, transformative power of the Spirit evident in Scripture."[25] To be a community that affirms *sola scriptura* as a guide for faith and life means that scripture comes alive in each person's life as he or she lives out the faith in community. Soliván does not deny the role of propositional statements, but they are of a "second order." It is only "after one has known in one's life the power of the Spirit in transformation," that one then moves "to this second order of discourse." Soliván depicts interactivity between faith and faith statements about scripture: "The dynamic, living authority of the Scriptures may be posited in a propositional form when its dynamic character has been attested by the one articulating the propositional claim." Faith experience and faith claims critique each other in order to attest to their fundamental authenticity. We cannot make claims about faith without experiencing the results of faith and scripture in our lives. Moreover, without the experience of faith, propositional truths around the authority of scripture become static and decontextualized. We need statements about scripture that recognize the impact of social status and cultural background in their formulation. The mutual critique between faith experience and faith statements, what Soliván calls "the existential aspect of biblical authority," sees scripture as both *logos* and *pneuma*—reason and Spirit—and thus helps "to transcend the cultural barriers inherent in propositional truths." Culture becomes a partner in the liberating enterprise of scripture rather than having an "approach that amalgamates the cultural perspectives, reducing it all to some common denominator, usually under the definitional power of the dominant culture."[26]

In fact, Soliván concludes, Latino/a Pentecostalism has learned to read scripture from the perspective of the non-dominant, the poor, who often eschew the focus on literary aspects of scripture. "A Pentecostal understanding of Scripture tempered by critical study also questions the other side of Fundamentalism that is enamored of the letter of the text." This is the case of fundamentalisms of both right and left, whether focused on literary inerrancy (the "right") or cultural analyses (the "left") that limit the conversation to mere literary interpretation. Poor, non-literate cultures have taught us to experience scripture, not just study it or make static claims about it. "When the Scriptures are reduced to a literary genre entrapped in history, the results are similar—a dead, lifeless word, far from the living creative Word of God spoken of by the prophets and experienced by the apostles and the church of the poor."[27] Thus in Hispanic Pentecostalism, as understood by Soliván, *sola scriptura* has an expansive understanding that encompasses the written text, a community's experience and living interpretation of that text, and its ultimate goal of personal and community transformation. In addition, the poor lead the way toward such a liberating perspective on the authority of scripture.

THE PRACTICE OF COMMUNITY INTERPRETATION: A "COMMUNAL READING"

How are such scriptural values of justice and community represented practically in actual Latino/a communities of faith? An example described by the Rev. Aida Irizarry-Fernández, a district superintendent of the United Methodist Church, offers a "communal reading" of the Bible that encompasses a see-judge-act paradigm of biblical study.[28] Irizarry-Fernández affirms that the study of scripture in Latino/a communities of faith should offer a prime opportunity for "building community" and "undergoing transforming moments." The see-judge-act methodology offers maximum "fluidity and adaptability" in biblical study because it is "an action/reflection process rooted in liberation theology and thinking."[29] Moreover, as "an empowering process," especially for communities of color, it "promotes team ministry, team analysis and unity in the Spirit among highly diverse communities, such as the Latino/a/Hispanic American population in the United States."[30]

Irizarry-Fernández affirms that although there is great ethnic, national, socioeconomic, and religious diversity among Hispanics/Latino/as in the United States, there are still many unifying forces. Traditionally, language has been one such unifying force among all Hispanics, but that is changing as third- and fourth-generation Hispanics begin to lose their Spanish. Skin color is also not a unifying force, because of the many hues and colors we Latino/as represent as the "cosmic race." Rather, it is our shared "historical memory" that should promote Latino/a/Hispanic unity in the United States. "In one way or another, we are all children of the sufferings and pains of conquest and colonization; we are siblings in exile from the south to the north of the continent."[31] Such a "post-colonial optic," to borrow Fernando Segovia's term,[32] can be a source of community building among Latino/as.

Biblical inquiry can also be transforming for a community engaged in the see-judge-act model. "The expectation is that those who engage in its action-reflection process will become faithful agents of change within a church and a society that operate from the demands of the reign of God." Such change does not happen within the typical "linear thinking and value system of the Western European world." For transformation to take place, "the more circular movement of ideas, emotions and values of non-Westerners" must be taken into account. Echoing Solíván's discussion about static, propositional scriptural truth in contrast to dynamic interaction between ancient scriptures and current readers, Irizarry-Fernández argues that every time the community gathers to study the Bible, "a new epiphany may emerge," which "can open the door to a new understanding of ourselves and of God." Biblical study that is open to dynamic interaction between text and readers in community can create new paths of understanding.[33]

Moreover, the "corporate learning" of a see-judge-act model of biblical interpretation in community allows people of diverse background to contribute to the theology of biblical revelation. As Jean-Pierre Ruiz proposes in Chapter 3, a variety of voices is heard, whether male or female, young or old, literate or illiterate, expert or non-expert. Such diversity around the "table" of biblical interpretation, Irizarry-Fernández points out, allows each person to bring "her or his own gifts and experiences to the realm of community" and encourages theological thinking "that will sustain, rather than divide, the community."[34] Division around scriptural interpretation is often the greatest impediment to building community in many faith settings. However, by creating an open and safe space, and opportunities for all to read, reflect and engage the Bible together, the goals of authentic biblical interpretation—transformation, justice, and community building—could have a greater chance of success.

Irizarry-Fernández gives some specifics about the meaning of this hermeneutical model for community exegesis and transformative action. She also, of course, gives concrete examples with a variety of scriptures and group settings. I only briefly summarize here the meaning of see-judge-act before indicating the implications of such a model for our exploration of *sola scriptura* in Latina/o Protestant thought.

First, "seeing" is about a thorough examination of the selected biblical text in order to understand its characters, their history, and their social context. Questions about the concerns and problems of the characters in the text, as well as their feelings and emotions, to the extent they can be known, inform this initial exploration of the text. Trying to figure out, initially, what the author is attempting to communicate to his or her community drives "seeing" the text. In these ways the modern readers of the text connect to the characters in the text both as individuals and as members of a community.

In the second step of the model, "judge," readers are encouraged, through a process of "spiritual discernment" to determine where they see themselves in the text. "This movement provides opportunities for participants to discern and analyze their own circumstances in light of the biblical text. It is an invitation to evaluate the conditions of our lives." This corresponds very much to the "reader-oriented criticism" that Fernando Segovia emphasizes in his writings.[35] The readers ask how the text speaks to them and to their community; where is the Good News in this text? To "judge" is also to explore the status of one's community in light of the scripture. These are not just matters of application of the text to the current situation, but contributors, as Segovia would say, to the whole task of understanding a text and its meaning. Segovia would also agree with Irizarry-Fernández here that transformation and liberation are ultimate goals of these reader-oriented readings of scripture, for the step asks the community "to reconsider corporate decisions" so that our study might make "a difference in the life of our church, our denomination, our community and our world."[36]

Accordingly, the last step of this biblical interpretation process involves .action. To "act" is to engage transformation through some sort of organized spiritual, political, or social effort at change. "We move from reflection into action. In this step, the text is re-read and reformulated in order to assist us in moving from assessment into commitment."[37] Notice the close relation to the text in this model. One is reading, analyzing and acting, and then starting the cycle again in order to inform transformative action. *Sola scriptura* entails not just the data in the text, but the movement of the text from static words and sentences to community discernment, action, and transformation. The model understands that there is an invitation in the text to which we as a community respond. The text as a faithful witness to God's word always moves in the direction of anticipatory, positive action that is just, liberative, and loving—in other words, that is "good news" for all. Irizarry-Fernández, in her employment of the method, shows that there is room for scholarly interaction with the text, but only as the community tries to "see" what is in the text. There is also social and political community analysis as the community tries to understand its place in the ancient text in light of current situations. Finally, the community looks at its own past action, just as it looked at the past action of the characters and communities reflected in the ancient text, in order to organize appropriate community action in response to the invitation of the text.

Irizarry-Fernández coheres with the thought of Samuel SolivÁn about the role of the Spirit in this process of biblical interpretation. In order to carry out this model each participant will need to have "an open mind and a willing heart in order to truly listen to the Spirit's voice in our midst." The table fellowship around which this biblical and community analysis takes place invites all—whether old or new to the community—"to enter sacred ground together in a journey of faith."[38]

Thus, two Latino/a Pentecostal scholars and one mainline Protestant Latina religious leader challenge their readers and their communities to consider wide-ranging understandings of the value and readings of the Bible as scripture. In each case, matters of justice for the "least of these" and community-building for all are celebrated as fundamental to the authentic appropriation of scripture. Experience and critical study are guiding lights to their notions of scriptural authority. *Sola scriptura* means that scripture helps interpret experience and that the search for justice and community informs the correct understanding of scripture. It is a two-way street.

PRINCIPLES OF COMMUNITY INTERPRETATION— JUSTO GONZÁLEZ

Given these specific strategies of Pentecostal scholarship and community oriented biblical study in a Latino/a mainline Protestant setting, perhaps we need some overarching principles in our search for a Latino/a biblical hermeneutic that takes *sola scriptura* seriously, but also takes into account the nature and experience of the Latino/a community in biblical interpretation. Justo González suggests five paradigms of Latino/a biblical interpretation in his work of Latino/a hermeneutics, *La Santa Biblia*.[39] Let me briefly review these paradigms in light of our search for a Latino/a Protestant response to the nature of *sola scriptura* for our day.

González posits that biblical hermeneutics through Latino/a eyes includes the paradigms of marginality, poverty, *mestizaje* and *mulatez*, exiles and aliens, and solidarity, all of which correspond in one way or another to the experience of Latino/as today. Thus González has added to the notion of *sola scriptura* paradigms of biblical interpretation that incorporate the experience of current-day readers, a community of interpretation, to cite the phrase invoked earlier in this essay from the work of Francisco García-Treto. By marginality, González refers to those on the margins of society, who can often see things in the biblical text that those in power, or at the center of a society, cannot. For example, in the Gospels and Acts we read stories about Jesus, the apostles, and those who opposed them, oftentimes referred to in the text as "the Jews." Those who stand outside the center of power today can understand how such references do not somehow indict a whole race, but rather refer to the problems people on the margins of a society (Jesus and the peasant population he served; the earliest Christians) often face with those who hold power, such as the Jewish and Roman leadership in Jerusalem.[40] As such, current-day experience of readers informs the interpretation of the ancient text and thus complements the notion that only in the words of scripture do we find the word of God. Without the experience of the reader, in this case the experience of marginality, we might miss this aspect of the biblical witness.

With regard to poverty, González emphasizes that a Latino/a reading of the Bible, given the economic status of so many Hispanics in the United States, is not just about what the Bible says about the poor, but more about what the poor have to say about the Bible. Echoing Fernando Segovia, González posits that "what one finds in the Bible depends to a large degree on one's perspective from which one reads the Bible." Therefore, the question is, What does the Bible say when read from the perspective of the poor? Put another way: What do the poor find in the Bible that the non-poor miss? Ultimately, it is not just a question of helping the poor by telling them what the Bible says about them (and thereby employing a truncated sense of *sola scriptura*), but realizing that the reading of the Bible by the poor can contribute to the whole church.[41] Thus Latino/a hermeneutics, as posited by González as well as other Latino/a interpreters, including the Protestants studied above, argues for wide-ranging opportunities in terms of who can read the text and give viable interpretative guidelines to it.

González also explores *mestizaje* and *mulatez*. These key terms in Latino/a theology refer to the status of many Latino/a groups as mixed races. For example, Mexican Americans are called *mestizos* because of their mixture with native peoples and the conquering Spaniards, and people of Caribbean background experience *mulatez*, the mixture of African black and European white races. Living as a *mestizo* or a mulatto brings to the fore the struggle of identity and, of course, racism. Referring to the New Testament book of Acts, González cites the example of the apostle Paul as a cultural *mestizo*. He has two names: Saul, reflecting his Jewish heritage, and Paul, the name he used when relating to Roman and Greek culture. In Acts, when the Pauline mission turns to the Gentiles, Saul becomes Paul and his cultural *mestizaje* as a Hellenistic Jew helps Paul accomplish his mission in the diverse world of the first century.[42] Latino/a readers of the New Testament more often than not understand the challenges and opportunities of having a multicultural identity because of our own experience as bilingual and bicultural beings.

Being "exiles and aliens," González's fourth set of interpretive lenses, also fits naturally in the lived experience of Latino/as today. Often cited with regard to Israel's Babylonian exile, theses terms speak to the fact and feeling of leaving one's center to enter somebody else's center. Thus, the state of being in exile and being called aliens represents "a strange sort of marginalization" precisely because one leaves a center to enter the periphery. However, González reminds us that, among Latino/as, that move often implies that one's beloved center, a homeland, has deteriorated due to "outside invasion or intervention, civil strife, economic disorder and decline, or economic and political oppression." Thus "the land our eyes first saw can no longer sustain the life of peace and joy that God intends."[43] We must leave it for somebody's center. Being an exile and an alien implies, therefore, that difficult experiences await those in this state, as expressed in the Psalmist's lament over the Babylonian exile: "By the rivers of Babylon—there we sat down and there we wept" (Ps 137:1). This scripture emphasizing an ancient experience of exile resonates in a major way with the Latino/a experience of exile today.[44]

Yet, the Bible also emphasizes several positive aspects and challenges with regard to exile. Thus scripture bears a diverse witness to ancient and modern experience of exile. First, the notion of caring for the "stranger" is important in the Bible, especially because, in a sense, we are all "exiles and aliens" in one form or another. Israel, formed out of a band of nomads, needed constantly to remember that history by its just treatment of the immigrant, the "stranger."[45] Second, the Bible encourages the exile to make the best of his or her new situation. González cites Jeremiah's challenge to the exiles in Babylon: "Build houses and live in them; plant gardens and eat what they produce. . . . But seek the welfare of the city where I have sent you into, and pray to the Lord on its behalf, for in its welfare you will find your welfare" (Jer 29:5, 7). This is a challenge to Latino/a immigrants as well to make their new home, a safe and just one, confronting those in power to make the changes necessary to ensure the well-being of the new immigrant.

Third, the Bible teaches that those in the center must understand the opportunity they now have with the influx of new peoples who can help bless the land and improve it, rather than considering these outsiders a burden. González recounts the story of Ruth and Naomi, "the story of a woman who becomes an alien for the sake of her husband, and another woman who becomes an alien for the sake of her mother-in-law." Further, "the alien who followed Naomi to Bethlehem became the great-grandmother of the great king of Israel." Thus it is of utmost importance, given such a reading of the biblical text, for "the powerful—particularly if they seek to do the will of God—[to] seek the alien, discover their gifts, and seek whatever wisdom and guidance those gifts might offer." The immigrant today is also a "giver," who can "bring enhanced meaning to freedom," and can "also contribute significantly to the economic well-being of the whole."[46]

González has thus shown us how this interaction between the ancient and the modern immigrant enriches the notion of *sola scriptura* beyond the one-way conversation that the term implies for many Protestant theologians today. For the Latino/a interpreter, biblical interpretation and authority engender dialogue. The immigrant reader, in particular, can teach us the contours of the immigrant experience in scripture, and in turn we learn to treat the "stranger" among us in just and empowering ways.

Solidarity is the last of González's hermeneutical paradigms for reading the Bible through Hispanic eyes. Unlike the other terms, which reflect in many ways the negative experiences of Hispanics in the United States, solidarity is at the heart of the Good News of Jesus Christ. The companion terms of *family* and *community* constitute ways in which both the New Testament and the Latino/a also express solidarity. *Unity* is another related term. González cites the community to which the author of 1 Peter writes, an exile community, for whom the Christian assembly provides a "'spiritual house' for the homeless (1 Peter 2.5); a 'chosen race' for those with no family; a 'holy nation' for those with no country (1 Peter 2.9)." Thus the church becomes "a home for the homeless."[47] We are reminded of the focus on community-building found both in the Bible and in the theological foci of Latino/a theologians, as noted above.

The theme of family is prevalent throughout the scriptures. It is an important theme for Latino/as as well, especially for many who have immigrated and lost the sense of *extended* family that is so important to us. For many Latino/as the church becomes the extended family that we have lost by coming to the United States, with its focus on the nuclear family. We also search the Bible for scriptures that affirm this need for a sense of family. In the New Testament, the Christian assembly becomes a home and a family for many who otherwise do not have a place that gives them a measure of status and community. González describes the church, as understood especially by Latino/a participants today, as an integral part of the gospel; it is not a mere "instrument" or "vehicle" or an add-on. For many Latino/as it is the "extended family" that we miss so much as a result of our immigrant status, as "aliens" in a new land.[48]

Indeed, González adds that the Bible is "the story of our family, the people of God." In it we find out who we are as a spiritual community.[49] We also find out what we are supposed to do. Solidarity creates a sense of community, family, and belonging, a home. Therefore, we become more capable of returning to our people, like Moses after the experience of the burning bush and the Samaritan woman after the encounter with Jesus at the well, "to do the work of God with and among them."[50] In short, solidarity creates mission. As Aida Irizarry-Fernández suggested, "seeing" what's in the Bible and "judging" its meaning for us creates the opportunity for just action as a community of faith both inside the community and outside in the world. A notion of *sola scriptura* that is merely an intellectual assent to a static doctrine, as Pentecostal scholars and activists such as Villafañe and Soliván argued against, leaves us with information about scripture but not action in response to it.

González concludes his chapter on solidarity by quoting from one of his sermons: "By means of solidarity between those who have and those who have not, between those who can and those who cannot, a new people shall be born, a new holy nation unto the Lord our God."[51] The Bible points to this picture of a community of haves and have-nots joined together in a spirit of liberation (see, for example, 1 Cor 1:26–31; 11:17–34). Any notion of biblical authority that does not promote this vision of solidarity falls short of the very internal witness of scripture.

Thus these paradigms of biblical interpretation that Justo González outlines for us—marginality, poverty, race, exile, and solidarity—are underlying principles for expanding the Protestant teaching about the authority of scripture. The Bible models these issues; Hispanic/Latino/as experience them. Together, the biblical witness and the Latino/a interpreter create an authoritative "scripture" that serves as a guide for the faithful, just living in community and in the world. That may be the understanding of *sola scriptura* that will inch us closer to an ecumenical Latino/a theology of revelation. In the conversation between past and present, we re-create scripture, not necessarily in our own image, but in the image of the community that God wants us to create, as exemplified by the Bible and by our experience as Latino/as of faith.

CONCLUSION: A PROPOSAL FOR A LATINO/A PROTESTANT THEOLOGY OF *SOLA SCRIPTURA*

In this chapter we have studied briefly the Reformation principle of *sola scriptura* and suggested that it was never meant to exclude the role of tradition, reason, and experience in the unfolding story of what is scripture and what it teaches. We have seen several examples of Protestant biblical interpretation and hermeneutics in Latino/a Pentecostal and mainline traditions. Invariably these traditions have celebrated the role of experience, the presence of the Spirit, and the quest for justice and community-building as fundamental signposts for biblical interpretation and authority. In other words, Latino/as in particular, if not Euro-centric Protestants and Pentecostals, have moved us closer to an understanding of biblical revelation and authority that goes beyond the letter of the law or a mere literary or literal interpretation of the Bible. Rather, they have tended to put Latino/a experience, especially around issues of identity, language, race, ethnicity, family, socioeconomic status, solidarity, and community, at the forefront of biblical interpretation. These matters are present in the Bible in a variety of ways, and they are present in the lives of Hispanics, for good or for bad. Why not put the two realities into conversation, rather than pit one against the other, or privilege one over the other?

In proposing a dialogue, we are not proposing anything new. In fact, we are returning to a notion of *sola scriptura* that engenders the kind of dynamic conversation between faith experience and faith statements that the Reformers intended. Scripture cannot be scripture unless a community says it is, as Jean-Pierre Ruiz reminds us in citing Wilfred Cantwell Smith. Moreover, we must de-center the biblical tradition, especially as it undermines alternative voices, and reinscribe the role of tradition and experience in ways that inform our readings of scripture, as suggested by Francisco Lozada, also cited by Ruiz.[52] What is interesting about this process of de-centering biblical authority that is exclusive of the minority voices is that Latino/a Pentecostals, who often talk like fundamentalists and literalists in their interpretation of the Bible, but act like Latino/a Roman Catholics in their celebration of spirituality and experience, as applied to biblical interpretation, might be helpful conversation partners in a movement toward an ecumenical Latino/a theology of revelation.

Moreover, as conversation partners, Latino/a Pentecostal scholars and practitioners will join mainline Latino/a Protestants and Roman Catholics in the joint quest for the "beloved community" and the justice that this community, also known as the kingdom of God, seeks to engender in our world, especially for the poor. For such goals—justice for the poor and community building for all—are clearly ensconced in the biblical tradition, and only the joint efforts of like-minded communities, influenced by the lack of justice, like Latino/a Pentecostals, mainline Protestants, and Roman Catholics, can bring about the transformation that our biblical hermeneutics ultimately pursues. The concept of *sola scriptura*, however we finally define it, must also promote the agenda of justice, community, and transformation that the biblical tradition teaches and our Latino/a community needs.

NOTES

[1] Justo L. González, *Mañana: Christian Theology from a Hispanic Perspective* (Nashville, TN: Abingdon Press, 1990), 52.

[2] See Fernando Segovia and Mary Ann Tolbert, *Reading from This Place,* vol. 1: *Social Location and Biblical Interpretation in the United States* (Minneapolis: Fortress Press, 1995); and Fernando Segovia, *Decolonizing Biblical Studies: A View from the Margins* (Maryknoll, NY: Orbis Books, 2000).

[3] Eldin Villafañe, *The Liberating Spirit: Toward an Hispanic American Pentecostal Social Ethic* (Grand Rapids, MI: Eerdmans, 1993), 123.

[4] Ibid., 205, 206.

[5] Francisco García-Treto, "Reading the Hyphens: An Emerging Biblical Hermeneutics for Latino/a/Hispanic U.S. Protestants," in *Protestantes/Protestants: Hispanic Christianity within Mainline Traditions*, ed. David Maldonado, Jr. (Nashville, TN: Abingdon Press, 1999), 164.

[6] Ibid.

[7] Jack E. Lindquist, "Sola Scriptura," in *An Introductory Dictionary of Theology and Religious Studies*, ed. Orlando O. Espín and James B. Nickoloff (Collegeville, MN: The Liturgical Press, 2007), 1305–1306.

[8] Ibid.

[9] Ibid., 1306.

[10] Vincent Bacote, Laura C. Miguelez, and Dennis L. Okholm, eds., *Evangelicals and Scripture: Tradition, Authority, and Hermeneutics* (Downers Grove, IL: InterVarsity Press, 2004), 10.

[11] Stanley J. Grenz, "Nurturing the Soul, Informing the Mind: The Genesis of the Evangelical Scripture Principle," in Bacote, Miguelez, and Okholm, *Evangelicals and Scripture*, 23.

[12] García-Treto, "Reading the Hyphens," 161.

[13] Eldin Villafañe, *Beyond Cheap Grace: A Call to Radical Discipleship, Incarnation, and Justice* (Grand Rapids, MI: Eerdmans, 2006), 57–81.

[14] Ibid., 66.

[15] Ibid., 75–76.

[16] Samuel Solivan, *The Spirit, Pathos, and Liberation: Toward an Hispanic Pentecostal Theology* (Sheffield: Sheffield Academic Press, 1998), 72.

[17] Ibid.

[18] Ibid., 93.

[19] Ibid., 93–94.

[20] Ibid., 93n1.

[21] Ibid.

[22] Ibid., 95.

[23] Ibid.

[24] Ibid.

[25] Ibid., 96.

[26] Ibid.

[27] Ibid., 96–97.

[28] Aida Irizarry-Fernández, "A Communal Reading. See-Judge-Act: A Different Approach to Bible Study," in *Engaging the Bible: Critical Readings from Contemporary Women*, ed. Choi Hee An and Katheryn Pfisterer Darr, 47–80 (Minneapolis: Fortress Press, 2006).

[29] Ibid., 47.

[30] Ibid., 48.

[31] Ibid.

[32] Fernando Segovia, "Biblical Criticism and Postcolonial Studies: Toward a Postcolonial Optic," in Segovia, *Decolonizing Biblical Studies*, 119–132.

[33] Irizarry-Fernández, "A Communal Reading," 48–49.

[34] Ibid.

[35] See, for example, Fernando Segovia, "'And They Began to Speak in Other Tongues': Competing Modes of Discourse in Contemporary Biblical Criticism," in Segovia, *Decolonizing Biblical Studies*, 3–33, especially 29–33.

[36] Irizarry-Fernández, "A Communal Reading," 50–51. See also Fernando Segovia, "Towards a Hermeneutics of the Diaspora: A Hermeneutics of Otherness and Engagement," in Segovia and Tolbert, *Reading from This Place*, 57–73, esp. 72, where Segovia posits that "an understanding of the [biblical] text as an other to us demands critical engagement with it—a thorough evaluation of its world, strategy, and applicability in terms of the reader's own historical and cultural context; the goal of such an engagement is none other than that of liberation itself."

[37] Irizarry-Fernández, "A Communal Reading," 51.

[38] Ibid.

[39] Justo González, *Santa Biblia: The Bible through Hispanic Eyes* (Nashville, TN: Abingdon Press, 1996).

[40] For examples of this with regard to Acts 13, see ibid., 41–42.

[41] See ibid., 58.

[42] For detailed development of Paul's *mestizaje*, see ibid., 80–84.

[43] Ibid., 91.

[44] For an analysis of this psalm from the perspective of the Cuban diaspora, see Ada María Isasi-Díaz, "'By the Rivers of Babylon': Exile as a Way of Life," in Segovia and Tolbert, *Reading from This Place*, 149–163.

[45] Ibid., 93–95, citing the work of Francisco García-Treto, "El Señor guarda a los emigrantes," *Apuntes* 1, no. 4 (Winter 1981), 4–7.

[46] González, *Santa Biblia*, 95–98.

[47] Ibid., 104, citing a sermon by Pablo Jiménez and the book by John Elliott, *Home for the Homeless: A Social Scientific Criticism of 1 Peter, Its Situation and Strategy* (Minneapolis: Fortress Press, 1990).

[48] González, *Santa Biblia,* 108–110, 113.

[49] Ibid., 110–111.

[50] Ibid., 111–112.

[51] Ibid., 112–113.

[52] See Francisco Lozada, Jr., "Reinventing the Biblical Tradition: An Exploration of Social Location Hermeneutics," in *Futuring Our Past: Explorations in the Theology of Tradition*, ed. Orlando Espín and Gary Macy, 113–140 (Maryknoll, NY: Orbis Books, 2006).

PART III

GRACE AND JUSTIFICATION

Soteriology and Theological Anthropology Shaped
a la latina

5

Outside the Survival of Community There Is No Salvation

A U.S. Hispanic Catholic Contribution to Soteriology

Miguel H. Díaz

INTRODUCTION

On the feast day of Our Lady of Guadalupe in 2006, immigration agents descended on six meat-processing plants in Minnesota belonging to Swift & Co. and arrested 1,297 illegal workers. In one of these plants, in Worthington, there were at least 360 children of illegal immigrants affected by the raids.[1] Prompt condemnation came from the seven Catholic bishops in Minnesota, including Archbishop Harry Flynn of the archdiocese of St. Paul and Minneapolis. In their statement the bishops specifically noted that immigration officials had exacerbated the entire ordeal by choosing to perform these raids on the feast day of Our Lady of Guadalupe:

> As the Catholic Bishops of the State of Minnesota, we are distressed and disheartened by the work place raids that took place in Worthington, Minnesota and other communities this past week. To add insult to injury, immigration officials chose the feast day of Our Lady of Guadalupe, patron saint of the Americas, as the day to target these workers and their families. . . .
>
> The raids did nothing to advance needed reform. Instead, the raids heartlessly divided families, disrupted the whole community of Worthington and undermined progress that that city had made toward bridging racial and cultural differences.
>
> We call for an end to such raids which violate the rights of workers and the dignity of work. These men and women are our brothers and sisters; as workers, they provide our food; as residents, they support our local businesses and communities. We must always remember that their dignity as human beings must be foremost in our thinking as we

address the critical issues surrounding immigration. Our faith calls us to overcome all forms of discrimination and violence so that we may build relationships that are just and loving.[2]

Unfortunately, what took place in Worthington, Minnesota, is symptomatic of ongoing raids on immigrant communities throughout this nation. Tragically, as the Minnesota bishops point out, negative consequences of these raids include the breakup of families, which particularly affects the lives of thousands of Latino/a children.

Recently, a woman named Tapia voiced the anxiety and fear that many undocumented Latino/a parents confront today.[3] Tapia and her husband were arrested after immigration authorities found them to be illegally employed in a Dixie Printing and Packaging Corporation plant in Baltimore. She was released under partial house arrest pending final decision by the courts (until the decision she has to wear a black monitoring bracelet around her ankle). Tapia and her husband faced a daunting decision: if they are deported to Ecuador, they either have to leave their daughter, Jessica, in the United States to be raised by relatives or take her to an unfamiliar country where socioeconomic conditions will seriously threaten the survival of their family. As Tapia expressed in Spanish to the reporter conducting the interview, "I do not know how my husband and I are going to survive there, let alone support Jessica."[4]

Issues related to the survival of communal identity have been central in the emergence and development of U.S. Hispanic theologies. In this essay the survival of particular communities, and all that this implies with respect to social, cultural, gender, political, economic, and religious factors that contribute to or hinder this survival, provides a starting point for envisioning a U.S. Hispanic Catholic soteriology. Though primarily envisioned from a Catholic perspective, this soteriology draws from the communal struggles to survive that most Latino/a Catholics and Protestants currently experience. It is my hope that this shared sociocultural location will contribute to ongoing efforts to birth what Justo González has characterized as a new ecumenism.

Consistent with recent developments in Catholic theologies of grace, my reflections do not separate the survival of community that results from the work of human hands from the ultimate salvation of community that emerges from the work of divine hands (through Christ and in the Spirit of God). In so doing, I hold in creative and analogical relationship temporal and historical efforts to preserve human communities with their eternal and God-given preservation that comes about as a result of God's triune presence in history.[5]

Some distinction between human community and divine community is inevitable in order to preserve the grace-filled initiative of divine life. But as the reflections of contemporary Catholic theologians have underscored, there is no experience of God for human beings "that has not been mediated through an experience of the world."[6] One might find it appropriate at this time to recall the oft-cited Barthian belief that Christians should read the bible with one hand and a newspaper with the other. In a similar way, González expresses the new U.S. Hispanic ecumenical vision that seeks to relate the gospel and the world and thereby draw out the concrete social implications of this Good News:

> This new ecumenism is not limited to issues of "life and work." It also includes what have traditionally been called matters of "faith and order." Indeed, it is our contention that there can be no division between life and work on the one hand and faith and order on the other, for as we work and live out the gospel we gain new insights into the meaning of our faith and the proper order for the church.[7]

In what follows I first briefly explore how contemporary Catholic thought understands the relationship between nature and grace, especially with respect to the way that this understanding affects notions of salvation and history. In particular, I rely on Karl Rahner's ground-breaking reflections on the triune life of grace and its salvific presence within the history of the world. Second, I briefly discuss how Latin American liberation theology has appropriated, critiqued, and gone beyond Rahner's contribution in its understanding of the historicity of salvation and its focus on the liberation of oppressed persons. Third, I argue how Latino/a theology parallels and differs from Rahnerian and Latin American liberation perspectives with its emphasis on the survival of Latino/a communal identities. Echoing, but re-visioning the ancient axiom *Extra ecclesiam, nulla salus,*[8] I propose the following axiom: Outside the survival of community, there is no salvation. To support my argument from a U.S. Hispanic Catholic perspective, I reflect upon the soteriological significance of the "Marys" of U.S. Hispanic popular devotions.[9] Finally, I conclude with a synthesis that reviews the main ideas presented in this paper.

SALVATION HISTORY AND HUMAN HISTORY:
THE CONTRIBUTION OF KARL RAHNER

No serious study in contemporary Catholic soteriolology can be done without considering the work of Karl Rahner. Among his central contributions to Catholic theological anthropology is his notion of the "supernatural existential." Parting ways with neo-Scholastic extrinsicism, and resisting his European context of secularization, Rahner proposes this key category of grace as a way to affirm the "always and everywhere" presence of God's self-offer (grace) in history.[10] Strongly influenced by a medieval Spanish spirituality, especially the Ignatian principle of the discernment of the Spirit in the ordinariness of life, Rahner sees human persons constituted within a historical and existential offer of grace.[11] Rahner argues that in the concrete state of affairs, the human being is already elevated to the "supernatural" gift of grace that comes from God's gratuitous, universal, and salvific will.[12]

Rahner's theology engages and develops the classic Thomistic principle that has become foundational in Catholic anthropology: "Gratia non tollit, non destruit, sed perficit naturam" (Grace does not destroy but perfects human nature).[13] Echoing the basic Catholic theology of grace, which this principle synthesizes, from a Christo-centric perspective, Rahner argues that human nature is what comes into existence when God expresses Godself in history. For Rahner, this self-expression is ontologically traced to Jesus Christ, whom Rahner sees as the Word through whom all other "human words" come into existence. Rahner argues that the humanity of Jesus is the ultimate symbolic realization of the communion between human and divine life.[14] In this way, human persons have existence because "God's self-expression, his Word, is uttered into the emptiness of the Godless void in love."[15]

Early in Rahner's thought, in an essay entitled "History of the World and Salvation History," Rahner expands his theology of grace from the perspective of salvation history.[16] This essay, which has been cited by a number of Latin American liberation theologians, seeks to understand the history of salvation as the climactic chapter in the creation, development, and fulfillment of human history. Rahner proposes the following three principles: (1) Salvation history takes place within the history of this world, (2) salvation history is distinct from profane history (note that Rahner argues for a distinction, not a separation), and (3) salvation history explains profane history. Rahner argues in favor of this last point in order to safeguard the ultimate reality (God), which grounds, sustains, and explains human history. "Salvation," writes Rahner, "is God and his grace and God's grace is not simply identical with the reality which is engaged in evolving history. . . . History is not simply the history of God himself—a theogony—and so does not find its ultimate basis in itself and is not self explanatory."[17]

While he strongly affirms the historical mediation of salvation, Rahner wants to avoid the danger of anthropological reductionism that might too closely associate the ultimate gift of human realization and life with any particular historical reality. In this sense, Rahner considers history "the realm of the provisional, the unfinished, the ambiguous, the dialectical."[18] However, this ambiguity with respect to history has led some of his critics to charge that his theology does not embrace a single approach to history. Even while acknowledging that Rahner recognizes one history in the sense that "there are no isolated sectors" of human existence that "are in no way co-determined by the history of grace and faith (or vice versa),"[19] such critics charge that, in his thought, salvation history remains qualitatively and quantitatively different from the history of the world.[20]

Undoubtedly, there is some ambiguity with respect to Rahner's arguments on the nature of history. His arguments appear to have been shaped with the following two objectives in mind: (1) the desire to preserve the absolute gratuity of the triune life of grace with respect to historical and all other created realities, and (2) his understanding of history as a creature of God and as such a created reality that encounters its true origin and future only when understood in light of the history of God's triune self-communication.[21]

With respect to both of these, the reader should note that Rahner upholds that the freedom of the "corporeal, social, and historical creature" to accept or refuse the gratuitous gift of salvation occurs "in all the dimensions of human existence with the world and not merely in the confined sector of the sacred or of worship and 'religion' in the narrow sense; it occurs in encounters with one's neighbor, with one's historical task, with the so-called world of every-day life, in and with what we call the history of the individual and of communities."[22] In this sense Rahner clearly intends to root salvation (understood as God's triune reality) in human history. But even while underscoring the historical mediation of salvation, Rahner does not want to turn history into a final arbitrator or judge of reality. Thus, he writes:

> Yet according to Christian eschatology, the decisions taken in salvation-history will be enacted in ever clearer forms and signs; they will fashion their own embodiments and expressions *in the most profound depths of existence within the history of the world,* even though final judgment, which will make a clear distinction between the wheat and the cockle within these objectifications belongs to God alone. (italics added)[23]

In Rahner's view the final judgment of historical events is in God's hands. While he insists that there is only *one* call to salvation comprised of human and divine communal expressions, and while he argues that there is no isolated sector of human existence that is not co-determined by grace,[24] he also wants to highlight that one "can only surmise, hope, or fear—but one cannot judge. The history of the world is not itself the judgment of the world, no matter how true it is that this judgment really takes place in that history."[25]

As noted earlier, Rahner's theology of grace conceives history in light of a fundamental openness to share in the life of God. For Rahner, God's saving history is a special and climactic chapter within the history of the world that entails God's triune self-communication.[26] "The Trinity is a mystery of *salvation,* otherwise it would not have been revealed" (italics in original).[27] In this latter sense, "theology (the doctrine of God) is inseparable from soteriology."[28] To know the "how" of our salvation is to know the historical manifestation of the mystery of God.

As Christians, we do not simply confess belief in an abstract God but in the God of life-giving accompaniment. Or, as Walter Kasper underscores, "The Christian concern is not with God in himself but with God-for-us, the God of

Jesus Christ, who is a God of human beings (Heb. 11.16)."[29] Thus, any Christian attempt to understand issues of grace and soteriology must somehow delve into the subject of trinitarian theology.

Rahner's axiom, which affirms the economic Trinity as the immanent Trinity (and vice versa), affirms that it is Godself that has been offered in history for the sake of human salvation. Seen from this perspective, the history of communal life among divine Persons is necessarily tied up with the history of communal life among human persons.[30] Or, to put it another way, salvation necessarily entails a social reality because God is a social being. Just as the divine community guarantees the eternal survival of divine Persons (God the Father/Mother is forever begetting the Word and breathing forth the Spirit in communal *perichoresis*),[31] so does human community guarantee the temporal survival and eternal mediation of salvation. While it is true that human communities cannot ultimately survive without God, God is encountered in the faith–filled human responses that actualize salvation.

Following the classic Thomistic theology of grace noted above, it is important to underscore that God's saving life cannot be conceived apart (separate) from human life. God's saving triune life presupposes, is encountered within, and perfects human communities. Or, as Catherine LaCugna underscores in her ground-breaking reflections on the Trinity, the life of God does not belong to God alone but is shared with us so that, accompanied by God, human and divine communities might eternally move to and from each other. Echoing Rahner's economic, soteriological, and utterly trinitarian starting point, LaCugna writes:

> The starting point in the economy of redemption, in contrast to the intradivine starting point, locates *perichoresis* not in God's inner life but in the mystery of the *one communion of all persons, divine as well as human.* From this standpoint 'the divine dance' is indeed an apt image of persons in communion: not for an intradivine communion but for divine life as all creatures partake and literally exist in it. Not through its own merit but through God's election from all eternity (Eph 1:3–14), humanity has been made a partner in the divine dance. Everything comes from God, and everything returns to God, through Christ in the Spirit. This *exitus* and *reditus* is the choreography of the divine dance which takes place from all eternity and is manifest at every moment of creation. There are not two sets of communion—one among the divine persons, the other among human persons, with the latter supposed to replicate the former. The one *perichoresis,* the one mystery of communion includes God and humanity as beloved partners in the dance. This is what Jesus prayed for in the high-priestly prayer in John's gospel (John 17:20–21).[32]

To summarize, Rahner's theology of grace, which assumes and develops basic Thomistic foundations in theological anthropology, offers a central source in contemporary Catholic thought for the unity of divine and human history. Rahner's theology makes clear that there is one God, whose saving and triune self-communication is historically manifested. Accordingly, God's offer of salvation takes place in all the communal dimensions of human existence within the world and as such cannot be confined to what would be characterized as simply "sacred" or "religious" activity. Most important with respect to arguments in this essay is the relationship between the eternal and soteriological nature of God's communal life and the historical and transcendental openness of human communities to receive and respond to that life.

There is little doubt that contemporary Catholic theological anthropology is much indebted to Karl Rahner. Among others, Latin American liberation theologies have deeply benefited from his contributions. In this chapter I cannot fully expand upon this insight. Suffice it for now to point out that the theological underpinnings for understanding salvation as liberation in the work of a number of Latin American liberation theologians can be found in the integral approach to nature and grace (salvation history and human history) that was prepared by theologians such as Karl Rahner.[33] I now turn to the historicity of salvation and the notion of liberation in Latin American theology and its relation to the life of God.

THE LATIN AMERICAN CONTRIBUTION: THE HISTORICITY OF SALVATION AND THE NOTION OF SALVATION AS LIBERATION

In his essay entitled "The Historicity of Christian Salvation" Ignacio Ellacuría offers two approaches to understanding the relationship between salvation history and human history. On the one hand, he notes there are those who see the "historical character of the salvific acts," and on the other hand, those who see "the salvific character of historical acts." Ellacuría points out how those in the first group are "mainly concerned with historically grounding and objectively proving fundamental acts of faith," while those in the second group are "especially concerned with which historical acts bring salvation and which bring condemnation, which acts make God more present, and how that presence is actualized and made effective in them."[34]

In an insightful discussion Ellacuría highlights how Latin American liberation theologies approach the relationship between salvation history and the history of the world. This approach can be summarized as follows: (1) There is but one history that includes salvation history and the so-called profane history; (2) this history is part of God's history and comprises what God has done with all of nature, what God has done in human history, and what God wants to come from God's eternal and constant self-giving; (3) the history of salvation is offered as a salvation in history; (4) salvation *in* history is a salvation *of* history; and (5) the history of salvation includes but goes beyond political liberation.[35]

It might be good to recall at this time our previous discussion of Rahner's notion of the "supernatural existential," and how the theological presuppositions of this notion have affected how Catholic theologians, including Latin American liberation theologians, have come to relate divine and human life. Ellacuría's discussion captures the Latin American desire to give greater weight to particular histories and understand with greater unity (greater than the unity exemplified in Rahner) the relationship between these historical realities and the triune life of God. As Ellacuría argues, it is not simply history in the abstract but all historical reality that is rooted *in* the very being of God:

> It would not be that God is in all things, as essence, presence, and potential depending on the character of those things; it would be that all things, each in its own way, have been grafted with the triune life and refer essentially to that life. The *theologal* dimension of the created world, which should not be confused with the *theological* dimension, would reside in that presence of the trinitarian life, which is intrinsic to all things, but which in human beings can be apprehended as reality and as principle of personality. There is a strict experience of this theologal dimension, and through it there is a strict personal, social, and historical experience of God. This experience has different degrees and forms; but when it is a true experience of the real theologal dimension of human beings, of society, of history, and in a different measure, of purely material things, it is an experience and physical probing of the triune life itself, however mediated, incarnated, and historicized.[36]

Similar arguments relating divine life with particular human histories can be found in the writings of Leonardo Boff and Gustavo Gutiérrez. For instance, Boff associates salvation with "an existential actualization of the mystery of communion," and Gutiérrez speaks of salvation as a process of entering into the charity that unites the three Persons of the Trinity."[37] For Boff, liberation entails the struggle against oppression that keeps persons from participation and communion, "the realities that most closely mirror the very mystery of trinitarian communion in human history."[38] For Gutiérrez, liberation entails the practice of charity, and charity "does not exist outside" the ethical choice of placing oneself in the path of neighbor so as to build "a just and friendly world." "To work, to transform this world, is to become a man and to build the human community; it is also to save."[39]

These various arguments from Latin American liberation theology assume and develop the basic theological premise regarding the communion that "always and everywhere" exists between divine and human life. Once again, at the heart of Rahner's theological contribution to contemporary theological anthropology is the notion that human nature is an intrinsic moment of the life of grace. There is in this sense no pure nature, no pure human activity, and no mere historical reality. Particular human realities exist already gratuitously elevated to a "supernatural" order. In this sense liberation theology historicizes from a Latin American context of poverty and marginalization the human encounter with God.

The existential openness of human nature and persons embraced in Rahner's notion of the supernatural existential becomes in liberation theologies a transcendental openness of historical reality.[40] This enables liberation theologians to speak not merely of political, historical, or ethical praxis but "a transcendent historical praxis, which makes manifest the God who becomes present in the acts of history."[41] This fundamental premise in liberation theology allows for salvation to be understood as truly human, truly historical—salvation is human liberation, though this is not all that it is! Salvation breaks forth within the human story that ordinarily begins, though does not end, with the historical liberation of persons. Conversely, human history, which salvation history presupposes, is an open history that finds its future and fulfillment in God's life.

Within this integral approach to history, God's history is conceived as *one*, "as nothing but the structural unity" in the Ellacurían sense "of salvation history and the history of the world."[42] No mere divine act, salvation is necessarily also a human response to the presence of God in history. The divine and human are brought together; salvation history and the history of the world co-determine and birth one another as one single history: God's history. This enables the economy *(oikonomia)* where God comes to dwell historically with us to be conceived as the expression of the human-divine communion, or, to be more theologically precise, as "the concrete realization of the mystery of *theologia* in time, space, history, and personality."[43] From this perspective of integral communion, salvation cannot exist without a history of liberation. For indeed, as liberation theologians underscore, God's saving/liberative praxis is "sown in the fields of the world and in history, so as to make it a history of God, of a God who is definitively all in all."[44] This is what liberation theologians intend when they give primacy to the salvation mediated in the historical liberation of the people of Israel.

THE U.S. HISPANIC CONTRIBUTION:
THE CULTURAL FACE OF SALVATION
AND SALVATION AS SURVIVAL OF COMMUNITY

"The challenge for those of us who have been inspired and influenced by liberation theology," writes Roberto Goizueta, "is to appreciate the fundamental insights of that movement while, at the same time, drawing from our different experiences and historical contexts in order to engage Latin Americans in a dialogue that will foster the further developments and deepening of those fundamental insights."[45] A brief perusal of the writings of Latino/a theologians would suffice to recognize the centrality of communal survival. Perhaps Ada María Isasi-Díaz captures the meaning of this central U.S. Hispanic theme best when she writes, "'Being fully' or 'not being' is what survival is all about. As Hispanic Women, 'being' designates existence in time and space; it means physical survival, and it means cultural survival, which depends to a large extent on self-determination and self-identity."[46] Survival starts with the physical but must also include the social and cultural dimensions of life.[47]

Survival, understood in this integral sense, is the key anthropological piece to construct a Latino/a soteriology. If in Latin American theology salvation is linked to the liberation of the oppressed, then in Latina/o theology salvation must be linked to the survival of our Latino/a identity.[48] Without abandoning the preferential option for the poor (in the socioeconomic sense of the term) Latino/a theologies witness to what we have named the preferential option for culture.[49] "This option does not exclude other socioeconomic, racial, and historical dimensions but in fact presupposes them, since culture cannot exist without them."[50]

I began these reflections noting the most recent and ongoing type of survival that a number of Latinos/as face, namely, survival of the most basic and ordinary expression of being church and community—the family. Challenged by the reality of deportation, thousands of illegal immigrants (not only Latinos/as) struggle to keep this communal reality alive. As the illegal immigrant named Tapia suggests in the story noted at the beginning of this essay, she and her husband struggle to preserve their family in the midst of various political and socioeconomic threats. Her story witnesses to cultural and socioeconomic human conditions that must be in place for the survival of community. But from another point of view, Tapia's story is not just about the mere preservation of communal identity. Read against a Christian theology that understands the historical mediation of God's life, the survival of human community, and, in particular, the family (in its various familial expressions) becomes the most ordinary means for humans to encounter God's salvation.

Many other social and ecclesial conditions exist that also threaten the survival of Latino/a families and communities. On the social side, poverty, unemployment, poor education, drug use, AIDS, hate crimes, and domestic violence toward women and children (in a recent study 70 percent of three hundred Latina women reported domestic victimization) all threaten the stability of Latina/o families. On the religious side, Latino/a families often find themselves alienated in churches and in sacramental "cerebrations" (rather than "celebrations"). A great number of pastoral agents (lay and ordained) simply lack adequate freedom and preparation relative to the ways that God's life crosses over and relates racially and culturally speaking. Thus, whether we speak of social or ecclesial life, survival is the most common human challenge facing Latinos/as in this country.

The notion of salvation as survival of community lies at the heart of Latino/a theologies and, more specifically, is a central theme in Latina/o popular Catholicism. To date, the theological interpretations of various symbols and narratives associated with Latino/a popular Catholicism exemplify how survival is understood as a kind of communal preservation, liberation, and "healing" (to use the most basic term associated with Augustine's soteriology) essential for the mediation of salvation. It is not by chance that some of the great voices in European and Latin American theologies have argued for the integral relationship between salvation history and human history on the basis of the experience of popular Catholicism: "The affirmation of God's history as the true history embracing everything that happens in history . . . comes to us through popular religion and also through pre-Christian religious traditions."[51]

Unlike European Western cultures, where modernity has birthed forth secularism and what Rahner characterizes as the "exiling" of God from ordinary human experiences, Latino/a popular Catholicism, steeped in pre-modern traditions and medieval Catholic roots, evidences the historical omnipresence of God.[52] The attention given by Latino/a theologians to the presence of God in *lo cotidiano* suggests how Latino/a theology "localizes" even more than Latin American theology the historicity of salvation. No other theological loci within the Latino/a popular Catholic world evidence this localization more than popular "Marian" devotions. "Mary" is omnipresent in the Latino/a Catholic world. She can be found in home altars, in the streets, in businesses, and tattooed on the bodies of Latinos/as. For a great number of Latino/a Catholics, she is the sociocultural sign of God's face turned to save and preserve communal identity in the ordinariness of history.

For me as a Cuban American, this ordinary encounter with God's saving presence was most evident in the yearly popular celebrations that accompany the feast day of Our Lady of Charity in Miami. These celebrations, which take place every September 8, are packed with cultural and sociopolitical significance.[53] The cry uttered by thousands of exiled Cubans to the "exiled" Virgin of Charity does not merely, or primarily, intend a "spiritual" outcome.[54] "Virgen de la Caridad, salva a Cuba" (Virgin of Charity, save Cuba) is a cry that expresses the conviction of those gathered to see God's salvific hand at work manifested *in* the survival of the homeland and *in* the cultural survival of the exiled community.[55]

Without erasing particular sociocultural and political differences related to U.S. Hispanic communities, and the many ways that these particular differences get sacramentally expressed and celebrated, other U.S. Hispanic devotions to the Virgin also exemplify the notion of salvation as survival of communal identity. This is certainly the case with the most widely known of all U.S. Hispanic "Marian" devotions—the devotion to *la morenita,* Virgin of Guadalupe. As the guardian of cultural memory and as a sociocultural expression of God's life with us, Guadalupe represents the survival/salvation of particular communities.[56]

If, as Espín argues, "the term *grace* labels not a thing but an experience—the human experience of God-for-and-within-us—and if it is true that it is the relational divine being (Trinity) that Christians find in the human experience of grace, and if it is necessary that all experiences of God and of God's grace be culturally mediated,"[57] then Guadalupe or any of the other "Marys" of Latino/a Catholicism can be understood as theological signs of grace, and more specifically in light of this essay, communal signs of grace that point to God's intention to preserve and save particular human communities.

Within Latino/a popular Catholicism any of the U.S. Hispanic "Marian" devotions offers a powerful reminder that God's salvific desire includes communal survival and all that this entails with respect to the transformation of unjust social, economic, political, cultural, racial, and gender experiences. These popular "Marian" devotions offer a visible manifestation of salvation where Latinos/as can *see* themselves overshadowed by the life of grace. Seeing Guadalupe, or seeing Our Lady of Charity, for instance, offers Mexican Americans and Cuban Americans respectively an understanding of how God's saving history has been at work in their history. To behold Our Lady of Guadalupe or Our Lady of Charity is to behold culturally God's saving hand stretched out to the Juan Diegos and Juan Morenos of this world. The consequence of beholding God's salvation is nothing less than life.[58]

From this vantage point, these "Marian" devotions offer the possibility of seeing the mystery of God *(theologia)* as a sociocultural "economized" reality. God's will in administering human history is socioculturally expressed through this woman whose most common and communal identity is within marginalized, oppressed, and suffering communities—communities who struggle daily for survival.

Because this woman has been "grafted" with God's life, the sociocultural realities that she embodies within the Latino/a world are challenged by and refer essentially to that life. This woman re-presents the historicity of salvation because, analogous to the divine Persons whose existence emerges from "community," her human identity emerges from and depends upon the relationship of divine and particular human communities. The "Marys" of Latino/a popular Catholicism are "of God," but they are also of particular Latino/a communities. In this sense, this woman serves as a sacramental sign of particular and "supernaturally" elevated communities of faith.[59] In her various ways of embodying distinct communal identities she witnesses to the communal and historical nature of God's salvific self-communication.

U.S. Hispanic Catholic theologians are not alone in highlighting the importance of popular religion, particularly U.S. Hispanic "Marian" devotions. For instance, in her insightful article "Ignored Virgin or Unaware Women," Nora Lozano-Díaz comments on the importance of Guadalupe as a "cultural symbol that affects all people of Mexican descent." Even while recognizing the oppressive history of this devotion with respect to women, Lozano-Díaz argues that "if Mexican and Mexican-American Protestant women cannot approach the Lady of Guadalupe as a religious symbol, they can look at her through other liberating efforts approached from cultural and feminist perspectives."[60]

Beyond the anthropological significance of serving as a guardian of culture, other Latino/a Protestant theologians have recognized the theological significance of these popular "Marian" devotions. Justo González, widely considered the leading voice of Latino/a Protestant theologies, underscores that "for generation upon generation of oppressed Indian people, told by word and deed that they were inferior, the Virgin has been a reminder that there is vindication for the Juan Diegos." He goes on to argue how "that is indeed part of the gospel message, even if it has not always been part of our message."[61]

Perhaps even more important for our present discussion, and especially with the intent of precipitating conversation around a more ecumenically minded U.S. Hispanic soteriology, is González's discussion about how "Protestant alienation in Latin America has usually been not only other worldly but also foreign oriented."[62] In many ways the "Marys" of U.S. Hispanic popular Catholicism can be for Protestants both otherworldly and foreign. For some Protestant U.S. Hispanics, she may come across as being divinely otherworldly as a result of Catholic theologies and popular practices that have presented her as if she were God. For others, she could be perceived to be humanly foreign when she has been presented primarily as a cultural sign of the Roman Catholic faith. In a similar way, Lozano-Díaz comments on the relationship between earthly and heavenly citizenship, especially in light of the many ways this relationship affects the ways Latino/a Protestants relate to "Marian" devotions:

> Protestants have been taught to live primarily as citizens from heaven and not from earth. Thus many Protestants have been encouraged to live their Protestantism outside their culture. This idea of living outside the culture is related to the anti-Catholic perspective mentioned above. Since the culture is seen as permeated with Catholic views, it is necessary, as much as possible, to withdraw oneself from it. In many cases, as soon as a person converts to the Protestant faith, he or she is required to stop dancing, smoking, drinking, playing cards, watching movies, seeing plays, attending bull fights or horse races. The new believer is taught to see life dualistically: the church and the world are opposite and conflicting realities. Thus new believers are required to retreat from the world, from any political or social commitment, and from culture in general. Although this idea of a heavenly citizenship is a valid one, it is also true that while Mexican and Mexican-American Protestants are on earth, they are also citizens and members of an earthly culture: the Latino one. Even though some Protestants have

tried to live outside earthly culture, this is not feasible. Every human being lives in a culture, and even if a person does not want to acknowledge it, the culture affects her.[63]

In light of what I have been arguing up to this point—the principle that outside survival of community there is no salvation—González's and Lozano-Díaz's observations carry enormous implications for ecumenical conversations. Whether or not the Virgin or any other popular religious expression is the locus of ecumenical conversations in soteriology is ultimately not what is most important (however important this locus might be for socioculturally mediating salvation for a given Latino/a community). What *is* essential is whether or not Latino/a Catholics and Protestants come to a consensus with respect to the *theologal* nature of our earthly citizenship. Or, to be more precise, can we see our earthly communal citizenship as an embodiment of our heavenly communal citizenship? Can we understand our temporal efforts to preserve community as being consistent with the eternal plan and life of God? Could we agree that the survival of our particular communal identities is essential because what is at risk is the encounter with God? How we represent that accompaniment is secondary and particular to our distinct religious histories.

Arriving at consensus around these issues may raise some ancient questions with respect to how Catholics and Protestants conceive the origin, present state, and destiny of history and all created reality. It may precipitate anew conversations around grace, human reality, the nature of salvation, and the human response. In the past, Catholics have tended to underscore the human response, whereas Protestants have tended to underscore the divine initiative.[64] But in our Latino/a way of embracing both/and approaches, can we opt for both grace and human effort, both survival and salvation? Can we can foster new ecumenical approaches that uphold the human efforts to preserve our communal identities as legitimate responses to the gospel and God's offer of salvation?

José Rodriguez suggests the possibility of this ecumenical vision when he engages the literary works of Piri Thomas in Chapter 6 of this volume. Thomas writes about the kind of evangelization that often proclaims Christ but forgets the identity and dignity of the hearers of this word, or the Christian proclamation that comes fully "armed with all the knowledge of the Bible," but lacks understanding of what makes Latino/a communities "tick." In such cases one wonders how the gospel can be received as good and saving news. Such lack of attentiveness to the particularity encountered within Latino/a communities is not only an issue within Anglo Protestant Churches. Even within Catholic communities in the U.S., where one might expect a more "sacramental" or analogical approach to faith and culture, there are plenty of examples where Latinos/as have been left "hanging on the cross," denied their particular saving ways of encountering the mystery of God.

CONCLUSION:
THE LATINO/A SOTERIOLOGICAL CONTRIBUTION
IN THE NEW REFORMATION

In this essay I have underscored an integral approach to survival of communities and their salvation. Salvation cannot be understood in "merely" religious terms, as a divine promise that concerns the world to come, bearing no relationship to the survival of and transformation of the present one. God's radical activity in the world, especially God's presence in Jesus, where human reality is not destroyed but rather "assumed," "raised," "perfected," and "transformed," underscores the theological referent of all created and historical reality. As Rahner has rightly noted, from this christological perspective, anthropology is for all eternity theology.[65]

After an introduction focusing on the social and political threats that face a number of immigrant families and suggesting the theological implications entailed in the physical, social, and cultural survival of these communities, this essay examined the relationship between nature and grace, and, more specifically, salvation history and the history of the world. I highlighted the contribution of Karl Rahner and argued for the integral way of relating human and divine communities, especially noting the classic Thomistic principle that affirms that God's triune life of grace presupposes, is manifested in, and completes human life. In particular, the economy of salvation (God's work through Christ and in the Spirit) is "proof" that God's reality is eternally communal. In turn, the central call of human reality is to participate in this reality, to remain historically anchored in God at all times.

The chapter turned next to an examination of the historicity of salvation, highlighting the work of a number of Latin American theologians. The notion of salvation as liberation has prevailed in this theology and points to the fundamental way in which liberation theologians conceive the oneness of historical reality and its transcendental function. The transcendental nature of historical reality is the reason why sin in Latin American liberation theology is conceived as a form of idolatry—sin makes absolute a given historical reality. The consequence of sin is a "hold back" at the level of creaturehood of the openness that historical reality has with respect to the life of God.[66]

Finally, turning to the U.S. Hispanic context, this essay proposed and examined the notion of survival as salvation. Survival should not be understood as a mere "getting by" with respect to ordinary life challenges. Indeed, in Spanish the word *sobrevivir* suggests not only the human struggle to survive in the midst of difficult situations but also a life experience of plenitude and abundance (in an eschatological sense of the term). Celia Cruz's rendition of Frederick Perren's and Dino Fekaris's song "I Will Survive" suggests both of these approaches to survival. Cruz's rendition uses only the word *sobrevivir* not only in reference to ordinary life struggles that have sustained her, but also with respect to the eschatological fullness that awaits her. In this life she sings, "I am surviving so that my people can hear me. . . . Breaking out of chains, I go on surviving. Crossing borders, I go on surviving." The song ends with her emphatic declaration that she will not only survive *(Yo viviré)*, but that she will indeed live in abundance *(Yo sobreviré)!*[67]

Grounded in the communal life of God and its communal worldly manifestation, and rooted in the widely accepted premise that theology (critical reflection on the reality of God) cannot be separated from soteriology (critical reflection on the saving reality of God), I argued for the principle that outside the survival of community there is no salvation. If we take seriously the communal life of God and its historical "incarnation," we must consider the importance of human communities and the impact of racial, cultural, gender, social, and religious experiences on these communities. Echoing a basic Thomistic principle, I argued that God does not destroy but rather desires, presupposes, and perfects the survival of particular life-giving communal realities in God's own eternal image.[68] As a way to exemplify my arguments I offered the "Marys" of U.S. Hispanic popular Catholicism as visible signs of the historicity of God's salvific communal manifestation.

At the beginning of my reflections I mentioned the raids on immigrant communities in Minnesota that took place on the feast day of Our Lady of Guadalupe. As the bishops from Minnesota point out in their statement, government officials added insult to injury by choosing to act on this significant religious feast day. To coopt the feast of Guadalupe in this way was tragic. But these cruel human actions paradoxically reveal the integral approach to survival proposed in this chapter. Because these raids occurred precisely on this feast day, they offer a powerful reminder of the connection that exists between social experiences and the life of God. If, as I have stated above, Guadalupe offers a sociocultural sign of God's communal self-offering to particular human communities, then, among other things, she witnesses that actions against the Juan Diegos of this world are actions that concern God. In her, survival of particular communities and God's desire to save are inextricably bound.

The theology of survival embraced in this chapter invites Latino/a Catholics and Protestants to join hands in what González has called the New Reformation. In this New Reformation earthly concerns can be understood to be "always and everywhere" under the shadow of God's triune life of grace. Any struggle in favor of the survival of our communities, whether we speak of defending the rights of illegal immigrant families, who face in their daily life *(lo cotidiano)* multiple forms of survival, or of standing in solidarity with more established Latino/a communities that still struggle to maintain their particular social, cultural, and religious identity in hostile ecclesial and social environments, must be seen as more than just a human struggle—it is also an ethical struggle to preserve historical links to the life of God. In our efforts to bridge heavenly and earthly realities, we might do well to listen to Christ's words embodying his practice of divine hospitality toward his human family:

Whenever you did it to the least of my earthly bodily community, you did it unto me (Mt 25:45).

NOTES

[1] According to a study conducted by PEW Hispanic Center in 2005, there were 3.1 million children living in the United States in homes in which the head of the household was unauthorized. Available on the pewhispanic.org website.

[2] "Minnesota Bishops Statement on Immigration," December 22, 2006. Available on the mncc.org website.

[3] N. C. Aizenman, "Pleading to Stay a Family," *Washington Post*, April 2, 2007.

[4] Ibid.

[5] It is customary in Catholic theology to draw comparisons between Creator and creature. Even while recognizing such similarities between Creator and creature, Catholic theology also affirms the dissimilarity that exists between human life and divine life. Because of the theology of grace implied in this teaching (one that sees a certain continuity between God and creature and differences in understanding the sovereignty of God over all creation), this Catholic teaching has at times been distinguished from what has been characterized as the Protestant dialectical imagination. This analogical approach has been characterized as a "similarity in difference" approach. See Richard McBrien, *Catholicism* (New York: HarperCollins, 1994), 15.

[6] Karl Rahner, "The Church's Commission to Bring Salvation and the Humanization of the World," in *Theological Investigations* 4 (New York: Seabury Press, 1976), 304.

[7] Justo L. González, *Mañana: Christian Theology from a Hispanic Perspective* (Nashville, TN: Abingdon Press, 1990), 74.

[8] See Francis A. Sullivan, *Salvation Outside the Church? Tracing the History of the Catholic Response* (New York: Paulist Press, 1992).

[9] Throughout this paper the proper noun *Mary* and its adjective *Marian* have been placed in quotes to suggest the theological complexity of this symbol within Latino/a theologies. As has already been pointed out by others, it would be a mistake to identify any of the U.S. Hispanic popular "Marys" simply with Mary of Nazareth.

[10] See Karl Rahner, "Nature and Grace," in Rahner, *Theological Investigations* 4 (New York: Crossroad, 1982), 165–188.

[11] Note that when asked to list the ideas and persons that influenced his theology, Rahner stated: "The spirituality of Ignatius, which we receive through the practice of prayer and religious formation, has been undoubtedly more important to me than all the specialized philosophy and theology both within and outside the Society." In P. Imhof and H. Biallowons, *Karl Rahner in Dialogue: Conversations and Interviews 1965–1982* (New York: Crossroad, 1986), 251.

[12] See Karl Rahner, "The Church's Commission to Bring Salvation and the Humanization of the World," 304.

[13] See Stephen J. Duffy, *The Dynamics of Grace: Perspectives in Theological Anthropology* (Collegeville, MN: The Liturgical Press, 1993), 167–172. See also Bernard Quelquejeu, "Anthropological Presuppositions of Human Existence," in *Is Being Human a Criterion of Being Christian?*, ed. Marcus Lefébure (New York: Seabury Press, 1982), 58–64.

[14] For a discussion of Rahner's theology of symbol, see Miguel H. Díaz, *On Being Human: U.S. Hispanic and Rahnerian Perspectives* (Maryknoll, NY: Orbis Books, 2001), 92–94.

[15] Karl Rahner, *Foundations of Christian Faith: An Introduction to the Idea of Christianity* (New York: Crossroad, 1990), 224–225.

[16] Karl Rahner, "History of the World and Salvation History," in *Theological Investigations* 5 (London: Darton, Longman, and Todd, 1966), 97–114. As Ignacio Ellacuría has observed, this essay comes at a time when Rahner has not developed the kind of political sensitivity shown later in his writings. Still, Rahner's essay evidences the mediating role he ascribes to history. For Ellacuría's comments, "The Historicity of Christian Salvation," in *Mysterium Liberationis: Fundamental Concepts of Liberation Theology*, ed. Ignacio Ellacuría and Jon Sobrino (Maryknoll, NY: Orbis Books, 1993), 271.

[17] Rahner, "History of the World and Salvation History," 110.

[18] Ibid., 97.

[19] Ibid., 100.

[20] See José Sols Lucia, *La Teología Histórica de Ignacio Ellacuría* (Madrid: Editorial Trotta, 1999), 107–109.

[21] Note Gustavo Gutiérrez's comment that Rahner's position seems ambiguous (*A Theology of Liberation* [Maryknoll, NY: Orbis Books, 1988], note 14).

[22] Rahner's philosophical basis for highlighting material reality as mediator of grace is laid out in his epistemological approach to Thomas's sense-based metaphysics. See Rahner, *Spirit in the World* (New York: Continuum, 1994).

[23] Rahner, "History of the World and Salvation History," 112.

[24] Ibid., 100.

[25] Ibid., 101.

[26] See Karl Rahner, *The Trinity* (New York: Crossroad, 1997), esp. 88–102. See also Thomas F. O'Meara, "A History of Grace," in *A World of Grace: An Introduction to the Themes and Foundations of Karl Rahner's Theology*, ed. Leo O'Donovan (New York: Crossroad, 1984), esp. 84–87.

[27] Rahner, *The Trinity*, 21.

[28] Catherine LaCugna, *God for Us: The Trinity and Christian Life* (New York: HarperCollins, 1973), 8.

[29] Walter Kasper, *The God of Jesus Christ* (New York: Crossroad, 1986), 158.

[30] LaCugna, *God for Us*, 228.

[31] *Perichoresis* is a term that has been used to define the "divine dance" or communal life of God comprised of mutual giving and receiving among the divine Persons. On this all-important notion, see ibid., 270–278.

[32] Ibid., 274.

[33] For instance, see Lucia, *La Teología Histórica de Ignacio Ellacuría*, 25–27; Martin Maier, "Karl Rahner: The Teacher of Ignacio Ellacuría," in *Love Produces Hope: The Thought of Ignacio Ellacuría* (Collegeville, MN: The Liturgical Press, 2006), 128–143; and Gutiérrez, *A Theology of Liberation*, 43–44.

[34] Ignacio Ellacuría, "The Historicity of Christian Salvation," 251. Philosophically speaking, Ellacuría's distinction with respect to Christian historical transcendence reflects his critique of what he conceived to have been the forgetfulness of the real in Western metaphysics in favor of being. Such forgetfulness has led European theologians to prioritize meaning over reality and, more important, of *rooting reality in being (ser) rather than being in reality*. To overcome this forgetfulness, Ellacuría proposes the "sensible apprehension" of reality "in its own right." Sensing and intellectual

are united in an open-ended process of apprehending. See Robert Lassalle-Klein, "Ignacio Ellacuría's Debt to Xavier Zubiri: Critical Principles and Theology of Liberation," in *Love Produces Hope,* 88–121, esp. 96, 103–104.

[35] For principles 3–5, I am indebted to the excellent summary provided in Lucia, *La Teología Histórica de Ignacio Ellacuría,* 119–126. The other two principles are derived from Ellacuría, "The Historicity of Christian Salvation," 272–274.

[36] Ellacuría, "The Historicity of Christian Salvation," 277. Note that consistent with his philosophical and theological criticism of Western thinkers' forgetfulness of the real and logification of intelligence, Ellacuría distinguishes between the theological (emphasis on reflection) and the theologal (emphasis on absolute and ultimate reality).

[37] Leonardo Boff, "Trinity," in *Systematic Theology: Perspectives from Liberation Theology,* ed. Jon Sobrino and Ignacio Ellacuría (Maryknoll, NY: Orbis Books, 1996), 77; Gutierrez, *A Theology of Liberation,* 115.

[38] Leonardo Boff, *Trinity and Society* (Maryknoll, NY: Orbis Books, 1988), 152.

[39] Gutiérrez, *A Theology of Liberation,* 113, 91. For a critique of the Latin American liberation anthropology that focuses on the human being as *homo faber,* and the notion that being human means being an agent of change engaged in the transformation of society, see Roberto S. Goizueta, *"Fiesta:* Life in the Subjunctive," in *From the Heart of Our People: Latino/a Explorations in Systematic Theology,* ed. Orlando O. Espín and Miguel H. Díaz (Maryknoll, NY: Orbis Books, 1999), 88.

[40] See Maier, "Karl Rahner: The Teacher of Ignacio Ellacuría," 138.

[41] Ellacuría, "The Historicity of Salvation," 264.

[42] Ibid., 274. Ellacuría borrows the notion of "structural unity" from Zubiri to refer to the way historical reality is organized. See Lucia, *La Teología Histórica de Ignacio Ellacuría,* 112–115.

[43] LaCugna, *God for Us,* 221–223. The reader should note how LaCugna assumes, critiques, and goes beyond Rahner's axiom ("economic Trinity is immanent Trinity and vice versa"). Briefly stated, LaCugna critiques the language of economic and immanent distinctions for its suggestion that "distinctions in the economy . . . originate in and are grounded in distinctions 'in' God." She proposes an alternative axiom ("*theologia* is fully revealed and bestowed in *oikonomia,* and *oikonomia* expresses the ineffable mystery of *theologia"*), whose main objective is to understand the economy as the comprehensive plan of God in which creatures and God coexist in the mystery of love and communion. From the perspective of this essay, the advantage of LaCugna's proposal is the potential to see the economy not simply (as she argues) as the Trinity *ad extra* but rather, as pointed out in the quotation cited in the body of the essay above, as the historical realization of the mystery of God.

[44] Ibid., 273.

[45] Goizueta, *"Fiesta,"* 89.

[46] Ada María Isasi-Diaz, *En la Lucha, In the Struggle: A Hispanic Woman's Liberation Theology* (Minneapolis: Fortress Press, 1993), 16.

[47] Ibid.

[48] On the theme of Latino/a identity, see articles that appeared in the 2006 issue of the *e-Journal of Hispanic/Latino Theology.* These articles reproduce rich conversations between black Catholic and Latino/a Catholic theologians on the subject of human identity on the occasion of the 2006 ACHTUS Annual Colloquium.

[49] "The preferential option for culture" is the expression that Espín and I have used to characterize Latina/o theology. See Espín and Díaz, "Introduction," in *From the Heart of Our People,* 3.

[50] Ibid.

[51] See Ellacuría, "The Historicity of Christian Salvation," 273. On a similar note, see Rahner's excellent article "The Relation between Theology and Popular Religion," *Theological Investigations* 16 (New York: Crossroad, 1984), esp. 144.

[52] See the various reflections of Orlando Espín on this topic in *The Faith of the People: Theological Reflections on Popular Catholicism* (Maryknoll, NY: Orbis Books, 1997).

[53] For a general discussion of religion and politics in Miami, see Miguel A. de La Torre, *La Lucha for Cuba: Religion and Politics on the Streets of Miami* (Berkeley and Los Angeles: University of California Press, 2003).

[54] On Friday, September 8, 1961, a statue of Our Lady of Charity was smuggled from Cuba through the Panamanian Embassy. This date has been described as the official beginning of the story of Cuban exile Catholicism in the United States. See Thomas Tweed, *Our Lady of the Exile: Diasporic Religion at a Cuban Shrine in Miami* (New York: Oxford University Press, 1997), 15.

[55] The architecture, art, homilies, and way of celebration in the Shrine of Our Lady of Charity in Miami convey a similar meaning. In a future work I hope to devote more time to examining theologically the worship space in the Shrine of Our Lady of Charity. I am particularly interested in the theological significance of the artistic centerpiece behind the altar drawn by self-taught muralist Teok Carrasco. It weaves Cuba's human history with the history of grace (represented by various religious events in the island). See Tweed, *Our Lady of the Exile,* esp. 107–115.

[56] For instance, see Jeanette Rodríguez, "Sangre llama a sangre: Cultural Memory as a Source of Theological Insight," in *Hispanic/Latino Theology: Challenge and Promise*, ed. Ada María Isasi-Díaz and Fernando Segovia, 117–133 (Minneapolis: Fortress Press, 1996); Virgilio Elizondo, "Our Lady of Guadalupe as Cultural Symbol: The Power and the Powerless," in *Liturgy and Cultural Religious Traditions,* ed. David Power and Herman Schmidt (New York: Seabury Press, 1977).

[57] Orlando O. Espín, "An Exploration into the Theology of Grace and Sin," in Espín and Díaz, *From the Heart of Our People,* 139.

[58] Note the parallel with Genesis 32:30, where Jacob sees the face of God and his life is preserved. In a forthcoming work, I intend to revisit and recast Rahner's central anthropological understanding of the human person as hearer of the word, proposing instead the salvific vision of the human person as *seer* of the word

[59] The reader may want to refer to Robert Lassalle-Klein's discussion of Rahner's "supernatural existential." Lassalle-Klein correctly observes how my communal reading of U.S. Hispanic anthropology in *On Being Human* leads to a more communal focus with respect to Rahner's "supernatural existential." See Robert Lassalle-Klein, "Rethinking Rahner on Grace and Symbol: New Proposals from the Americas," in *Rahner beyond Rahner: A Great Theologian Encounters the Pacific Rim,* ed. Paul Crowley (New York: Rowman and Littlefield Publishers, 2005), 88–89.

[60] See Nora O. Lozano-Díaz, "Ignored Virgin or Unaware Women: A Mexican-American Protestant Reflection on the Virgin of Guadalupe," in *A Reader in Latina Feminist Theology: Religion and Justice*, ed. María Pilar Aquino et al. (Austin: University of Texas Press, 2002), 207, 212.

[61] Justo L. González, *Mañana: Christian Theology from a Hispanic Perspective* (Nashville, TN: Abington Press, 1992), 61.

[62] Ibid., 71.

[63] Nora O. Lozano-Díaz, "Ignored Virgin or Unaware Women: A Mexican-American Protestant Reflection on the Virgin of Guadalupe," in *A Reader in Latina Feminist Theology: Religion and Justice,* ed. María Pilar Aquino et al. (Austin: University of Texas Press, 2002), 210–11.

[64] See "Joint Declaration on Justification by the Lutheran World Federation and Catholic Church," October 31, 1999. Available on the vatican.va website.

[65] Rahner, *Foundations of Christian Faith,* 225

[66] See Ellacuría, "The Historicity of Christian Salvation," 277–278. See also David Traverzo Galarza, "Sin: A Hispanic Perspective," in *Teología en Conjunto: A Collaborative Hispanic Protestant Theology*, ed. José David Rodríguez and Loida I. Martell-Otero (Louisville, KY: Westminster John Knox Press, 1997), 119–120.

[67] To listen to the song, visit the tsrocks.com website and search for "Celia Cruz." During the fruitful exchange of ideas at 2007 ACTHUS Annual Colloquium in Los Angeles a number of questions were raised relative to the issue of whether or not survival could connote more than merely getting by. I owe part of this insight to Michael Lee, who prompted me to consider the Spanish rather that the English sense of survival. For an African American perspective that underscores survival rather than liberation as the primary lens to understand the presence of God, see Delores S. Williams, *Sisters in the Wilderness: The Challenge of Womanist God-Talk* (Maryknoll, NY: Orbis Books, 1993).

[68] For a study of the notion of *imago Dei* from the perspective of feminist theological anthropology, see Michelle A. Gonzalez, *Created in God's Image: An Introduction to Feminist Theological Anthropology* (Maryknoll, NY: Orbis Books, 2007), esp. 133–160.

6

Shaping Soteriology *a la latina*

Christian Theology and Writer Piri Thomas

José D. Rodríguez

INTRODUCTION

While Christian teachings explore a great number of topics, such as the triune God, creation, providence, humanity, sin, the church, Christian life, Christian hope, and so on, the distinctiveness of Christian theology lies in the person and work of Jesus Christ. For Daniel L. Migliore, one of today's most distinguished North American Protestant theologians, this assumption is so important that it leads him to claim that "theological reflection on any topic is Christian to the extent that it recognizes the centrality of Jesus Christ and the salvation he brings."[1]

The reason for Jesus' central place in Christian faith lies in the fact that he was the person in whom the disciples and others encountered God. While the Christian's knowledge and encounter with God is not limited to the encounter with Jesus, he provides the central, but not exclusive symbol and norm for understanding God.[2]

One can summarize Jesus' message about God in terms of salvation.[3] Every aspect of Jesus' teaching presents God's gracious initiative of salvation for human existence and the whole of creation. Yet, despite the centrality and importance of salvation for Christianity, the fullness of the experience of salvation and the amplitude of its existential reality make evident that no single definition of salvation can confine its meaning.[4] While the full meaning of salvation remains elusive, and it is conceived specifically in a variety of ways, one can argue that it consists in a positive response to the negativities (sin, sickness, suffering, death, and so forth) that threaten the existence, meaning, purpose, fullness, and destiny of human life. Some contemporary theologians describe it as the "power for making whole and well that which is negative, corrosive, and damaging to human existence, all the way to death or extinction."[5] Others, as "the experience-acceptance of a releasement from the bondage of guilt-sin, the bondage of radical transitoriness and death, the bondage of radical anxiety in all its forms."[6] For Latino/a theologians in the United States, the Christian message of salvation is fundamentally related to the praxis of liberation and human fulfillment in the various dimensions of daily life.

> To be saved is 1) to be liberated from the sins of the individual through the acceptance of a new life in Christ; 2) to be liberated from the oppressive economic, political, and social conditions that constitute corporate sin; and 3) to take control of one's own destiny. In the deepest sense possible, liberation is salvation.[7]

Throughout the centuries the church has confessed that Jesus is Lord and that he brings salvation. Christian theologians have explored the meaning of the person and work of Jesus Christ under the headings of Christology (the doctrine of the person of Jesus Christ) and soteriology (the doctrine of his saving work). Yet for a great number of theologians, and this author as well, the person and work of Christ are inseparable.[8] One could even argue that personal identity is constituted by the cumulative expression of a person's history. In this sense a meaningful expression of anyone's identity, and particularly of Jesus' identity, needs to be closely related to that person's life and actions.[9]

Following this assumption, the early church communicated its understanding of Jesus in Gospel narratives recounting his message, ministry, passion, and resurrection.[10] In what is considered one of the earliest Lutheran dogmatic writings of the sixteenth century, Philip Melanchthon insisted that "to know Christ means to know his benefits."[11] In his explanation of the second article of the Creed in "The Small Catechism" Luther states: "I believe that Jesus Christ, true God, begotten of the Father in eternity, and also a true human being, born of the Virgin Mary, is my Lord. He has redeemed me, a lost and condemned human being."[12] More recently, the Jesuit North American theologian Roger Haight, in his monumental scholarly study of Christology, traces how through the centuries, from the time of the early primitive church to the present, theological reflection about Jesus Christ has been intimately connected to his salvific work of redemption.[13]

PLURALISM OF NEW TESTAMENT CHRISTOLOGIES

While those who came in contact with Jesus and tried to understand his teachings and actions made implicit christological interpretations of him, formal christological interpretations of Jesus developed as Christian interpretations of him were made on the basis of his impact on his disciples. These christological interpretations emerged after Jesus' death and in light of the Easter experience, nurturing the conviction that salvation from God came in a new way mediated through Jesus' resurrection.

In exploring the depth and extent of the pluralism of New Testament Christology, Roger Haight points to five types of Christology in the biblical writings.[14] For Haight, Jesus came to be interpreted as the last or new Adam (the new creation),[15] the Son of God,[16] the prophet animated by God as Spirit,[17] the sage or teacher of wisdom (the embodiment of God's wisdom),[18] and the Word of God the Father.[19]

The significance of the pluralism of Christologies present in the New Testament is twofold. First, it serves to establish the emerging consensus by both biblical and theological scholars that Christology began to develop, not by way of inference from Jesus' teachings and sayings, but out of an Easter experience continually nourished in a liturgical context by worshiping communities in different contexts, witnessing to their particular experience of the risen Jesus.[20] The principle that holds together the Christologies in the biblical writings is that all of them express an existential relationship to the person of Jesus as the bringer of salvation from God. But since this is something that ultimately deals with absolute transcendent mystery, with God, it necessarily yields to a variety of interpretations.[21]

Second, the New Testament witness to the genesis of Christology leads to a continuous historical effort of witnessing to this redemptive act of Jesus Christ among us. Lutheran North American theologian Michael Root argues for the constitutive nature of the narrative structure of soteriology. His claim is that to speak about the redemptive significance of Christian soteriology is to speak not only about the events depicted by the story—the saving work of Jesus Christ throughout his ministry, death, and resurrection as witnessed by his disciples in the New Testament writings—but also to the continuous redeeming narrative character of the story in different geographical and historical settings that illumine and transform the world and life of Christians throughout history.

> Neither simply the events nor simply their narration redeems. The events are redemptive as they grasp peoples and individuals through their depiction in narrative and ritual, Word and Sacrament, . . . The soteriological task within Christian theology is then to show how the Christian story is the story of human redemption. . . . Within soteriology, the theologian attempts to show how the Christian story has a particular kind of relation to the reader's life and world. This story is the story of the reader's redemption. The task within soteriology is to explicate that highly significant relation.[22]

For Root, the biblical story and the life and world of the believer do not exist in isolation but constitute one world and one story. The stories of Jesus and of the believer become related by the narrative connections that make them two sequences within a single larger story. The story becomes good news because redemption follows from the primary form of inclusion in the story. The task of soteriology, then, is to show how the reader is included in the story and how the story then is or can be the story of that reader's redemption.[23]

It is precisely this assumption that led Virgilio Elizondo to reflect on *mestizaje* as a central notion in a Latino/a soteriology aimed at providing a more concrete dimension of the scandalous significance of the redemptive work of God in Jesus Christ. By reflecting on the Galilean identity of Jesus, which for the author mirrors the experience of social and cultural discrimination of Mexican Americans and Latino/as from other cultural backgrounds in the United States, Elizondo calls attention to the conflictual character of Jesus' message of God's reign and his ministry among the marginalized, which came to a climax on the cross. This saving work of God, which incorporates as a central constitutive element Christ's resurrection, brings forth the promise of a new creation to confront idolatrous systems of evil that deprive human beings of their God-given dignity.[24]

DEVELOPMENT OF CLASSICAL SOTERIOLOGY

Christological interpretations were not limited to the New Testament writings. Some of the most important teachings of Christianity, still binding to the large majority of Christians, were articulated during a formative period of history stretching from the second century to the medieval and reformation periods.[25] Throughout this time some of the New Testament metaphors for the liberating and reconciling work of Christ—his ministry, death, and resurrection—were elaborated into theories of atonement.

One of these theories, a favorite among many patristic theologians, is called the cosmic-conflict or Christ the Victor theory. This perspective develops the battle metaphor found in some New Testament passages (see Col 2:15). The work of atonement is viewed as a dramatic struggle between God and the forces of evil in the world. The divine nature of Christ is deeply hidden in the human nature of Jesus of Nazareth, thus fooling the evil forces into thinking that he is an easy target. Gregory of Nyssa (330–395), a Cappadocian Christian theologian from east-central Asia Minor, uses the provocative image of a fish unsuspectingly swallowing the bait on a hook. Under cover of his human nature, Christ overcomes the forces of evil that hold human beings in bondage. By his cross and resurrection, Christ decisively triumphs over these powers and consequently frees their captives.[26]

> Hence it was that God, in order to make himself easily accessible to him who sought the ransom for us, veiled himself in our nature. In that way, as it is with greedy fish, he might swallow the Godhead like a fishhook along with the flesh, which was the bait. Thus, when life came to dwell with death and life shone upon darkness, their contraries might vanish away. For it is not in the nature of darkness to endure the presence of light, nor can death exist where life is active.[27]

Although this theory rightly emphasizes the reality and power of evil forces that keep human beings in bondage, as well as the costliness and assurance of God's victory, the description of Christ's atoning work with this image reduces Jesus' humanity to a mere disguise to deceive the evil powers, and the language of a cosmic battle undermines the awareness of human responsibility for its sinful condition. Other critics of this theory argue that its overly triumphalist expression may also lead to a denial of the continuing power of evil and sin in history and in our own lives.

Despite these limitations, the cosmic battle theory of atonement draws attention to two important Christian teachings: (1) God's redemptive work is a product of love and not of coercion or brute force; and (2) evil forces are self-destructive. "As morally offensive as the idea that God uses deception in the work of salvation may be, what the crude images of this theory intend to convey is that God's hidden or "foolish" way of redeeming humanity is wiser and stronger than the apparently invincible forces of evil."[28]

Another influential theory is the one provided by the medieval Scholastic theologian Anselm, Archbishop of Canterbury (1093–1109), in his now classic work *Cur Deus Homo* (Why God became human). The theory is commonly known as the *satisfaction* theory of atonement. Anselm's description of the story of salvation was so clearly reasoned that it became the foundation of Western soteriology. His theory is derived from biblical passages suggesting vicarious suffering as the way by which humankind is redeemed (Is 53; Gal 3:13). He attempts to show on purely rational grounds that the debt incurred by human sin can be suitably discharged, and the affront to God's infinite dignity can be suitably rectified only if one who is both fully divine and fully human took it upon himself to offer his life on our behalf.[29] For Anselm, if estranged human beings were to share fellowship with God once again, God's honor would first need to be satisfied. Given God's perfectly righteous character, it is inconsistent for God to tolerate sin. Since God wants to be in fellowship with us, but we are sinful and unable to satisfy God's honor, God became human. In the person, ministry, death, and resurrection of Jesus Christ the gap between our unrighteousness and God's righteousness is bridged.[30]

> No member of the human race except Christ ever gave to God, by dying, anything which that person was not at some time going to lose as a matter of necessity, Nor did anyone ever pay a debt to God, which he did not owe. But Christ of his own accord gave to his Father what he was never going to lose as a matter of necessity, and he paid, on behalf of sinners, a debt which he did not owe.[31]

Although in this theory the humanity of Christ is given a more significant regard, and both the seriousness of sin and the costliness of redemption find more intelligible expression to the medieval mindset[32] than in the earlier cosmic-conflict theory, the Anselmian theory's use of the juridical metaphors of the New Testament brings divine mercy and justice into collision, for grace is made conditional on satisfaction. On this point Migliore persuasively asserts:

> But the satisfaction theory as traditionally presented also raises serious questions. Most important of all, it seems to set God in contradiction to Godself. It draws upon the juridical metaphors of the New Testament in a way that brings mercy and justice into collision. In other words, the Anselmian theory makes the act of forgiveness something of a problem for God. Grace is made conditional on satisfaction. But is conditional grace still grace? According to the New Testament, it is not God but humanity who needs to be reconciled. In the New Testament God is not so much the object as the subject of reconciliation in Christ.[33]

Roughly thirty years after Anselm's publication, a third major theory of atonement, often called the subjective or *moral influence* theory, was proposed by Peter Abelard (Pierre Abélard). This French philosopher and theologian, whose fame as a teacher and intellectual made him one of the most renowned figures of the twelfth century, argued that Anselm's logic was defective. He drew from Anselm's premises to deny Satan any rights over humankind, thus, removing Satan from the drama of salvation, but posed the problem in terms of God and human beings in relation to each other. Abelard's proposal focused on God's loving initiative as the transformative cause for salvation:

> Now it seems to us that we have been justified by the blood of Christ and reconciled to God in this way: through this unique act of grace manifested to us—in that his Son has taken upon himself our nature and persevered therein in teaching us by word and example even unto death—he has more fully bound us to himself by love; with the result that our hearts should be enkindled by such a gift of divine grace, and true charity should not now shrink from enduring anything for him.[34]

Abelard's salvation theory consists in Jesus being a revelation and effective demonstration of God's love for humankind. In contrast to the two other theories mentioned, in which an objective emphasis on Christ's salvific work is established, either by some cosmic battle or some legal transaction,[35] in Abelard's theory the atoning work of Christ is produced only when it is appropriated in the act of faith and allowed to transform one's life. Through his teaching and witness of God's loving initiative, Jesus Christ enkindles our love of God and neighbor. For Gustav Aulén, the dynamics of Anselm's view underscore that the change effected in salvation is not on the part of God but in human beings engendering conversion.[36] On this score Haight argues that Aulén's contention that Abelard's view was extended further as a moral theory by nineteenth-century liberal thought misinterpreted Abelard's position by promoting a view in which salvation was understood as a human movement toward God. For Haight, as an Augustinian Anselm's position reiterated Augustine's understanding of the radical power of divine love and its transforming effect in the life of the believer.[37]

The sixteenth century brought renewed interest in the classical theories of atonement. In their denunciation of the Roman church's teaching that salvation was achieved, in part, through the mediation of the church,[38] Martin Luther and John Calvin described the redemptive work of Christ as the sole act of mediation for the salvation of humanity.

Luther emphasizes that salvation is a gift of grace. He describes a number of negativities from which human existence is saved (sin, death, Satan, God's curse, and even the law), but salvation is fundamentally envisioned as a gracious initiative of reconciliation with God, mediated through the gracious redeeming act of God in Jesus Christ, grasped only in faith.[39] Despite being divine, Christ becomes incarnate (a sinner) taking our place (being our representative) in obedience unto death, making satisfaction for our sinfulness. As our representative, Christ defeats the forces of evil as the innocent, obedient, holy, and divine one. Salvation is appropriated by the believer by clinging to Christ in faith, producing an existential union effecting a "wonderful exchange" in which what is ours becomes Christ's and vice versa.

> So long as sin, death and the curse remain in us, sin damns us, death kills us, and the curse curses us; but when these things are transferred to Christ, what is ours becomes His and what is His become ours. Let us learn, therefore, in every temptation to transfer sin, death, the curse, and all the evils that oppress us from ourselves to Christ, and, on the other hand, to transfer righteousness, life, and blessing from Him to us.[40]

Calvin stressed that the main purpose of Christ's incarnation was our redemption.[41] In contrast to Luther, for whom the dialectic between law and gospel is a fundamental axiom,[42] for Calvin the law is positive and, after justification, becomes a guide for the Christian life and an important resource for ordering the community. He emphasized that the Christian, once justified, should lead a holy life in the world, guided by the law, and within the context of the calling that was assigned to each of us by God's providence. Consequently, in Luther, salvation is conceived as an existential relationship of unity with God that takes place right now, a product of divine gracious initiative, appropriated in faith by the believer. In Calvin, however, salvation is understood as an experience of redemption comprehending the believer's whole life in the world.

To better articulate the breadth and benefits of our salvation in Christ, the Reformers used the classical atonement theories in light of the three offices of Christ:

Christ as prophet shows us the way to God, by his love forging a path on which we are called to follow behind (Abelardian atonement). Christ as priest bears the penalty for that which we cannot carry, taking upon himself the consequences for our sin (Anselmian atonement). Christ as king has won the battle over Satan, uplifting us to do good works in the kingdom of God *(Christus Victor)*.[43]

For the dissenting voices of the Radical Reformation, the atoning work of Jesus Christ was described with the image of the Prince of Peace. Their resistance against the violent governance of the temporal powers led them to conceive of Christ as the one surrendering to the world's cruelty, revealing its idolatry and transient nature, in order to transform it. This vicarious redemptive work of Christ called his followers to a life of peacemaking and reconciliation true to the original character of New Testament Christianity.[44]

The concern raised by Anabaptist Christians that the lordship of Christ had been transformed by dominant structures of power from its original peacemaking and reconciliation nature into a rationale for the brutal establishment of European nations, was also raised by faithful Christians during the period of the European (violent and/or nonviolent) conquest and evangelization of the Americas.[45] An important development of this European conquest was the imposition of slavery. Both Native American and African peoples were submitted to a condition of slavery by an appeal to triumphalistic Christologies. The prophetic stance of leaders such as Fray Bartolomé de Las Casas and a host of African American slaves[46] turned this faulty Christology on its head by declaring the presence of Christ in the suffering of the indigenous, and by laying claim to the coming arrival of Jesus to free them from their bondage.[47]

In his assessment of the significance of these and various other theories of atonement that emerged throughout Christian history, Luis G. Pedraja argues that while they show the need to understand the intimate relationship that exists between the person and work of Christ, they may also serve to demonstrate (1) how culture affects our theological interpretation,[48] (2) ways through which dominant sectors of society and power structures may use these theological constructions to marginalize and oppress others,[49] and (3) the need to emphasize that our knowledge of God's gracious initiative of salvation in Jesus Christ needs to be established on the whole of Jesus Christ's work and life, from his birth to his resurrection,[50] rather than based on just one single event (his ministry, his cross, his resurrection, and so on).

During the period of the Enlightenment (eighteenth and nineteenth centuries), christological discussions were focused through the lenses of history and logic, and it became common to distinguish between the person and the work of Jesus Christ. While Christologies of this period offered a protection against fideism,[51] their weakness lay in their inability to explore fully statements of faith. Enlightenment theologians John Wesley (1703–91), an Anglican clergyman and Christian theologian who was an early leader in the

Methodist movement, and Friedrich Schleiermacher (1768–1834), a Reformed pastor, philosopher, and theologian, aware of the benefits and limits of reason-based Christologies, aimed to improve upon the insight of the sixteenth-century reformers. Wesley's soteriological emphasis combined human reason and the effort for the completion of Christ's salvific work in the process of sanctification, encouraging attentiveness to spiritual disciplines and good works: "If we remain unrighteous, the righteousness of Christ will profit us nothing!"[52]

Friedrich Schleiermacher, often called the pioneer of modern theology, insisted on reestablishing the relationship between the person and the work of Christ. He argued that in the resurrection Jesus reveals not just who he really is, but also who we really are in him: "What we celebrate at Christmas is nothing other than ourselves as whole beings—that is, human nature . . . viewed and known from the perspective of the divine."[53]

For Schleiermacher, salvation is envisioned within a broad vision of human history in which Jesus Christ becomes the historical influence of God's power to draw people into a new God-consciousness, leading to the forgiveness and removal of sin. This state of God-consciousness is further described as one in which people are drawn into union with God by being united to Jesus Christ, which also leads them to both a new self-consciousness and a different relationship with the world.[54]

CHALLENGES OF THE TWENTIETH CENTURY

In the twentieth century christological reflections continued to privilege the supremacy of reason and Enlightenment ideals, but a commitment to a rediscovery and analysis of history led to a growing awareness of its limitations and misuse by the dominant sectors of society, moving to new methodological approaches in the effort to interpret and witness to the saving work of God through Jesus Christ.[55]

Late in the nineteenth century Walter Rauschenbusch, a Baptist minister and professor of church history at Rochester Theological Seminary (1902–1917),[56] argued that our service to Christ called us to a witness committed to correcting the pervasive social injustices in the world. As the leading figure of the Social Gospel movement, he grounded this United States–based movement in the teachings and example of Christ. While a number of prominent church leaders of his day became involved in the movement's vision to meet social needs through the ministrations of the institutional church, Rauschenbusch gave this special emphasis a theological perspective, legitimizing it in mainstream American Protestantism.[57]

The modern Catholic Incarnational theology represented by Karl Rahner (1904–1984), the German Jesuit neo-scholastic theologian regarded by many as the foremost Roman Catholic theologian of the twentieth century, was an attempt to retrieve the original place of theological thought in the service of

Christian life by confronting the problems posed by modern philosophy and science. Rahner established his understanding of Jesus Christ within a broad and rich discernment of God's self-communication in history and creation. From the origins of creation to the end of time (eschaton), God's saving will is revealed in the world through self-giving love, animating the world's response at every moment. Jesus Christ, conceived not only as God's absolute promise, but also as the acceptance of God's self-communication, is revealed as creation's own fulfillment. This approach is both evolutionary, as it grounds Christology in a prior understanding of creation and God's self-communication with humanity, and eschatological, as it postulates that creation reaches it climax in Christ, and emphasizes the close relationship in Christology between the creature and the redeemer. Pierre Teilhard of Chardin (1881–1955), the twentieth-century visionary French Jesuit, philosopher, and scientist who spent the bulk of his life trying to integrate religious experience with natural science, most specifically with theories of evolution, suggests that the movement of the universe anticipates mystical communion in Christ in what he calls the "Omega point," where the coalescence of consciousness will lead us to a new state of peace and planetary unity.[58]

In response to the crisis in Western culture following the two World Wars, Karl Barth (1886–1968), Emil Brunner (1889–1966), Dietrich Bonhoeffer (1906–1945), Reinhold Niebuhr (1892–1971), and H. Richard Niebuhr (1894–1962), along with a number of other Christian theologians in Europe and North America, emerged to counteract the prevailing optimism with regard to natural theology and human reason, emphasizing both the transcendence of God and the impact of sinfulness on creaturely existence. These neo-Orthodox theologians reestablished in their works and teachings the sixteenth-century Reformation principle of the centrality of Christ to Christian belief, arguing that the knowledge of God's will can only be ascertained on the basis of God's self-revelation in Jesus Christ. "Emphasizing divine transcendence, sinfulness, and the centrality of Christ, they believed, would counteract the tendency of their contemporary religious and political leaders to project an understanding of God founded in their own image and preferences."[59]

Building from the insights of modern Roman Catholic thought, the spirit of Vatican II, and the neo-Orthodox movement, while simultaneously being critical of various aspects of these developments, Latin American theologians emerged in the lead with their writings and sociopolitical experience of a liberationist movement. In his ground-breaking text *A Theology of Liberation,* Peruvian Roman Catholic theologian and Dominican priest Gustavo Gutiérrez (1928–) presents Jesus Christ as liberator of a sinful condition that, when perceived from the experience of the marginalized and oppressed, emerges as a systemic condition demanding a radical liberation encompassing the various interrelated dimensions of oppression.[60] As Jones and Lakeland argue, the Christologies of Gustavo Gutiérrez, Leonardo Boff, Jon Sobrino, Elsa Tamez, and other contemporary Latin American theologians sought, in part, to challenge European and North American privilege, exhorting wealthy

Christians across the globe to repent of their excesses and to join in solidarity with the poor.[61]

Other liberation Christologies have emerged outside the Latin American context. Feminist theologians such as Rosemary Radford Ruether and Elizabeth Johnson in North America and Elisabeth Moltmann-Wendel and Maria Kassel in Europe argue that the teachings and witness of Jesus Christ challenge the sexist and patriarchal assumptions about the character of God's power. For them, God's incarnation in the person of Jesus of Nazareth represents the "*kenosis* of the Father," the emptying of the patriarchal throne,[62] the condemnation of oppressive hierarchies. Christ's death on the cross, rather than being an expression of satisfaction for God's honor, is conceived as God's compassion poured out in the person of Christ, who, not for being sexually identified as a man, but given his full participation in human nature, enters fully into the suffering of the marginalized and oppressed.[63]

African American liberation theologians, led by the provocative works of James Cone (1939–), hold that "Jesus Christ is black," arguing that God is the "God of the Oppressed" because Jesus' life, death, and resurrection established a radical solidarity with the oppressed to liberate them from their multidimensional bondage. That is to say, "Christ is black . . . not because of some cultural or psychological need of black people, but because and only because Christ really enters into our world where the poor, the despised, and the black are, disclosing that he is with them, enduring their humiliation and pain and transforming oppressed slaves into liberated servants."[64]

Among the most recent contextual Christologies in North America are those representing the Asian American community. Like their counterparts in Asia,[65] representatives of these perspectives, such as Kevin Park, Kosuke Koyama, and C. S. Song, draw upon Eastern philosophical, religious, and literary traditions, articulating their theological reflections in a style more suitable to people from Asian descent than to those with typical Western categories and styles of thinking. A key concept in the works of most of these theologians is the notion of marginality, comparing the marginalization of Asian Americans in the United States, as well as the masses of poor people in Asia, to the incarnation as an expression of divine marginalization. An authentic Asian Christology must also take seriously the soteriological implications of non-Christian religions.[66]

Given the pervasive experience of globalization in our world, and the increasing awareness of the religious factor in national and international affairs, one of the most important tasks facing the church and theology in the twenty-first century is the need to give serious reflection to the relationship between the Christian faith and the beliefs of other religions. A central dimension of this task is to clarify our conviction that Jesus Christ is Lord and Savior of the world, while at the same time honoring and respecting the integrity and value of the teachings of other religions.[67]

Mark W. Thomsen, a contemporary Lutheran missiologist, argues that, in spite of the usual limitations of interpretative models,[68] they can provide valuable insights for interpreting the current theological discussion on this topic. In his study of this subject he mentions three models often used in interpreting the relationships between Christianity and other faiths. The first is the *exclusivist* model, which assumes that there is one final revelation and one saving event of God, namely, Jesus Christ. Therefore, salvation is not possible outside the preaching of Christ and faith in Jesus Christ.[69] The second, or *inclusivist* model, in contrast to the first one, argues that while Jesus Christ is the savior and Lord of the world, the fullness of God's truth and grace, God's revealing and saving power is also present within all history and within every culture and people.[70] The third is the *pluralist* model, which contends that since the core of Christianity lies in its theocentric perspective, that is, in the reality and particular experience of the mystery of God, Jesus Christ is only one of the many revealing and saving events that originate and spring forth from the one reality of God.[71] In this perspective there is no normative Christology, thus other religions can establish ways of salvation without reference to Christ.[72]

Thomsen positions himself somewhere within the inclusivist camp. For him, there are three important factors that always need to be held for an adequate understanding of the saving work of Jesus Christ. First, one needs to trust that the costly, vulnerable, serving, all-embracing, and transforming love that comes to expression in the Jesus of flesh and blood flows from the heart of God; second, that the heart of God and Jesus' Spirit are present and active within all creation and all people; and third, that the destiny of all reality and of all humanity is one in God, who raised Jesus from the dead and poured out God's Spirit for the sake of all creation.[73]

A HISPANIC/LATINO/A SOTERIOLOGY

Hispanic/Latino/a[74] soteriology emerges and is contextually conditioned as an effort to articulate the witness of faith of Hispanic/Latino/a people in their history of struggle and experience of discrimination in North America. While its method is closely related to Latin American liberation Christology in its emphasis on social location, a focus on the historical Jesus, its conception of God's preferential option for the poor and excluded, and the inseparability of faith and practice, it also provides its own distinctive emphasis and themes.[75] Several important christological proposals have been produced by a number of distinguished Hispanic/Latino/a theologians.[76] In this study I propose my own.

My interest in popular religion has led to the quest for those resources that witness to the spiritual and religious expressions of the Latino people in the United States and its territories. This area of interest has captured the attention of an increasing number of Latino scholars, providing a rich and provocative documentation.[77] This knowledge has challenged important tenets of traditional epistemological and theological reflection, as well as dominant trends in the past and present mission and ministry with Latinos by mainline expressions of the Christian church in North America.

In this study I explore some valuable contributions of the Latino Protestant religious perspective by analyzing a selection of examples from the literary work of the Afro–Puerto Rican author Piri Thomas. My preference for the contributions of this author lies in the fact that his work stands as an important and provocative genre in what is labeled Latino literature. Thomas is also one of the few Latino authors who have written about their personal experience and convictions in order to stimulate a critical examination of the religious and spiritual expression of traditionally underrepresented constituencies in North American society.

LITERATURE AS A LOCUS OF RELIGIOUS EXPRESSION

In several of his recent publications Luis N. Rivera-Pagán regrets the negligible attention given by most theologians to exploring literature as a focus of our creative and spiritual imagination.[78] To be sure, while the homiletical exposition of religious leaders has paid attention to the images of humanity and the sacred in literature, modern theological reflection has been mostly nurtured by the intellectual dialogue with representatives in the fields of philosophy and the social sciences. With few exceptions, theologians have neglected a thoughtful reflection on the contributions of literature in exploring the dilemmas, enigmas, and yearnings of humanity.[79]

For Latin American theologians, this usual disregard of literature becomes unacceptable, given its significance as the focal expression of the Latin American existential drama in all of its manifold complexities. For Rivera-Pagán, the need for a serious theological exploration of Latin American literature derives not only from the relevance that the creative symbolic expressions of this literature provides in response to the queries of religious and ecclesiastical concerns, but also, as Vitor Westhelle and Hanna Betina Götz claim, from the fact that the exploration of the myths, the utopias, and the faith immersed in our literature might be one of the ways to overcome the difficult predicament in which Latin American liberation theology finds itself, that is, in a historical period aptly described by Elsa Tamez as one of messianic drought in which the horizons seem too close.[80]

Hispanic/Latina religious leaders in the United States view this dialogue between literature and theology as an important source of Hispanic/Latino theology. Yet, given the recent emergence of this theological perspective, studies available in this area are few and are mostly from a sociological or literary perspective.[81] In addition, while Latino authors usually follow an interdisciplinary approach, most of the studies of Protestant popular religion explore this topic from a theological perspective or a viewpoint that takes one's own denominational tradition as a lens from which to interpret the significance of this religious expression.[82]

My choice of the literary work of Piri Thomas[83] aims at enriching these efforts, not only by selecting a Latino author for whom literature becomes a preferential vehicle of expression, but also because his particular contributions challenge not only a dominant literary genre in Latino literature, but other theological efforts at this task.

PIRI THOMAS AND HIS LITERARY CONTRIBUTIONS

Born of Puerto Rican and Cuban parents in New York City's Spanish Harlem in 1928, Piri Thomas's struggle for survival, identity, and recognition began at a very early age. The vicious and cruel street environment of poverty, racism, and street crime experienced in New York City's ghetto streets led to his involvement with crime. In 1955 he ended up in prison for armed robbery. After serving seven years of incarceration and hard labor, he rose above his violent background of drugs and gang warfare, using his street and prison experience to reach out to young people and turn them away from a life of crime. In 1967 he published *Down These Mean Streets*, now considered a classic of its kind. This provocative and psychologically penetrating autobiographical novel launched his career and fame as an author, winning him both instant and lasting acclaim.[84]

Thomas's literary contributions are part of what Puerto Rican cultural critic Juan Flores describes as the literature of lowercase people. In U.S. Latino literature, lowercase literature is that derived from sources other than those identified with formal education and cultural literacy. While authors of this literary genre are clearly familiar with the works of classical and contemporary literature, their perspective never leaves the world of the Latino bordering on destitution and intricately associated with blackness and the African American experience. For Flores, there is a significant distinction between this type of literature and other variants of Latino literary expression. The distinctive feature of Latino lowercase literature lies not in its thematic concerns or stylistic features, but on the differential sociological placement and grounding of the writing and social identity of its subjects. For lowercase Latino writers, their work stands face to face with social experience, however harsh and saturated with mass culture, with its characters, voices, and story lines, all recognizable inhabitants of the mean but real streets.[85]

My interest in the works of Piri Thomas originated in the late 1980s, when I read Antonio M. Stevens Arroyo's excellent anthology of writings, speeches, prayers, hymns, and other documents offering a profile of the powerful forces summoning the Latino people in the United States to a new articulation of their faith.[86] In my estimation, the particular contribution of

Thomas in this continuing project lies in provoking a more comprehensive exploration of Latino Protestant popular religious beliefs.

The Enduring Contribution of Protestant Popular Beliefs

I don't think one can assume that the literary work of Piri Thomas is a clear and undisputed representation of mainline Protestantism in the United States. While in several interviews he has affirmed the importance of spirituality in his life, his respect for all religious expressions, including a preference for Pentecostalism,[87] the fact remains that his bitter and pervasive experience of discrimination, even from what he calls the white church, led him to part company with institutionalized forms of religion. However, one of the most significant contributions of Piri Thomas's works is his ability to communicate what Vitor Westhelle describes as the two particular and important dimensions of the word *Protestant* from a popular perspective. For Westhelle, one of these important dimensions is an expression of protest. The other is an unequivocal profession of faith. Concurrently, they communicate the good news through the dynamics of announcing together with denouncing the pain produced by this proclamation.[88] In this regard Thomas's legacy is an important witness to the enduring contribution of Latino Protestant popular beliefs in the United States.

Confessing the Faith, Nitty-Gritty

In his anthology Stevens Arroyo places various selections from Thomas's writings in a section where he highlights some crucial challenges for the development of a Hispanic Church in the United States. For Stevens Arroyo, one of these fundamental challenges is the articulation of a theological perspective that in its affirmation of the faith and cultural identity of Latinos provides the grounds for the recognition of a sociohistorical subject both challenging and enriching the witness of the whole church in North America.

The selections of Thomas's writings are taken from his second book, *Savior, Savior, Hold My Hand,* in which he continues his autobiographical narrative, focusing on his religious conversion to Pentecostalism and concluding with a description of his present commitment to people rather than institutionalized forms of religion.[89] These segments recount the author's vivid encounters with the arrogant and racist attitudes portrayed by representatives of the religious establishment, along with his painful yet determined efforts for a witness of faith true to his understanding of the gospel.

In one of the stories he is challenged by Lenny, a young white minister from the South coming to work with the youngsters in the ghetto. Thomas is asked to introduce him to the kids and their families. Yet Lenny's attitude in relating with Puerto Rican and black kids of the neighborhood raises the concern of the author who confronts him:

> "For God's sake, Lenny," I continued. "The Bible and Christianity aren't nothing new here in El Barrio. We got more storefront churches than Carter has liver pills. They may be poor but they are beau-coup sincere. The trouble is with the outside people from nice well-to-do churches who sincerely send people to work among us armed with all the knowledge of the Bible and a complete lack of understanding about what makes us tick. Christ sakes, Lenny, if you come to spread God's word, then just come and let us teach you about our humanity, and don't look on us like something that lived in the Stone Age."[90]

Another and more crucial encounter takes place with John, originally his partner in a project with hard-core teenage gangs, aimed at changing their lives by way of Christian practice and teaching. Taking the kids from the club to worship services at churches in the suburbs led the author to experience both the piety and the contempt of the middle-class white church in relating to the faithful from the ghetto. His reaction is to confront John, who encouraged this proselytizing initiative, with the racist and contemptuous approach. John reproves what he perceives as the author's insolent comments and suggests bringing his angry feelings to God in prayer. The author responds:

> Prayers gotta be strengthened with some king of action, John. Without disrespect, amigo, if you've read history, too, you'd know many people have been taught to pray and when they finished praying and looked around, their land and respect was gone—taken away by the ones who had taught them to pray.[91]

In a witty and penetrating reflection on the nature of this predicament, the author points to the heart of the problem. Those from the ghetto are treated with disdain because they are considered inferior.

> I had noticed things I hadn't dug before or perhaps hadn't wanted to dig in the white Christian/ghetto relationship. It was like we weren't equals. It was as if they were the chosen ones—despite the teachings in their Bibles—like they were sent to save us by getting us a hearing with Christ. But like it had to be on their own terms.[92]

For the author, our witness of faith demands integrity and showing respect for the dignity of human beings, who are *all* a product of God's gracious creative initiative. Those living in the ghetto are not *basura* (litter) or inferior. They are, rather, the ones suffering the consequences of human greed and injustice. They should be considered equals and treated with fairness. They are our brothers and sisters and, as such, deserve our love and affection. In fact, their witness of faith is not merely informed by the gospel; the integrity and endurance of their convictions under the severe and burdensome context of the ghetto recovers the fundamental confessing dimension of Christianity characteristic of its emergence as a marginalized and persecuted community in the first century, and the stance of some of its prophetic leaders, who throughout history have challenged the church to remain faithful to God's word in the midst of ideological manipulation, oppression, prejudice, and idolatry.

HANGING ON A GHETTO CROSS

The last part of the book reveals some valuable insights of the author in responding to this difficult condition. As the narrative continues, the relationship between him and John keeps deteriorating. Becoming aware of the growing animosity between him and his partner, Piri decides to leave the job. His decision to resign leads to a climactic experience with John, who resents what he sees as the author's irrational and insolent attitude.

> "Look, if you are angry at something, we can talk it out. Haven't we always been able to reason things out?"
> "John," I cried, putting all kinds of brakes on my voice 'cause it was jumping into all kinds of different angry octaves. "I didn't mind you copping credit every time I turned in some guns. I even accepted a lot of the other crap you were putting down as long it helped the kids. But it's game time now. . . . Pure and simple, I QUIT."
> "You never had it so good, Piri." John's voice lost its cool.
> "Well I'm going to have it better, man. I QUIT."
> "If you quit, I'll see to it you never work around this area again."[93]

John's sinister threat escalates as he fails in his various attempts to change Piri's mind. Shortly after leaving the job, Piri received a call from the mother of one of the kids. After her son was taken to the police station she discovered some guns in his room, and she asked Piri to dispose of the weapons. Even though he wasn't with the club anymore, he decided to help her. He called John to bring the guns to the club so they could be taken to the police station. In his response, John revealed his contempt for Piri:

> "You're not with the club anymore, so you don't have our backing. You're violating the law by having those weapons in your possession." His voice had a lot of innuendos in it. . . . "I'll be home. Bring all of them." His voice sounded like some friendly undertaker.[94]

Piri gets the weapons and drives to John's house in the suburbs. John is waiting for him. Piri gives the guns to John, who surprisingly responds by turning them back to him.

"Why are you giving them back to me for? You said it was the club's responsibility and I brought them to you. Where you at John?"

"I've already notified the state troopers and also the precinct in New York that you are carrying a bag full of weapons. So I would advise you to turn yourself in with them."

I stood there stunned. Checking out my hearing, like I couldn't believe what was coming out of his mouth. His face had sheer hate on it. And I knew my face had contorted into some mask of hurting rage. My voice came out between my teeth, "You know I'm on parole. You know I owe over six years to the state."

"You should have thought of that before you picked them up."[95]

John's betrayal provokes Piri to rage, but, containing his anger, he responds:

"You got it your way up to now, John, but it won't always be like that. People will know where you are at some day." My words just bounced off his door closing behind him.[96]

Realizing his dilemma, Piri calls Carl, the producer of a Christian film crew with whom he had made a documentary to promote the club's work with the kids of the neighborhood; he asks Carl to help him bring the weapons to the police station. When they arrive at the precinct, the officers in charged took the guns and handed Piri a summons for a court appearance to respond to his participation in this incident. The thought of being imprisoned once again for parole violation drove Piri to a frenzy. While his earlier prison sentence was the consequence of embracing the violence of the streets, now he was being punished for doing something right, and for him that was wrong.

The day of the trial Piri was tormented with anxiety, and when his name was called, he made his way up to the judge. Listening to the magistrate, he wondered if he was in the wrong court. The judge commended him for his fine civic performance and bade him to continue with his good work. Shocked by the gracious and unexpected outcome of the trial, he reflected:

I swear to the hole in my one shoe, I just nodded and said something like *chevere* to the judge and walked out of that court, *mucho* tall and knowing deep inside me that for a short while there, I had hung between walking out of that court with my pride and dignity as a man intact and being sent back to prison for some more years of dehumanization. And I knew that not everybody, except those like me, could ever fully understand the agony of what had gone down for me these last seven days.[97]

Deliverance comes as a gift. It's not the product of our own doing. For Piri, this central teaching of faith became true at the point when he felt fatally destined to return to the horrible experience of prison. Hanging on a ghetto cross, torn by the scorn and deceit of evil forces, he encounters once again the gracious initiative of God that he had experienced in the past through the loving care of his mother. Rather than seeking revenge from John and from those whose religious commitment cannot hide their prejudice, he goes back to the streets, walking tall, to continue his loving struggle against racism, poverty, and injustice.

Hanging on the Cross as a Practice of Faith

Vitor Westhelle argues that the most significant contribution of Protestantism in Latin America lies in witnessing to what Luther understood as *teologia crucis*. For Luther, it is this central understanding of the gospel rather than a description of a dogmatic tenet that depicts a fundamental experience of the gospel. In fact, Luther preferred the phrase "a theologian of the cross" to that of a "theology of the cross" in order to emphasize that this theological notion referred to a theological praxis rather than a theological locus.[98]

Furthermore, it is Westhelle's conviction that the *Protestant* nature of Latin American liberation movements provides a more adequate understanding of Luther's teaching of the cross, as a theological perspective enabling our comprehension of God's self-revelation in history. His claim is that the sixteenth-century Protestant Reformation and these Latin American militant movements share a common eschatological vision in which their mutual experience of exclusion and condemnation leads to the possibility of a truly liberating experience.[99]

The final section of Piri Thomas's autobiographical text serves as a powerful and persuasive witness to this conviction of faith. While the concern of his wife, Nita, for Piri's irregular and decreasing participation in church services led her to perceive in him an apparent spiritual decline produced by his unfortunate experience with John, a final conversation with her husband helps clarify his unwavering expression of vital and resolute faith.

A Million Ghetto Crosses out There

For most of those who read Piri Thomas's autobiography from a pious religious perspective, the author's final rejection of institutionalized forms of religion may appear to be a setback or a type of reversal to his old ways. To be sure, his experiences with Lenny, John, and a host of other church-going Christians from the white middle-class church who could not witness in their practice what they preached or taught about their faith, were more than wanting. The product of such religious testimony continued to lead to a prejudiced, intolerant, and dehumanizing relationship with those that, given their skin color, culture, economic status, and a host of other differences, were considered of lesser value and treated as inferior.[100] For Piri, this was a sort of Babylonian captivity of the church, its leaders, and its institutional forms that needed to be radically transformed. His strong belief in the gospel, mediated through a variety of religious institutional forms and living witnesses, helped him resist the temptation of falling into this hypocritical stand, a return to the violence of his former life, or the downfall of nihilism. Having experienced the gracious and liberating gift of God's love in his own life, he was committed to a faith active in love through traditional or nontraditional forms of institutional religion. His choice to continue his witness of love through his street ministry with kids, their families and friends, as well as with those already in prison, led to creative forms of being the church as a sign and proleptic anticipation of God's eschatological reign in history.[101]

At the end of the book, as his wife Nita leaves for a church service, Piri remains in their house along with their son looking out the window and reflecting on the future ahead.

> "We are going to walk tall or not at all, World," I told myself. Then I smiled and half aloud whispered, "Hey, Jesus Christ, I betcha' there must be a million ghetto crosses out there."[102]

For those of us for whom Westhelle's insights, mentioned above, as well as the reflection and proposals made by a host of other emerging voices of faithful and committed Christians today reflecting on these and similar issues, with the conviction that they constitute an important recovery of the spirit of the sixteenth-century Reformation for our present context, Piri's contribution becomes an eloquent expression of the vital and enduring contribution of the spirit of Protestantism from a popular perspective.

NOTES

[1] Daniel L. Migliore, *Faith Seeking Understanding: An Introduction to Christian Theology,* 2d ed. (Grand Rapids, MI: Eerdmans 2004), 163.

[2] While Jesus' representation of God is distinctively his, Jesus' God is in no substantial way other than the God of Israel (Robert Haight, *Jesus: Symbol of God* [Maryknoll, NY: Orbis Books, 2005], 88–118).

[3] Haight's examination of the perception of God conveyed through Jesus includes God's personal experience as parent (Father), God's transcendent nature, God's benevolence and love for the whole creation, and God's absolute will for the salvation of all, which is also qualified by God's interest in justice and judgment (ibid.).

[4] For Haight, salvation as mediated by Jesus Christ has also been defined in Christian tradition as redemption and atonement (ibid, 335–336).

[5] For Haight, "Such power on the level of being itself can only be God's power. Thus Tillich speaks of salvation as New Being, or the power that overcomes being that is sick and estranged" (Haight, *Jesus,* 337).

[6] David Tracy, "The Christian Understanding of Salvation-Liberation," in *Face to Face* 14 (1988), 39, quoted in ibid., 355.

[7] Miguel A. De La Torre and Edwin David Aponte, *Introducing Latino/a Theologies* (Maryknoll, NY: Orbis Books, 2001), 86.

[8] An important element of the christological works of Latino/a theologians is to bring together our understanding of the person and work of Christ. For Ada María Isasi-Díaz, the distinction between the historical Jesus and the work of Christ is not just alien to popular wisdom, which tends to meld the two words into one (Jesucristo), but this folding into one word the name of Jesus and the title Christ serves to sustain and motivate Hispana/Latina women in their everyday struggles against what limits liberation–fullness of life and all that promotes justice and peace (Ada María Isasi-Díaz, *La Lucha Continues: Mujerista Theology* [Maryknoll, NY: Orbis Books, 2004], 242–243).

[9] For Luis G. Pedraja, the insistence of Latino/a Christologies to maintain together the person of Jesus with the work of Christ is what reveals the fullness of Jesus' divine nature. "For Hispanic Christologies, the work and the person of Christ actually come together, so that you know who Jesus is by what Jesus does. Jesus' actions revealed his divinity. But what is it that Jesus does? If you were to ask most Latinos/as the answer would be a resounding 'Jesus saves'" (Luis G. Pedraja, *Teología: An Introduction to Hispanic Theology* [Nashville, TN: Abingdon Press, 2003], 145).

[10] In the New Testament the person and work of Jesus Christ are intimately related. This is evident in its interpretation of his name—"'Call his name Jesus for he will save people from their sins' (Mt 1:21)" (ibid., 168).

[11] The original Latin expression is *hoc est Christum cognoscere beneficium eius cognoscere* (Philip Melanchthon, *Loci communes Theologici,* in *Melanchthon and Bucer,* ed. Wilhelm Pauck, Library of Christian Classics 19 [Philadelphia: Westminster, 1969], 21).

[12] Martin Luther, "The Small Catechism," in *The Book of Concord,* ed. Robert Kolb, Timothy J. Wengert, and Charles P. Arand (Minneapolis: Fortress Press, 2000), 355.

[13] In his book the author aims at providing a study of this subject to provoke the interest of our present postmodern culture.

[14] One of Haight's goals in choosing these five typologies is to show that, "from a theological standpoint one can move from a pluralism that first appears as a confusing morass of different interpretations to a recognition that the pluralism in New Testament Christology is valuable and freeing, it has positive constructive implications" (Haight, *Jesus,* 154).

[15] This is a reference to Paul's metaphor of the "final Adam," in which Jesus saves humankind by being obedient (Rom 5:12–21; 1 Cor 15:21–23, 45–49) (ibid., 156–159).

[16] This is a reference to Mark's soteriology, in which Jesus is a chosen and anointed agent of God who acts with God's authority and saves by being the object of faith and, especially, the hope for the future (Mk 1:1; 1:11; 9:7; 14:61; 15:39) (ibid., 159–163).

[17] This is a reference to Luke's soteriology, in which Jesus' very coming into being and historical career are the embodiment of God Spirit's power to work for salvation (Lk 1:35; 3:22; 4:1; 4:14; 4:21; Acts 10:38) (ibid., 163–168).

[18] This is a reference to wisdom Christologies in which a metaphorical identification of Jesus with God's Wisdom leads to a soteriology in which Jesus not only reveals God but is also the exemplar of human existence (Phil 2:6–11; Col 1:15–20; Mt 11:25–30) (ibid., 168–173).

[19] This is a reference to a Logos Christology in which Jesus saves by revealing and embodying God as Wisdom, that is, making it appear as real in the flesh (Jn 1:1–18) (ibid., 173–178).

[20] For Haight, this pluralism of New Testament Christologies is due to historical necessity, over and above the transcendent character of their subject matter. "As the Jesus movement spread to new peoples, and new communities were formed, one can imagine how christological development took on a certain life of its own in each community. Each community had its own culture into which it appropriated Jesus. Each had a distinctive set of problems that generated questions peculiar to it. Each possessed a particular religious tradition, which supplied a language to interpret Jesus. Different communities appreciated different aspects of the person or message of Jesus. In short, Jesus was interpreted from within the context of the specific tradition and language of the various communities to whom he was introduced, thereby producing of necessity different understandings of him" (ibid., 182).

[21] This assumption leads Haight to argue that every Christology that explains this existential and salvific relationship of the Christian to Jesus constitutes an orthodox Christology. However, for an objective criterion to establish the adequacy of christological expressions, he argues that "it must correspond to what we can know of Jesus and to the interpretations of him in the New Testament; it must attend to the classic doctrines which have been normative for the churches for so long; it must be in communion with other Christian churches and not isolated or idiosyncratic; it must be coherent and intelligible for the world of those to whom it would communicate and whose faith it would represent; it must posses an ethical credibility and the power to generate a Christian life" (ibid., 180–184).

[22] Michael Root, "The Narrative Structure of Soteriology," in *Modern Theology* 2, no. 2 (January 1986): 146–147.

[23] Ibid., 147.

[24] Virgilio Elizondo, *Galilean Journey: The Mexican-American Promise* (Maryknoll, NY: Orbis Books, 1983). Other Latino/a theologians incorporate the notion of *mulatez* as a new image that helps us understand various aspects of the incarnation, not through philosophical abstractions, as characteristic of the early ecumenical conciliar debates, but through culture and social location (see Pedraja, *Teología*, 138–142). As Pedraja mentions in his study, Loida Martell-Otero, arguing that in recent years *mestizaje* has lost its provocative edge, introduces instead the words *sata* and *sato* (mongrel) for the same purpose (ibid, 141). See also Loida I. Martell-Otero, "Of Satos and Saints: Salvation from the Periphery," in *Perspectivas* (Summer 2001), 7–38.

[25] Given the enormous amount of material available, I limit my focus in this study to a few important examples. Two of the most significant studies in this area are H. E. W. Turner, *The Patristic Doctrine of Redemption: A Study of the Development of Doctrine during the First Five Centuries* (London: A. R. Mobray, 1952); and the famous study of types of "atonement theories" by Gustav Aulén, *Christus Victor: An Historical Study of the Three Types of the Idea of Atonement* (London: SPCK, 1950).

[26] Alister E. McGrath mentions that Rufinus of Aquilea (345–410) also used this metaphor (Alister E. McGrath, *The Christian Theology Reader* [Oxford: Blackwell, 2001], 334–335).

[27] Gregory of Nyssa, "Address on Religious Instruction," in *Christology of the Later Fathers,* Library of Christian Classics 3, ed. Edward Rochie Hardy (Philadelphia: Westminster, 1954), 301.

[28] Migliore, *Faith Seeking Understanding,* 183.

[29] Thomas Williams, "Saint Anselm," in *Stanford Encyclopedia of Philosophy,* available online. Roger Haight argues that, according to Anselm, the need for God to become incarnate for our salvation lies with original sin, which was an infinite offense against God. The offense of sin could not be forgiven by God by gratuitous amnesty because it would not restore human beings to their original dignity. Satisfaction was impossible for human beings because sin required eternal punishment or infinite satisfaction. The saving work of Jesus consisted in surrendering his life freely; his choosing death was an act not owed to God because he was sinless. The God-man Jesus Christ as confessed by Chalcedon rendered satisfaction to God because his act was that of a representative of all humanity and simultaneously an act of God (Haight, *Jesus,* 227–228).

[30] Serene Jones and Paul Lakeland, *Constructive Theology: A Contemporary Approach to Classical Themes* (Minneapolis: Fortress Press, 205), 170.

[31] Anselm of Canterbury, "Why God Became Man," in *Oxford World's Classics: Anselm of Canterbury, The Major Works* (Oxford: Oxford University Press, 1998), 349.

[32] Migliore contends that "Anselm's reflections on this question arise out of the medieval thought world and presuppose then-current understandings of law, offense, reparations, and social obligations. God and humans are related like feudal lords and their serfs. Since disobedience dishonors the lord, either satisfaction must be given or punishment must follow" (Migliore, *Faith Seeking Understanding,* 184).

[33] Ibid.

[34] Peter Abelard, "Exposition of the Epistle to the Romans (An Excerpt from the Second Book)," in *A Scholastic Miscellany: Anselm to Ockham,* ed. and trans. Eugene R. Fairweather (New York: Macmillan, 1970), 283.

[35] Both of which would appear to be complete apart from any participation of those on behalf of whom the action is performed.

[36] Aulén, *Christus Victor,* 112–113.

[37] "First of all, Abelard embraces a high christology; the Logos is incarnate in Jesus. Thus, God's approach to human existence is ontological. It is love incarnate, a love of God for human existence and the world that is realized or effected in action. Moreover, the love that is aroused in the human person to respond to God is also ontologically caused by God. It is the effect of the gift of God as Spirit. Abelard is an Augustinian: where there is love of God, it is the effect of the work of God as Spirit or grace. And Abelard explicitly refers to this working of the Spirit by citing Paul: 'Because the charity of God is poured forth in our hearts, by the Holy Ghost, who is given to us' In the end, Aulén slights the interpretation of Abelard because he has another interpretation as his standard, one closer to that of the reformers (Haight, *Jesus,* 231–232).

[38] They disagreed that confessing to a priest, engaging in acts of penitence, praying to the saints, and purchasing indulgences could help ensure that souls would ultimately find rest in God (Jones and Lakeland, *Constructive Theology,* 173).

[39] Martin Luther, *Lectures on Galatians,* vol. 26 of *Luther's Works,* ed. Jaroslav Pelikan (St. Louis: Concordia, 1963; Philadelphia: Fortress Press, 1963), 276–296, 359–374. "In a way, the work of Christ is God reconciling God's self in order to accept human beings in love. The larger framework for understanding God is as a God of love and mercy. But this can be grasped only in faith. While in sin, the conscience of the sinner can only see God's justified anger at sin" (Haight, *Jesus,* 232).

[40] Luther, *Lecture on Galatians,* 292.

[41] John Calvin, *Institutes of the Christian Religion,* ed. John T. McNeill, trans. Ford Lewis Battles, Library of Christian Classics (Philadelphia: Westminster, 1960), II.12.1, II.12.4.

[42] In Luther, the law, although in itself good and from God, becomes a negative category because it exposes and condemns our sin and, by appealing to our will, is a temptation to further sin and a curse.

[43] Jones and Lakeland, *Constructive Theology*, 173–174.

[44] "These early Anabaptist Christians wishing to restore 'New Testament Christianity' were inspired by their belief in a Christ whose lordship stood in direct opposition to temporal authorities who extended rule by the sword. Jesus Christ is the one who submits to the world's violence and exposes its idolatry and ephemeral nature through his cross and resurrection. He thus calls his followers to a fundamental reorientation in life away from false powers that enforce belief and subservience through violence, toward the power of peace making and reconciliation made real in Jesus' flesh. The tragedy of 'establishment' christology, in the eyes of the Radical Reformers, is that the One who rejected the sword becomes a tool for the empire's self-aggrandizement. Violent atonement theories (such as Anselm's) can readily be twisted into justification for the state's ruthless extension of power. Anabaptist dissent with the politico-theological establishment often resulted in martyrdom. Between 1525 and 1528 most of the movement's early leaders had been tortured and executed. Their enduring witness compels us to ask in what ways the Prince of Peace has been twisted into a Lord of Empire in our time" (ibid, 174–175).

[45] For a valuable investigation of this topic, see Luis N. Rivera Pagán, *A Violent Evangelism: The Political and Religious Conquest of the Americas* (Louisville, KY: Westminster/John Knox Press, 1992).

[46] For an important study on this subject, see Dwight N. Hopkins and George C. L. Cummings, eds., *Cut Loose Your Stammering Tongues: Black Theology in the Slave Narratives* (Maryknoll, NY: Orbis Books, 1991).

[47] Jones and Lakeland, *Constructive Theology*, 175–177.

[48] "For instance, during a time where people often sold themselves into slavery and had to be ransomed from it, the ransom theory made good sense. . . . Anselm, living in a time where duels were fought to satisfy injuries to one's honor, could easily understand how sin could damage God's honor and how this debt would have had to be satisfied through the shedding of blood. . . . It should not surprise us that Abelard, whose tragic love for his student Eloise, led to dire consequences and a life of unfulfilled love, would develop a theory of the Atonement based on love and sacrifice" (Pedraja, *Teología*, 150).

[49] "This is the flip side of the Atonement theories. Those in power can use the theories to claim that our oppression comes because of our sin and debt to God (Anselm) or because we do not love God enough (Abelard)" (ibid.).

[50] "Latina theologian Loida Martell-Otero, drawing in part from Irenaeus, argues that it is not the cross that saves us, but the whole work of Jesus' life—the Incarnation, who he was, his ministry, his death, and resurrection—that is salvific. Hence, it is not the crucifixion itself that saves us, but the Incarnation, which initiates God's work of reconciliation that becomes manifest through his whole life" (ibid., 151). In his recent study of Christology, Alberto L. García argues for an atonement theory in which the saving work of Jesus Christ, rather than being focused only on liberating us from the forces of Satan and evil (whether of a spiritual or social nature), also becomes the liberating center and empowering force of our community in its daily struggles (Alberto L. García, *Cristología: Cristo Jesús, Centro y Praxis del Pueblo de Dios* [St. Louis: Concordia Publishing House, 2006], 106, 110–138).

[51] Fervent belief that claims to be self-evident to those in the "know," refusing discussion or debate.

[52] John Wesley, "The Lord Our Righteousness," in *The Sermons of John Wesley*, ed. Albert C. Outler and Richard P. Heitzenrater (Nashville, TN: Abingdon Press, 1987), 390.

[53] Friedrich Schleiermacher, "Christmas Eve Dialogue on the Incarnation," in *Friedrich Schleiermacher: Pioneer of Modern Theology*, ed. Keith W. Clements (Minneapolis: Fortress Press), 200.

[54] Friedrich Schleiermacher, *The Christian Faith* (New York: Harper Torchbooks, 1963), 431–433.

[55] "The most pronounced twentieth-century example of the misuse of human reason is the Holocaust and its associated christological exclusionism. The heinous murder of six million Jewish people was justified christologically. Consider this statement, made by the German Christian Church of the 1930's: 'Christ, as God the helper and saviour, has, through Hitler, become mighty among us. . . . Hitler [National Socialism] is now the way of the Spirit and Will of God for the Church of Christ among the German nation'" (Jones and Lakeland, *Constructive Theology*, 179–180). Given the limited nature of this study, I will limit myself to some brief remarks about the significance of these various perspectives, suggesting in the footnotes additional bibliographical resources where the reader may find a more detailed examination of these perspectives.

[56] Son of a Lutheran pastor, Karl August Rauschenbusch, a Lutheran missionary who taught German at Rochester Theological Seminary, Walter, after an extensive experience of theological and historical studies in the United States and Europe, took a three-month summer pastorate at a German Baptist Church in Louisville, Kentucky. On June 1, 1886, he began his eleven-year pastoral call at the Second German Baptist Church in a poor and dangerous neighborhood in New York City known as Hell's Kitchen. (A number of biographies of Rauschenbusch are available online.)

[57] In *In His Steps* (1896), Charles Sheldon, a novelist and follower of Rauschenbusch's perspective, "describes the transformation of a town whose community members follow their pastor's suggestion to ask 'What would Jesus do?' before each of their actions. Sheldon's conviction that social behaviors founded in the person and teachings of Christ can actually improve society continues to reverberate in today's popular 'What Would Jesus Do?' movement" (Jones and Lakeland, *Constructive Theology*, 180–181).

[58] Ibid. 181.

[59] Ibid. "The charge to discern who God is by looking to Jesus Christ was used by Barth and Bonhoeffer (leaders of the Confessing Church Movement) to condemn the German Christians for treating Hitler as a Messiah-figure" (ibid.).

[60] "The conclusion to be drawn from all the above is clear: salvation embraces all persons and the whole person; the liberating action of Christ—made human in this history and not in a history marginal to real human life—is at the heart of the historical current of humanity; the struggle for a just society is in its own right very much a part of salvation history" (Gustavo Gutiérrez, *A Theology of Liberation*, 15th anniv. ed. [Maryknoll, NY: Orbis Books, 1988], 97).

[61] Jones and Lakeland, *Constructive Theology*, 182. See also Migliore, *Faith Seeking Understanding*, 200–204; and Haight, *Jesus*, 363–394.

[62] Rosemary Radford Ruether, *Sexism and God-Talk: Toward a Feminist Theology* (Boston: Beacon, 1993), 1–11.

[63] Elizabeth A. Johnson, *She Who Is: The Mystery of God in Feminist Theological Discourse* (New York: Crossroad, 1993), chap. 12. See also Elisabeth Moltmann-Wendell,

"Is There a Feminist Theology of the Cross?" in *The Scandal of a Crucified World: Perspectives on the Cross and Suffering*, ed. Yacob Tesfai (Maryknoll, NY: Orbis Books, 1994), 87–98; Maria Kassel, "Tod und Auferstehung," in *Feministische Theologie: Perspektiven zur Orientierung* (Stuttgart, 1988); Migliore, *Faith Seeking Understanding*, 209–212.

[64] James Cone, *God of the Oppressed* (New York: Seabury, 1975), 136. Migliore, *Faith Seeking Understanding*, 204–208. See also *Black Theology: A Documentary History Vol. I (1966–1979)* and *Vol. II (1980–1992)*, ed. James H. Cone and Gayraud S. Wilmore (Maryknoll, NY: Orbis Books, 1993).

[65] For example, Jesuit theologian Aloysius Pieris (Sri Lanka) and feminist Presbyterian Korean theologian Chung Hyun Kyung.

[66] See also Migliore, *Faith Seeking Understanding*, 216–219.

[67] A valuable exploration of this topic can be found in Haight, *Jesus*, 395–423; and Migliore, *Faith Seeking Understanding*, 301–329.

[68] For Thomsen, interpretative models can oversimplify and fail to capture the nuances made by particular perspectives (see Mark W. Thomsen, *Christ Crucified: A Twenty-first-Century Missiology of the Cross* (Minneapolis: Lutheran University Press, 2004), 56.

[69] Thomsen sees this as the position taken by Billy Graham and other evangelical theologians, particularly manifested in "The Amsterdam Declaration of 2000" (ibid., 56–57).

[70] Inclusivism includes two types. One is the representative model in which other religions contain intrinsic values and possess authentic rays of truth about God, and they can thus be seen as preparations for the reception of the fullness of the truth of the Christian gospel. The other, the instrumental/constitutive model, in which other religions, while possessing revelatory knowledge of God's saving activity in creation (general revelation), lack the conviction that Christ remains as God's final revelation and ultimate saving event (final and ultimate revelation) (Migliore, *Faith Seeking Understanding*, 308–311). Some theologians would further claim that, while their conviction is that salvation is the saving act of God in Jesus Christ, the saving work of God is ultimately God's doing, and they leave the reality of God's inclusion into God's promised kingdom (reign) of people from other religions and faiths in God's hands (Thomsen, *Christ Crucified*, 60). Among Roman Catholic theologians an important exponent of this model is Karl Rahner (ibid.). In Lutheran circles Carl E. Braaten is a representative of this position: "God reveals himself in many ways, but there is salvation in the name of Jesus Christ alone" (Carl E. Braaten, "Hearing the Other: The Promise and Problem of Pluralism," *Currents in Theology and Mission* 24 [1997], 395).

[71] Two of the most important representatives of this position are John Hick and Paul Knitter.

[72] Migliore, *Faith Seeking Understanding*, 314–316; Thomsen, *Christ Crucified*, 61–64.

[73] Thomsen, *Christ Crucified*, 74.

[74] How to name the people from the Spanish-speaking Caribbean, Central America, South America, Latin America, and those of Latin American descent in North America has always been an issue of controversy. In this study I use the notion of *Hispanic/Latino/a* theological perspective to highlight the various nomenclatures used to describe our people; however, I use the terms *Hispanic, Latino, Latina,* or *Latino/a* to refer to the same subject. For a more detailed study of this issue, see Ada María

Isasi-Díaz, *En la Lucha: In the Struggle: A Hispanic Women's Liberation Theology* (Minneapolis: Fortress Press, 1993), 2–4; José D. Rodríguez and Loida I. Martell-Otero, eds., *Teología en Conjunto: A Collaborative Hispanic Protestant Theology* (Louisville, KY: Westminster/John Knox Press, 1997), 1–4, 9n3.

[75] See, Eduardo C. Fernández, *La Cosecha: Harvesting Contemporary United States Hispanic Theology (1972–1998)* (Collegeville, MN: The Liturgical Press, 2000); Miguel A. De La Torre and Edwin David Aponte, eds., *Introducing Latino/a Theologies* (Maryknoll, NY: Orbis Books, 2001); Orlando O. Espín, "The State of US Latino/a Theology: An Understanding," in *Hispanic Christian Thought at the Dawn of the Twenty-first Century: Apuntes in Honor of Justo L. González,* ed. Alvin Padilla, Roberto Goizueta, and Eldin Villafañe, 98–116 (Nashville, TN: Abingdon Press, 2006).

[76] For some of the most important contributions of Hispanic/Latino/a theologians in this area of research, see Sixto J. García, "A Hispanic Approach to Trinitarian Theology: The Dynamic of Celebration, Reflection, and Praxis," in *We Are a People: Initiatives in Hispanic American Theology,* ed. Roberto S. Goizueta, 107–132 (Minneapolis: Fortress Press, 1992); Virgilio Elizondo, "The *Mestizo* Jesus," in *Galilean Journey: The Mexican-American Promise* (Maryknoll, NY: Orbis Books, 1983); idem, *The Future Is Mestizo: Life Where Cultures Meet* (New York: Crossroad, 1988); Justo L. González "The *minority* God" in *Mañana: Christian Theology from a Hispanic Perspective* (Nashville, TN: Abingdon Press, 1990); Luis G. Pedraja, "The *Mestizo-Mulato* Christ," in *Teología: An Introduction to Hispanic Theology* (Nashville, TN: Abingdon Press, 2003); idem, *Jesus Is My Uncle: Christology from a Hispanic Perspective* (Nashville, TN: Abingdon Press, 1999); Ada María Isasi-Díaz, *La Lucha Continues: Mujerista Theology* (Maryknoll, NY: Orbis Books, 2004); Migliore, *Faith Seeking Understanding,* 212–216; and finally, the recent work in Spanish by Alberto L. García, *Cristología Cristo Jesús: Centro y Práxis del Pueblo de Dios* (St. Louis: Editorial Concordia, 2006), in which Jesus Christ is described in his liberating redeeming work as the center and empowering force for the daily struggles of our Latino/a community.

[77] See Orlando Espín, *The Faith of the People: Theological Reflections on Popular Catholicism* (Maryknoll, NY: Orbis Books, 1997).

[78] See Luis N. Rivera-Pagán, *Mito, exilio y demonios: Literatura y teología en América Latina* (Hato Rey: Publicaciones Puertorriqueñas, 1996) and *Essays from the Diaspora* (Chicago: Lutheran School of Theology at Chicago, 2002).

[79] For Rivera-Pagán, some of these attempts have been unfortunately limited to a mere rhetorical decoration (*Mito, exilio y demonios,* 8). The following are a number of publications that explore the dialogue between religion and literature; see their suggestions for significant literature in this area of research. Robert Detweiler, ed. *Art/Literature/Religion: Life on the Borders* (Chico, CA: Scholars Press, 1983); David Jasper, *The Study of Literature and Religion* (Basingstoke: Macmillan, 1989); Robert Detweiler and David Jasper, eds., *Religion and Literature: A Reader* (Louisville, KY: Westminster John Knox Press, 2000). Among the works focusing on the Latin American context, see Gustavo Gutiérrez, *Entre las calandrias: un ensayo sobre José María Arguedas* (Lima: Instituto Bartolomé de Las Casas, 1990); Reinero Arce Valentín, *Religión: Poesía del mundo venidero: Las implicaciones teológicas en la obra de José Martí* (Quito: Consejo Latinoamericano de Iglesias, 1996); Raúl Fornet Betancourt, *Filosofía, teología, literatura: aportes cubanos en los últimos 50 años* (Aachen: Concordia Reihe Nonographien, Band 25, 1999); Antonio Melo Magalhães, "Notas introdutórias sobre teologia e literatura," in *Cuadernos de Pós-Graduação* (Instituto

de Encino Superior, São Paulo) 9 (1997), 7–40. An important recent work in the study of religion and U.S. Latino/a literature is Hector Avalos, *Strangers in Our Own Land: Religion in U.S. Latina/o Literature* (Nashville, TN: Abingdon Press, 2005). This last book has a study of the relevance of the works of Piri Thomas and other Latino/a writers for Latino/a theological reflection (ibid., 57–115). Another recent and very valuable publication in this area of research is Michelle González, *Sor Juana: Beauty and Justice in the Americas* (Maryknoll, NY: Orbis Books, 2003).

[80] Rivera-Pagán, *Essays from the Diaspora,* 27. See also Vitor Westhelle and Hanna Betina Götz, "In Quest of a Myth: Latin American Literature and Theology," *Journal of Hispanic/Latino Theology* 3, no. 1 (August 1995): 5–22; and Elsa Tamez, "Cuando los horizontes se cierran: Una reflexión sobre la razón utópica de Qohélet," *Cristianismo y sociedad* 33, no. 123 (1995): 7. The above-mentioned works by Rivera-Pagán are important contributions in addressing this challenge. They provide a valuable historical and analytical survey of mostly (but not limited to) Latin American authors, bibliographical resources, and significant stages in this area of study. They also stand as some of his constructive contributions in provoking and moving forward this area of research. My goal in this study is to join Rivera-Pagán, Götz, Westhelle, and others in this important effort by highlighting the contributions of Latino/a authors in the United States.

[81] See, for example, the suggestive study by Ana María Diaz-Stevens, "In the Image and Likeness of God: Literature as Theological Reflection," in *Hispanic/Latino Theology: Challenge and Promise,* ed. Ada María Isasi-Díaz and Fernando F. Segovia, 86–103 (Minneapolis: Fortress Press, 1996); or Elena Olazagasti-Segovia, "Judith Ortiz Cofer's *Silent Dancing:* The Self-Portrait of the Artist as a Young, Bicultural Girl," in Isasi-Díaz and Segovia, *Hispanic/Latino Theology,* 45–62.

[82] See, for example, the work of Samuel Solivan, "Sources of a Hispanic/Latino American Theology: A Pentecostal Perspective," in Isasi-Díaz and Segovia, *Hispanic/Latino Theology,* 134–148; Angel Santiago-Vendrell, "Popular Religion as a Unifying Factor in the Latino/a Religious Community: A Pentecostal Proposal in US Latino/a Ecumenical Theology," *Journal of Pentecostal Theology* 12, no. 1 (2003): 129–141; and David Maldonado, ed., *Protestantes/Protestant: Hispanic Christianity within Mainline Traditions* (Nashville, TN: Abingdon Press, 1999).

[83] Piri Thomas was born John Thomas, Jr. According to an interview with Thomas, the name Peter was added later by his father, who thought an Anglo-sounding name would give him a better opportunity to succeed (see also Carmen Dolores Hernández, *Puerto Rican Voices in English: Interviews with Writers* [Westport: Greenwood Press, 1997], 172.). The name Piri (Pee-ree) reflects the Puerto Rican Spanish pronunciation of Petey, a hypocoristic form of the more formal Peter. (Avalos, *Strangers in Our Own Land*, 99).

[84] For more detailed information about his life and writings, see his website, www.cheverote.com.

[85] Juan Flores, *From Bomba to Hip-Hop: Puerto Rican Culture and Latino Identity* (New York: Columbia University Press, 2000), 167–188. In an earlier study on this subject Flores provides a history of Puerto Rican literature in the United States in which he argues that the contributions of Piri Thomas, Nicholasa Mohr, Edward Rivera, Pedro Pietri, and others belong to a literary genre that he calls popular, ethnic, minority, testimonial, or non-canonical literature. This literature produced by Nuyorrican authors (Puerto Ricans living in the United States) shares with the literature of other traditionally under-represented communities in the United States (Chicanos/as,

African Americans, and so forth) its resistance to assimilation of the social, economic, political, and cultural values of the dominant sectors of North American society, along with an intentional interchange and collective affirmation of the complementary nature of their struggles (Juan Flores, *La Venganza de Cortijo y otros ensayos* [Rio Piedras: Ediciones Huracán, 1997], 131–155).

[86] Antonio M. Stevens Arroyo, *Prophets Denied Honor: An Anthology of the Hispanic Church in the United States* (Maryknoll, NY: Orbis Books, 1980).

[87] See the interview Piri Thomas had with Dorothee von Huene Greenberg, available at www.cheverote.com.

[88] Vitor Westhelle, "Prefacio," in José D. Rodríguez, *Justicia en nombre de Dios: Confesando la fe desde la perspectiva hispano/Latina* (Chicago: Lutheran School of Theology Hispanic/Latino Ministry Program, 2002), xii. It might be interesting to explore whether this notion, rather than being a reference to the word *Protestant,* which may be limited to an allusion to the sixteenth-century Reformation movement, can be expanded to describe an important characteristic of our Latino/a heritage, affirming our Catholic roots along with a prophetic vocation.

[89] Piri Thomas, *Savior, Savior, Hold My Hand* (New York: Doubleday and Company, 1972).

[90] Ibid., 325–326.

[91] Ibid., 259.

[92] Ibid., 257.

[93] Ibid., 333–334.

[94] Ibid., 343.

[95] Ibid., 344–345.

[96] Ibid., 345.

[97] Ibid., 348–349.

[98] Vitor Westhelle, *Voces de Protesta en América Latina* (Chicago: Lutheran School of Theology at Chicago, 2000), 111–120.

[99] Ibid., 107–127.

[100] In a recent conversation with the Puerto Rican anthropologist and Metropolitan Community Church pastor Rev. Dr. Pablo Navarro, I was persuaded that today we need to add to these differences gender, sexual orientation, and non-Christian religious convictions.

[101] In his thoughtful study on the church as a sign and present anticipation of God's reign, José D. Rodríguez-Rivera provides a persuasive and provocative study from a Latino Protestant perspective on the temptation felt by church leaders throughout history to confuse institutional forms of the Christian church with God's promised reign in history. For this author, the experiences of grassroots Christian communities emerging in Latin America and other third-world countries constitute creative forms of being the church today led by the power of God's Spirit, challenging institutional forms of religion and its leaders to a new reformation (José D. Rodríguez, *La Iglesia, signo y primicia del reino: Reflexiones pastorales desde el Caribe y América Latina* [Chicago: Lutheran School of Theology at Chicago, Hispanic/Latino Ministry Program, 2003]).

[102] Thomas, *Savior, Savior, Hold My Hand,* 361.

PART IV

ECCESIOLOGY *A LO MESTIZO/A Y MULATO/A*

What Happens to "Church" When We Move *Latinamente* beyond Inherited Ecclesiologies?

7

Corpus Verum

Toward a Borderland Ecclesiology

Roberto S. Goizueta

Over the past twenty years U.S. Latino/a theology has emerged as an important movement whose questions and insights have had a significant impact on the life of the church and the academy in the United States. Whether in biblical studies, theological anthropology, theological method, ethics, or Christology, U.S. Latino/a theologians have made creative, groundbreaking contributions to the ongoing development of the Christian intellectual tradition. As some have noted, however, we have done relatively little sustained scholarly reflection in the area of ecclesiology.[1] This has certainly been true of my own work. While numerous ecclesiological insights are implicit in and can be gleaned from the work of U.S. Latino/a theologians, the task of systematically articulating the implications of U.S. Latino/a experience for Christian ecclesiological reflection remains largely before us.

In this chapter I suggest some possible avenues for reflecting on ecclesiology in the context of U.S. Latino/a theology. Drawing on the work already done by U.S. Latino/a and Latin American theologians, I argue that certain aspects of U.S. Latino/a experience, as well as central insights of these theologians, have important implications for Christian ecclesiology in the twenty-first century.

I begin with a brief outline of *communion ecclesiology.* Among the most important contemporary ecclesiological paradigms, communion ecclesiology posits an understanding of church grounded in a world view and theological anthropology that should be very attractive to Latino/a Christians. At the same time I suggest that lacunae inherent in this paradigm demand an opening to other ecclesiological models, models that have emerged in or been adapted by Latino/a and Latin American theologians and that involve a retrieval of aspects of ecclesial history and tradition heretofore under-appreciated. Such models represent a process whereby ecclesiology becomes increasingly concrete sociohistorically.

COMMUNION ECCLESIOLOGY

Among ecclesiological movements over the past several decades one of the most influential is communion ecclesiology. It would be difficult to address ecclesiological issues today without addressing the issues raised by communion ecclesiology. At the same time, the term itself remains ambiguous, often functioning more as a heuristic device than a term that actually specifies a particular intellectual movement:

> Communion ecclesiology is an approach to understanding the church. It represents an attempt to move beyond the merely juridical and institutional understandings by emphasizing the mystical, sacramental, and historical dimensions of the Church. It focuses on relationships, whether among the persons of the Trinity, among human beings and God, among the members of the Communion of Saints, among members of a parish, or among the bishops dispersed throughout the world. It emphasizes the dynamic interplay between the Church universal and the local churches. Communion ecclesiology stresses that the Church is not simply the receiver of revelation, but as the Mystical Body of Christ is bound up with revelation itself.[2]

As an "approach" that emphasizes the intrinsically social or relational character of Christian life, communion ecclesiology resonates with what Gary Riebe-Estrella has called the "sociocentric organic" nature of Latino/a culture.[3] As he and other Latino/a theologians have pointed out, the world view and theological anthropology of Latino/as reflects a profoundly communal understanding of the person, the cosmos, and the divine. Drawing on premodern historical roots, Latino/a popular religion gives expression to a participatory world view in which person, cosmos, and Creator are integrally and inextricably related. What Riebe-Estrella calls the "egocentric contractual" world view—which posits a self-made, autonomous individual as the foundation of society—is thus perceived as alien and often, indeed, inhuman.[4]

There thus exists a patent, natural affinity between communion ecclesiology and the lived faith of Latino/as. Precisely as an approach rather than a clearly delineated ecclesiological theory, however, communion ecclesiology is and has been susceptible to a wide array of interpretations and practical applications. Much rides, for instance, on how one actually interprets the very notion of relationship or interplay. It is here, I suggest, that Latino/a theology has a great deal to contribute, precisely in its ability to concretize and historicize what remains undefined, vague, and abstract in communion ecclesiology. Indeed, the failure to specify and make concrete what is meant by *relationships* and *interplay* is precisely what has made communion ecclesiology susceptible to manipulation in the service of ideological agendas that, in the end, undermine rather than promote authentic communion.[5]

Among the numerous insights of Latino/a theologians and Latin American theologians that can contribute to a more historically grounded communion ecclesiology I want to highlight four: (1) the community of faith as *Pueblo de Dios,* (2) the community of faith as *Pueblo Crucificado,* (3) the ecclesiological implications of a Galilean Christology, and (4) popular religion as integral to a Latino/a ecclesiology.

In each of these cases, I suggest, U.S. Latino/a theological reflection can address the inherent ambiguity of communion ecclesiologies by making increasingly concrete the very notion of communion. This process of concretization will move in two directions simultaneously: back to the Jesus Christ of the Gospels, and forward to the contemporary historical context of a global church "on the border." In other words, the ambiguities of a communion ecclesiology can be addressed through a retrieval of the intrinsic connection between Christology and ecclesiology, on the one hand, and (I argue) between ecclesiology and popular religion, on the other. Latino/a popular religion, in turn, incarnates a lived ecclesiology that retrieves not only the medieval and baroque roots of Latin American Christianity but, as well, the border-crossing, "multi-discursive" religious practices of the earliest Christian communities. A Latino/a ecclesiology will ultimately be a praxis-based, lived ecclesiology and, as such, give contemporary expression to aspects of the Christian tradition, from Paul to Trent, that have received relatively little attention and that may thus contribute to the development of a fuller, more adequate communion ecclesiology.

PUEBLO DE DIOS

Gary Riebe-Estrella has noted that "one of the great advances in ecclesiology promoted by the Second Vatican Council is its use of people of God as the primary image for its understanding of church."[6] He goes on to argue—quite appropriately and convincingly—for the significance of this image in the articulation of a U.S. Latino/a ecclesiology. The image of *populus Dei* certainly reflects the sociocentric world view of U.S. Latino/a culture. At the same time, that world view becomes a lens through which the people of God can be interpreted in a particular context that lends the image greater specificity. Analogously, Latin American theologians have interpreted the image with greater attention to sociohistorical context. For instance, notes Riebe-Estrella:

Alvaro Quiroz Magaña emphasizes that the socioeconomic categories in Latin America have determined the direction of the reflections these theologians have made on their self-understanding as People of God and on the particular role in church that Latin American Catholics are called upon to play. He posits that there are core facets to the concept of church as the People of God: 1) the priority of Christian existence over the organization; 2) the pilgrim people, sacrament of God's Reign; and 3) church as called to be a permanent historical incarnation.[7]

José Comblin contends that "the concept 'people of God' offered the gateway to a church of the poor. . . . The perspective of the people of God helped bring a new appreciation for the historic character of the church's earthly pilgrimage, the fundamental equality of all Christians, the recognition of the value of every human creature, the revaluing of local churches—with some hints of a priority of the poor."[8]

Riebe-Estrella then asks what the specifically U.S. Latino/a experience of cultural oppression might contribute to a further concretization of the people of God image. Looking to the Hebrew Bible, he draws on the experience of Israel as a model for understanding the historical experience of Latino/as as people of God. The foundation of Israel as people of God is the extended familial relationships that, though circumscribed geographically, radiate outward concentrically through the family's relationships with other families in the community. Likewise, in the Latino/a world view, "all relationships use family as their paradigm."[9] This is true not only of Latino/a Catholics but of Protestants as well: "Although Catholics and Protestants have differing, even at times competing, ecclesiologies, both have a common understanding of the church based on the Hispanic experience of *familia*. The family is an archetype of the church."[10] As helpful as the paradigm of *la familia* may be, however, the use of such a model must avoid romanticization and remain attentive to the historically ambiguous character of Latino/a familial relationships. Latina scholars, for instance, have examined how, for Latinas, family relationships can be sites of both the liberating development of human agency and the oppressive exploitation of women's labor.[11]

At the same time, when these familial relationships are developed in the context of conflict with a larger, aggressive dominant culture, they are capable of forming the basis for a sense of peoplehood that defines itself not only *ad intra*, but also *ad extra*, as other in relation to the dominant culture. This sense of otherness "creates a fertile ground for a sense of *latinidad* and for a less biological and more analogous sense of *pueblo*."[12] Thus, the *Pueblo de Dios* gains a historical concreteness rooted in its socioeconomic and racial-cultural otherness. At the heart of this interpretation of people of God, then, is the insistence that, precisely as a distinct community and pilgrim people, the *Pueblo de Dios* always constitutes itself *over against* a dominant other; for better or worse, confrontation and conflict are at the very heart of the *Pueblo de Dios*. If the people of God represents the sacrament of God's reign, the sacrament of the kingdom, then the moment that sacrament incarnates itself historically, it provokes resistance and confrontation. To paraphrase Jon Sobrino, the people of God as sacrament of the kingdom cannot be understood apart from the counter image of the anti-kingdom.[13]

Despite the advantages of the *Pueblo de Dios* ecclesiological model for U.S. Latinos/as, however, Riebe-Estrella notes some latent ambiguities: "The limitations of the sociocentric perspective also have their play, as the sense of church is rather narrowly restricted to the *Pueblo de Dios en Marcha* (the Latino segment of the church in the United States), or to the local parish, to which there is often a high sense of allegiance, or even more narrowly to the groups of families within the parish to which one is related."[14] To address these limitations he turns to the central gospel symbol of God's reign. That is, the church as people of God, or even as a pilgrim church, cannot be properly understood apart from its intrinsic relationship to the kingdom. To be people of God necessarily implies a practical commitment to the coming of God's reign:

> People of God now becomes the result of personal commitment, yet it is a commitment to a reality that predates the commitment of every individual. . . . The way this people lives out with each other the mystery of costly love, embodied in Jesus' death and resurrection, becomes revelatory of the vocation of all humanity to form a single people who live in sisterhood and brotherhood with one another. However, this sisterhood and brotherhood of humanity is neither created nor constituted by the free choice of individuals. Rather, this relationship mirrors how humanity was originally created—not as unrelated individuals but as family (Gn 1:27–28). This relationship constitutes the fundamental identity of each human person. In addition, as family, the creation of humanity images who God is. The peoplehood of humanity, which is signified in the people of God, is revelatory of the communitarian nature of God. In this sense the church as the People of God is an icon of the divine.[15]

The church as people of God is thus sacrament of God's reign and icon of God's Trinitarian nature. Consequently, membership is never automatic (based on family ties or bloodlines) but demands a practical commitment to *be* what we already *are* by virtue of God's own creative-salvific activity in history. Such a commitment implies, in turn, a "costly love" insofar as the coming of God's reign always provokes violent resistance.

Riebe-Estrella intimates that such reading of ecclesiology *latinamente* will have implications not only for the church's understanding of itself as people of God but also for its self-understanding as body of Christ. He does not develop these reflections further but encourages others to pursue such avenues of research.[16]

PUEBLO CRUCIFICADO

Latin American theologians also have noted certain weaknesses or ambiguities in the image of people of God as a specification of communion ecclesiology. Sobrino, for instance, observes that *people* remains abstract so that, while the term may relativize distinctions between clergy and laity, it fails to highlight inequalities among the laity; the term thus historicizes the hierarchical dimensions of the church while retaining an ahistorical understanding of the laity. Moreover, contends Sobrino, while suggesting the possibility of a church of the poor (especially given the connotations of the Spanish *pueblo* and *popular*), the people of God fails to integrate a preferential option for the poor as an explicitly ecclesiological—not only ethical—category: "A Church *for* the poor represents an ethical and therefore necessary approach, but it is not necessarily an ecclesiological approach. . . . A Church *of* the poor . . . poses a strictly ecclesiological problem; it concerns the very being of the Church."[17] The ambiguity of the term *people* is alluded to as well by European political theologians such as Jürgen Moltmann, who notes that "because not all are 'people' in the same way, . . . the fellowship in which all are to see the glory of God 'together' is created through the choosing of the humble and through judgment on the violent."[18] Unfortunately, not even within the church are "all people in the same way," witness the exploitation suffered by so many women and children within the walls of the church over the centuries. So the term *people* has had an ambiguous history both in society and in the church.

The response Sobrino proposes to this problem is evangelical at its core:

> The Spirit of Jesus is in the poor and, with them as his point of departure, he re-creates the entire Church. If this truth is understood in all its depth and in an authentically Trinitarian perspective, it means that the history of God advances indefectibly by way of the poor; that the Spirit of Jesus takes historical flesh in the poor; and that the poor show the direction of history that is in accord with God's plan.[19]

In no way does the church of the poor suggest a parallel church; rather, it specifies the privileged (not exclusive) sociohistorical locus wherein the church *is* church and discovers what it means to *be* church. Neither does this understanding obviate the need for an official magisterium; rather, it proposes (again, based on the gospel) the way in which the magisterial authority ought to function, namely, in solidarity with the poor. The ecclesiological image of the church of the poor posits not a new church but "a new mode of being the church."[20]

Inspired by Archbishop Oscar Romero and Ignacio Ellacuría, friends who had shared the common fate of those who identify with the poor, Sobrino would later concretize the ecclesiological image of the people of God even further. If "the Spirit of Jesus takes historical flesh in the poor," if the poor are the privileged mediators of that Spirit not only in the world, but within the church itself (not because they are necessarily morally superior but simply because they are poor), then the very historicity and corporeality of the poor is itself the privileged locus for encountering Jesus' flesh, the body of Christ in the world today. The sociological category of "the poor" takes on an explicitly *theological* character. If the people of God remains insufficiently historical until specified sociologically as the church of the Poor, this latter remains insufficiently theological until specified as the crucified people, *el Pueblo Crucificado*.

The crucified people are the privileged historical mediation of the crucified and risen Christ in the world. As mediators of the crucified and risen Christ not only in the world, but also in the church, the crucified people also remind us that suffering is one of the marks of the church. Ecclesiological reflection undertaken in the context of a preferential option for the poor, for the crucified people, would thus retrieve for contemporary Christians the ancient notion of the *ecclesia crucis* (so central for Saint Paul and Luther):

> No other single ecclesiological theme receives the attention that the suffering of the church receives in our textual sources. For centuries theology has maintained that the true marks of the church are the four that are named in the Nicene Creed: "one, holy, catholic, and apostolic church." . . . Each of these *notae ecclesia* can find some biblical basis, but none of them can claim a fraction of the attention paid to the theme of the church's suffering in these sacred writings. . . . The earliest and most prominent manner of discerning the true church and distinguishing it from false claims to Christian identity was to observe the nature and extent of the suffering experienced by a community of faith. Why? Because, of course, as Paul makes clear . . . if you claim to be a disciple of the crucified one you must expect to participate in his sufferings; . . . you will have to become a *community* of the cross.[21]

To say that suffering is a mark of the church is to privilege the crucified people and to demand solidarity with the victims as the privileged praxis through which we demonstrate ourselves to be church. "Hence," as Shawn Copeland notes, "the community of believers, the *ekklesia*, the church ought to be recognizable in its willingness to stand beside the poor, injured, despised, and excluded sufferers in history, in its willingness to suffer."[22]

This is not to suggest, however, that the crucified people are themselves identical with the crucified and risen Christ. As Gustavo Gutiérrez warns, the poor themselves are called to make a preferential option for the poor; the poor themselves can be accomplices in victimization.[23] (In the U.S. Latino/a context, this imperative becomes especially important as Latinos/as assimilate and achieve "success" in the larger U.S. society.) Rather, again in the words of Copeland, "like Jesus, the church must be willing to risk fortune and future for the sake of those who are abandoned to the scrap heap of history. Above all, these children, women, and men must be loved, for in their suffering they bear the mark of the crucified Jesus, who is no one else than the Resurrected Lord."[24]

Here we have, then, the seeds of a rereading of the ecclesiological image of body of Christ that has been appropriately called for by Gary Riebe-Estrella. In this regard, I suggest that, since the late Middle Ages, the notion of body of Christ as applied to the community of the faithful has become increasingly spiritualized if not mystified. As Henri de Lubac and other scholars have observed, the term *corpus mysticum* (mystical body of Christ) was not widely used in reference to the church until the late twelfth and early thirteenth centuries. The term *mystical body of Christ* originally appeared in the fifth century and referred not to the church but to the eucharist; the church was the *verum corpus* (true, or real, body). The eucharistic controversies of the eleventh century made it necessary to apply this latter term to the eucharist.[25] If, as Joseph Cardinal Ratzinger has posited, the term *mysticum* was never intended to mean "mystical" but rather "referring to the mystery (of the eucharist)," it does not stretch the imagination to see how *corpus mysticum* could have led to a spiritualization of the term body as applied to the church, even as the same term, as applied to the eucharist, became increasingly literalized.[26] De Lubac argues that one result of this shift was an increasing identification of the eucharistic species with the historical body of Christ on the cross. The corollary, it would seem, was an increased gap between the historical body of Christ on the cross and the church. Referring to the Pauline notion of the body of Christ, Gutiérrez observes: "Readers often regard this theology of the church as simply a beautiful metaphor. However, we must, shocking though this idea may be, see through to the realism that characterizes the Pauline approach. He is speaking of the real body of Christ, which he looks upon as an extension of the incarnation."[27]

What Sobrino and Ellacuría are doing, therefore, is retrieving the original connection between the people of God and the historical body of Christ on the cross while, at the same time, concretizing and specifying that intrinsic connection; what unites the two is the cross or, more precisely, the crucified body. In an analysis of Ellacuría's ecclesiology, Kevin Burke writes:

> As Jesus' Body becomes the sacramental symbol of the salvation he mediates, so too the church's bodiliness enables it to continue making that salvation present in history. As Christology needs to approach the whole mystery of Jesus Christ by beginning from his historical corporeality, ecclesiology needs to approach the salvific sacramentality of the church from its historical corporeality. . . . For the church to be the Body of Christ in history, it must be present to history through particular historical actions that continue and correspond to the life of Jesus. . . . It means the church cannot fulfill its vocation with its back turned to the crucified peoples of our world. On the contrary, it must seek them out, live in solidarity with them, announce God's Good News to them, and reflect to them the truth that they are God's beloved ones.[28]

The *ecclesia crucis* identifies itself with the crucified people, seeks their liberation, and in so doing shares in their suffering. The Real Body of Christ is thus mediated by the real bodies of poor persons in history.[29]

Both outside and within the church the crucified people are the privileged locus for encountering today the crucified and risen Lord. In so mediating the wounded and resurrected body of Christ in the world, the church herself is called to a cruciform existence in history. This is true not because the cross is the goal of Christian discipleship but precisely because it *isn't*. Precisely because Christian discipleship is *ultimately* not about death but about life. The church thus demonstrates most fully its commitment to life to the extent that it, as Sobrino and Ellacuría say, "takes the crucified people down from the cross." Such solidarity leads to and is rooted in the cross not as an end in itself but as the inevitable consequence of the church's mission as sacrament of the reign of God:

> Consequently, the church fulfills its sacramental vocation to mediate salvation to history when it makes concrete both the critical and constructive demands of the reign of God in each historical situation. The church fulfills the critical demand of God's reign when it prophetically denounces the crucifying powers of the world. It takes up its constructive task when—in deed even more than word—it announces that the reign of God draws near as salvation/liberation of the poor in relation to their terrible situation of captivity and death.[30]

The church becomes a crucified church insofar as it embodies, makes present, and proclaims the reign of God as the continuation in history of Christ's own enactment of that reign. Just as the Risen Christ still bears the wounds of crucifixion, so too must the reign of God bear the wounds resulting from its proclamation and enactment in history.

Contemporary consumerist culture likewise fosters a mystification of the body that obfuscates the intrinsic connection between the crucified and risen Christ's body and the church as body of Christ. For all the dominant U.S. culture's obsession with the body, our culture is repulsed by any body that is wounded, which is to say, by any *real* body. The Western preoccupation with the body as an abstract ideal masks an underlying depreciation of imperfect, scarred, or wounded bodies—the wounded, if glorified, body of Christ as well as the wounded bodies of the poor. Gutiérrez notes:

> Some Christian milieus, usually in affluent countries, have promoted a reevaluation and "celebration" of the human body in cultural expressions—for example, some modern dances and other bodily forms of expression that are used in eucharistic celebrations. . . . Whatever the merits of this claim, I want to note here that the concern for the corporeal in Latin American spiritual experiences has come about in quite a different way. . . . It is not "*my* body," but the "body of the poor

person"—the weak and languishing body of the poor—that has made the material a part of a spiritual outlook.[31]

The failure to see the body of Christ *as it is*, as a crucified *and* risen Body, ultimately prevents us from truly appreciating, truly taking seriously, the lived faith of the poor, who do not flee from the wounded bodies in their midst to the illusory security of abstract, ideal bodies; they are not concerned with abstract ideals but with real persons, with the real Christ. The Crucified people of God make it possible for us—in Sobrino's words—to be "honest about the real," honest about the real body of Christ.

A BORDERLAND ECCLESIOLOGY

The renewed appreciation of church as *corpus verum*, that is, *real* body of Christ, thus demands a retrieval of the intrinsic connection between the body of the historical Christ, as crucified and risen, and the church. We have argued that this is precisely the ecclesiological significance of the notion of the crucified people. At the same time, the notion of crucified people itself demands concretization within the specifically U.S. Latino/a context. To this end, some Latino/a theologians, especially Virgilio Elizondo, have pointed to another aspect of the crucified and risen Christ with ecclesiological implications of special relevance to U.S. Latinos/as, namely, the historical Christ's social location and identity as a Galilean Jew. In the words of Elizondo, "The overwhelming originality of Christianity is the basic belief of our faith that not only did the Son of God become a *human being*, but he became *Jesus of Nazareth*. . . . Jesus was not simply a Jew, he was a Galilean Jew; throughout his life he and his disciples were identified as Galileans."[32] Consequently, argues Elizondo, any Christology that claims to be rooted in the Gospels—and that takes seriously the Christian doctrine of the incarnation—must take as its starting point the *historical-theological particularity* of Jesus Christ. That particularity, including his racial-cultural distinctiveness as a Galilean Jew, is not merely accidental to the Christian kerygma; it is at the very heart of the kerygma. That identity, moreover, has important implications for a twenty-first-century ecclesiology that speaks to the reality of a global church.

As Christianity becomes increasingly a third-world religion, shaped by the world views and cultures of those regions where the Christian faith is experiencing its greatest growth, the future of the church will not be determined by ecclesial and theological movements in Europe. For, unlike the "globalization" effected through violence and conquest, this new historical reality is taking root in and being nurtured by local churches and grassroots communities. The face of this global church is marked not so much by colonization as by immigration. This global Christianity finds its cradle not in the great cathedrals of Paris and Cologne but in the poor neighborhoods of Lima, Manila, and El Paso.

What does a Christian ecclesiology have to say to this reality? I have already suggested how the body of the crucified and risen Christ can ground an ecclesiology rooted in the historical experience of the crucified peoples of our societies. Now I want to suggest that the racial-cultural identity of that figure as a Galilean Jew can further ground an ecclesiology racially and culturally in the experience of those marginalized peoples who today represent the most vital segment of the Christian world. In other words, in the global context as well as in the U.S. context, one way of concretizing and historicizing the notion of crucified people is precisely by understanding the theological relationship between crucifixion and Galilee, both with respect to the body of the historical Christ and with respect to the church as *corpus verum*.

Galilee was and is a borderland. In the Gospels this borderland and its inhabitants take on theological significance. It is no mere coincidence that, in the Synoptic accounts, Jesus comes from Nazareth, in Galilee; meets his end in Jerusalem; and finally returns to Galilee, where he appears to the apostles after his resurrection (Mk 14:28; Mt 26:32, 28:7, 10, 16).

The theological significance ascribed to the Galilean borderland is rooted in the history, geography, and culture of the region. As Elizondo notes, Galilee "was an outer region, far from the center of Judaism in Jerusalem of Judea and a crossroads of the great caravan routes of the world. It was a region of mixed peoples and languages."[33] Contiguous with non-Jewish territories and geographically distant from Jerusalem, Galilee was often viewed by first-century Jews as "a Jewish enclave in the midst of 'unfriendly' gentile seas."[34] "The area as a whole," writes biblical sociologist Richard Horsley, "was a frontier between the great empires in their historical struggles."[35] The Roman administrative cities of Sepphoris and Tiberias were centers of Hellenistic-Roman culture. Consequently, Jewish worship in these cities was "dramatically affected by the influences of Hellenistic-Roman culture and political domination."[36] Their religious-cultural diversity, together with their economic wealth, made the Galilean urban centers objects of resentment and opposition throughout the Galilean countryside, where village life among the peasantry was "guided by Israelite customs and traditions."[37]

In the Gospels, this social, political, cultural, religious, and geographical reality takes on soteriological significance as the place that defines the very character of the Christian revelation, for the Good News is incarnated in the person of Jesus Christ, Jesus the *Galilean Jew*. His ministry and mission, especially, begin and end in Galilee.

In order to understand the Good News, insists Elizondo, we must understand the soteriological *value* (or, rather, anti-value) of Galilee, especially its villages, such as Nazareth. Like so many human societies throughout history, the ruling elites in Jesus' world attached a moral and indeed theological value to the racial-cultural differences of the Galileans:

In Galilee the Jews were looked down upon and despised by the others as they were in the rest of the world. They were considered to be

stubborn, backward, superstitious, clannish, and all the negative ste-
reotypes one could think of. Furthermore, the Jews of Judea looked
down upon the Galilean Jews, for they considered them ignorant about
the Law and the rules of the Temple, contaminated in many ways by
their daily contacts with the pagans, not capable of speaking correct
Greek since their language was being corrupted by the mixture with
the other languages of the region. In short, their own Jewish people
despised them as inferior and impure. Because of their mixture with
others, they were marginated by their own people.[38]

The Jewish establishment in Jerusalem could not conceive that God's word
could be revealed among the "impure" people of the borderland: "Search
and you will see that no prophet is to rise from Galilee" (Jn 7:52). Yet it is
precisely in the midst of a *mestizo* people, among "savages" and "barbar-
ians," that God takes on human flesh.

Moreover, it is precisely in the midst of those racial-cultural outcasts that
the resurrected Christ, the now-glorified witness to God's power and love, is
encountered: "He has risen from the dead, and behold, he is going before
you to Galilee; there you will see him" (Mt 28:7). Just as the ministry and
mission that define Jesus Christ as Son of God had begun in the villages and
countryside of Galilee, so will that ministry and mission find their
eschatological fulfillment in Galilee: "There you will see him." Jesus' ministry will end where it began; it is in Galilee that his disciples will see the
resurrected Jesus. The chosen place of God's self-revelation is there where
Israelites and Gentiles live side by side, where Jewish religious practices incorporate Hellenistic influences, where popular Judaism remains outside the
control of Jerusalem's "official" Judaism. The *mestizo,* "impure" culture of
the borderland is the privileged locus of God's self-revelation. God becomes
incarnate in a Galilean Jew, who is crucified in Jerusalem, is raised from the
dead, and, now in glorified form, returns to the Galilean borderland, where
his disciples are gathered and the new *ekklesia* is born:

> The point of bringing out all this is to appreciate the human beginnings
> of God's mission. God becomes not just a human being, but one of the
> shamed, lowly and rejected of the world. He comes to initiate a new
> human unity, but the all-important starting point is among the most
> segregated, untouchable and impure of the world. Among those whom
> the world has thrown out, God will begin the way to final unity.[39]

The crucified and risen Christ returns to the Galilean borderland to recon-
stitute the community of disciples that had disintegrated when the disciples
had abandoned Jesus on the way to Calvary. This renewed gathering, this
ekklesia, will be born not in Jerusalem but in Galilee, not at the center of
power but on the margins, not among the religiously and theologically "pure"
but among the "impure." Just as the glorified body of the crucified and risen

Christ is revealed to the disciples in the Galilean borderland, so is the church as body of Christ born on that day, on the border—among the crucified people.

POPULAR RELIGION:
A LIVED, MULTI-DISCURSIVE ECCLESIOLOGY

If the church is thus an intrinsically borderland church, born in the midst of multiple cultural, racial, and religious influences, these will necessarily influence the church's self-understanding as well as its ritual life and symbolic world. This is true of our own time and it was true of Jesus' time, when Galilean Judaism developed outside the complete control of the religious leadership in Jerusalem and alongside non-Jewish populations. "It is possible, perhaps even likely," observes Horsley, " . . . that some Jews considered themselves faithful even while they utilized what would be classified as pagan or Greco-Roman symbols as a matter of course in their everyday lives."[40] Their religious-cultural diversity, together with their economic wealth, made the Galilean urban centers objects of resentment and opposition throughout the Galilean countryside, where village life among the peasantry was "guided by Israelite customs and traditions."[41]

Yet even the Jewish traditions of the peasants were different from those practiced in Jerusalem:

> Galilee was heir in some form to the traditions of the Northern Kingdom. . . . Torah was important, as was circumcision in Galilean society, but not the written and oral Torah as interpreted by the Judean and Jerusalem retainer class and enforced where they could by the Temple aristocracy. Rather Galilee was home to popular legal and wisdom traditions. . . . Galilee was also ambivalent about Jerusalem, the Temple, the priestly aristocracy, temple dues and tithes.[42]

In short, as Horsley argues, Galilean Jewish practices could be described as a kind of popular religion:

> The distinction anthropologists often make between the "great tradition" and the "little traditions" may be of some help in formulating the issues. A "society" may develop cultural traditions at two levels: the traditions of origin and customary practice continue as a popular tradition cultivated orally in the villages, while specialists codify those same traditions in a standardized and centralized form as an official tradition, which is cultivated orally but perhaps also reduced to written form. Something like this distinction between official tradition and popular tradition may help explain the situation in Galilee as seen both in sources from the first century C.E. and in early rabbinic literature.[43]

The notion of popular religion—as religious traditions and practices that, though influenced by the larger tradition's codified and "official" texts and practices, nevertheless emerge from a borderland people whose lived faith incorporates influences from both sides of the border—is thus at the very heart of the Christian *ekklesia*, at the very heart of a Christian ecclesiology. These are the "little stories" that, notes Alejandro García-Rivera, make possible the "Big Story."[44] Or the "demotic discourses" that sociologist Martin Stringer compares with "dominant discourses" in Christian tradition.[45] This is where the body of Christ is incarnated today.

Latino/a popular Catholicism represents a retrieval of the borderland church and religiosity that global Christianity itself represents. If we avoid the modern, rationalist temptation to reduce tradition to texts, laws, concepts, or confessions, and instead include within our understanding of tradition the *lived* traditions of the poor, we can avoid an ecclesiastical revanchism that identifies tradition with only the relatively recent, modern, rationalist understanding of tradition that characterized Trent and Vatican I, and we can avoid a liberalism that assumes the same rationalist understanding of tradition, though in order to reject or deconstruct tradition.

What, in turn, makes possible such a recovery of traditional religious practices and traditional "ways of being religious" is the distinct history of Latin American and, hence, Latino/a Catholicism. That distinct history embodies a premodern understanding of religious practice, faith, and church; the roots of Latin American Catholicism are found in Iberian medieval and baroque Christianity. As historian William Christian has noted, the medieval Christian world view and faith were not seriously threatened in Spain until the late eighteenth century.[46] Consequently, Iberian Catholicism was not forced to develop a response to the Protestant reformers' arguments or rebut them point by point—as northern European Catholics and, later, European Catholics in the United States would be forced to do.[47]

In order to defend itself against the Protestant "threat" to orthodoxy, northern European Catholicism would become increasingly rationalist, demanding a clarity, precision, and uniformity in doctrinal formulations that were simply not necessary in areas where *Catholic* and *Christian* continued to be essentially interchangeable terms; in Spain, there was no urgent need to define, clarify, and distinguish Catholic belief, especially in the wake of the *reconquista* and the expulsion of the Jews in 1492.[48] (It is no coincidence that Thomas Cajetan, a father of modern neo-Scholasticism, was also the papal legate to Germany who, in the sixteenth century, examined Martin Luther and helped draft the papal bull *Exsurge Domine*, which condemned Luther.) It would be the more rationalist, northern European Catholicism that would take hold in the English colonies—and it is this understanding of Catholicism that continues to inform the U.S. Catholic establishment to this day, whether conservative or liberal.

The differences between Catholicism in the English and in the Spanish colonies were reinforced by the fact that, like the Iberian colonizers as a whole, Iberian Catholicism interacted—even if often violently—with an Amerindian culture that, in many ways, shared a world view quite similar to that of medieval Christianity. Conversely, like the English colonizers as a whole, Anglo-American Catholicism in the English colonies generally rejected any such intermingling with the indigenous culture, preferring to expel and exclude rather than subjugate and subdue that culture.

Drawing on his research into the historical origins of Latino/a popular Catholicism, Orlando Espín observes that the Iberian Christianity brought by the Spanish to Latin America

> was medieval and pre-Tridentine, and it was planted in the Americas approximately two generations before Trent's opening session. . . . While this faith was defined by traditional creedal beliefs as passed down through the church's magisterium, those beliefs were expressed primarily in and through symbol and rite, through devotions and liturgical practices. . . . The teaching of the gospel did not usually occur through the spoken, magisterial word, but through the symbolic, "performative" word.[49]

As yet, in their everyday lives, Christians did not clearly distinguish creedal traditions from liturgical and devotional traditions; both were assumed to be integral dimensions of *the* tradition. Espín avers that "until 1546 *traditio* included, without much reflective distinction *at the everyday level*, both the contents of Scripture and the dogmatic declarations of the councils of antiquity, as well as devotional practices (that often had a more ancient history than, for example, Chalcedon's Christological definitions)."[50] At the grassroots, medieval culture accepted, and even encouraged, the kind of complexity that would be perceived as threatening by later generations needing to draw clear and distinct confessional boundaries: "Many of the characteristic features of medieval culture come from the cultivation of complexity, from the enchantment and the challenge represented by contradictions, from the *yes and no* as this was expounded by Abelard, the Parisian intellectual and Christian theologian of the 12th Century."[51] According to Espín, the clear distinction between dogma (that is, the *content* of tradition) and worship (that is, the *form* in which that tradition was embodied in everyday life) did not become crystallized until the Council of Trent. He goes on to suggest that "on this side of the Atlantic the church was at least in its second generation, and it took approximately another century for Trent's theology and decrees to appear and become operative in our ecclesiastical scene."[52]

Its medieval roots also contribute to the peculiarly noninstitutional character of Latin American and Latino/a popular Catholicism. There is no doubt that popular Catholicism draws heavily from the symbolic, liturgical, and evangelical resources of "institutional" Catholicism and, indeed, contributes to the development of those broader traditional, "official" resources. Yet the vitality of popular Catholicism comes primarily from its intimate connection to the everyday life of the people, particularly its deep, intimate connection to domestic life. Likewise, religious leadership is not primarily male and clerical but female and lay; traditions are not passed down primarily through official ecclesiastical organs but through educational and catechetical structures that are quite tangential to the official, sacramental life of the parish. These two dimensions clearly intersect (especially in the celebration of important life events such as birth, marriage, and death), but they are not simply coextensive.

Once again, these characteristics reflect the premodern roots of Latino popular Catholicism. The exclusive identification of "the church" with the institution, hierarchy, juridical structure, and clergy only became widespread and entrenched in the wake of the Protestant Reformation, as a defense against the challenges it presented. Avery Dulles locates what he calls this "deformation of the true nature of the church" in the late Middle Ages:

> Catholic theology in the Patristic period and in the Middle Ages, down through the great Scholastic doctors of the thirteenth century, was relatively free of institutionalism. The strongly institutionalist development occurred in the late Middle Ages and the Counter-Reformation, when theologians and canonists, responding to attacks on the papacy and hierarchy, accented precisely those features that the adversaries were denying. . . . The institutional outlook reached its culmination in the second half of the nineteenth century, and was expressed with singular clarity in the first schema of the Dogmatic Constitution on the Church prepared for Vatican Council I.[53]

Dulles's point is reinforced by medieval historian Gary Macy: "In the late Middle Ages, in particular, claims for control of ecclesiastical governance became more strident."[54] Prior to that, the precise character of "the church" and of what constitutes Christian tradition, authority, and belief was broader and less clearly defined.[55] While in the medieval church "there certainly was a quite distinct clerical culture with its own set of laws and rituals," among the forces that helped define medieval Christianity were the laity, religious women, and popular religious practices; these are too often ignored by contemporary historians who read back into that period our contemporary ecclesiological assumptions (for example, that "the church" is identical with what we today might call the "official" or "institutional" church).[56]

The exclusion of the diverse forms of lay, popular religion from our definition of the church in the Middle Ages served the purposes of *both* the post-Tridentine papacy, which argued that "the one true church had always and everywhere agreed on the fundamental dogmas proclaimed at Trent . . . thus preserving a unified voice down through the centuries," *and* the Protestant Reformers, who argued that "the Roman Curia . . . used its totalitarian powers to ruthlessly enforce its heretical will."[57] Moreover, as Macy notes, "this mythology suited equally well the anti-clerical agendas of the Enlightenment and of the nineteenth century. In this scenario, religion—especially institutional religion—presented a unified opposition to science, education, and any form of liberation."[58]

In our contemporary ecclesial context, the identification of "the church" with the juridical structure and its official representatives has also served the purposes (whether wittingly or unwittingly) of both Catholic neo-conservatives and liberals—precisely inasmuch as both are operating within the framework of the fundamentally modern ecclesiology that emerged in the late Middle Ages and gained prominence in the Reformation, Trent, and Vatican I. Whether to promote or reject that ecclesiology, both neo-conservatives and liberals are dependent on it. Conservative and liberal Catholics share a common, thoroughly modern institutional*ist* (to use Dulles's term) identification of church with a monolithic structure, the former to affirm it and the latter to reject it.

In the United States one consequence has been that the important place of popular religion in the life of the church has been either depreciated or ignored altogether; in Latin America the enduring force of popular Catholicism has prevented its complete marginalization. As post-Enlightenment ecclesiologies gained greater influence in the nineteenth and twentieth centuries, the Latin American Catholic Church has developed on two separate but often overlapping levels: the popular Catholic practices that are central to the everyday lives of the vast majority of Latin American Catholics, and what many refer to as *la religión de los curas* (the religion of the priests). Precisely because this complexity retains similarities to medieval Christianity, a better understanding of this might contribute to a deeper appreciation of Latino Catholicism as a resource for ecclesiology.

This history also helps underline not only the similarities but also the differences between Latin American and European popular Catholicism. Liturgical theologian Mark Francis contents:

> Because it adhered more strictly to the spirit of the Council of Trent, the devotional life of most of the European immigrant groups . . . was regulated by the clergy, who were instrumental in its revival during the nineteenth century. Latin America never had a history of such clerical oversight, both because of a lack of native clergy and a policy toward popular religion that was much more laissez-faire on the part of the Church.[59]

Thus, Euro-American popular Catholicism has a different ecclesiastical history from that of U.S. Latino/a popular Catholicism, even though they share a similar emphasis on symbol and ritual as defining the way in which the faith is lived out.

As Catholicism in the United States becomes increasingly *Pan*-American, the historical argument of scholars like Dulles, Macy, Espín, and Francis becomes increasingly relevant for understanding our context both theologically and pastorally. The Catholicism that originally came to Latin America was essentially Iberian and medieval in character; the Catholicism that came to the English colonies was northern European and, as Jesuit historian John O'Malley has argued, essentially modern in character.[60] This distinction has important ramifications. For instance, the distinction helps explain why U.S. Latino/a Catholics, being of little real interest to either liberal or conservative "mainstream" Catholics, are generally invisible to scholars of "American Catholicism," whether these scholars are liberal or conservative; whether liberal or conservative, Euro-American Catholics in the United States share an essentially modern world view that tends to view Latino/a Catholicism with suspicion.

Ironically, the reasons for the suspicion are similar to those which legitimated anti-Catholic, nativist sentiments *against* Euro-American Catholics not long ago. In both cases underlying modern prejudice against anything *medieval* (the word itself often used as a synonym for *backward*) has engendered violent reactions against any group perceived as embodying a world view, values, or beliefs that in any way resemble those of medieval Christianity, which are themselves perceived as naively materialistic, superstitious, and infantile:

> The United States in the nineteenth century was Protestant and revolutionary, and Roman Catholic immigrants became the enemy. . . . [Matteo] Sanfilippo points out, for instance, that it became extremely important in the nineteenth century to prove that the medieval Vikings, not Columbus, discovered America, since Columbus was "Italian, Catholic and in the service of Spain," while the Vikings were the ancestors of the nordic democratic and Protestant world. It is from this thought-world that [Protestant *and* Catholic] medievalists draw when they unwittingly and uncritically paint "the medieval church" as a "Roman Catholic" monolith.[61]

Thus, if today Irish American Catholics are wary of Mexican American Catholics, it is because the latter embody a type of Catholicism similar to that which Irish American Catholics have long been trying mightily to live down in order to be accepted as full-fledged members of our modern democracy. Arguing that the prejudice against medieval Christianity is based on the anachronistic assumption that medieval Christianity was identical with post-Tridentine Roman Catholicism, Macy has perceptively diagnosed the problem facing Hispanic Catholics in the United States: "If the Church in the Middle Ages was tyrannical, corrupt, and immoral, and the Church in the Middle Ages was (and is) Roman Catholic, then Roman Catholics are immoral, corrupt, and tyrannical. Hispanics, as mostly Roman Catholics, can therefore be expected to be devious, immoral, lazy, technologically underdeveloped, and ignorant."[62] The irony lies in the fact that, whereas in the first half of the twentieth century Catholics as a whole were the objects of this modern prejudice, today it is Latino/a Catholics who are often the objects of prejudice at the hands of a thoroughly "Americanized," thoroughly modern U.S. Catholic establishment that has assimilated the modern prejudice against the Middle Ages.

The point here is not to suggest either that U.S. Latino/a popular Catholicism can simply be equated with medieval Christianity, which it cannot, or to suggest that we can or should somehow "return" to some romanticized version of medieval Christianity that was, after all, also characterized by a great deal of horrific violence, oppression, and corruption. Rather, I simply mean to suggest that an understanding of the historical influences of medieval Christianity on Latino/a popular Catholicism can contribute to a more differentiated understanding of church history and the history of Christian religious practices. A recovery of that history can, in turn, be an important resource for ecclesiological reflection in the concrete context of a global church.

Such a rereading of the diversity of ecclesial and liturgical practices need not, moreover, be limited to the study of medieval Christianity in its relationship to the contemporary context. So, for instance, if we reread early Christian religious practices through such a differentiated optic we would discover a fluid, dynamic panoply of religious practices that include but go beyond the "official" practices of the church. So, for instance, Christian religious practices have always extended beyond the ritual meal which evolved into the central sacrament of the eucharist. Martin Stringer writes:

> The meal has inevitably received most attention because this, in the form of the eucharist, has become the principal ritual event of the Christian church. However, by focusing on the eucharistic aspects of the meal at the expense of other ritual activity, the impression can be given that there is far more continuity and consistency within the early history of Christian worship than is perhaps the case.[63]

In his fascinating study of the history of Christian worship, Stringer argues that "for much of the first thousand years of Christian history official liturgical worship and lay devotion were largely indistinguishable, each fed off and into the other."[64] The same could be said of the distinction between eucharistic worship and Spirit-filled worship. That is, while Christian churches are today divided between those in which eucharistic worship of one form or another predominates ("mainline" and clerical) and those in which Spirit-filled worship predominates (Pentecostal or Charismatic, lay), this has not always been the case.

In its earliest years the Christian community worshiped in a variety of ways, including the shared meal and ecstatic, Spirit-filled practices that flowed in and out of the meals. So, in the Corinth of Paul's time, "worship was focused around a shared meal and a gathering of the community in which each individual brought hymns, words, songs and various forms of ecstatic gifts."[65] Gradually during the first generations, worship became increasingly formalized and "Paul's ecstatic and disordered gathering in which each person brought a hymn or a psalm or a spiritual experience had no part to play."[66] Though increasingly relegated to the periphery as worship became focused on formal, highly structured, clerically led worship, such forms of personalized, spontaneous, lay-identified devotion and worship continued into the Middle Ages. In medieval Spain, for instance, while "the dominant discourse was clearly that of the Catholic Church, with its reinforcement in the liturgy," there also proliferated

> local demotic discourses [that] could take many different forms, from the language of saints and devotion to particular images, to those of spiritual powers, local healers, and debates about the role of any number of local sprites, goblins and others. . . . Each level of religious discourse clearly interacts, to a greater or lesser extent, with all the others, but need not overlap in terms of perceived contradictions or tensions. Most ordinary people can have dual or even multi-discursive competence and can switch from discourse to discourse depending on circumstances.[67]

Articulating a more concrete notion of church in our contemporary context would also entail, therefore, an openness to the ecumenical character of a borderland church as "multi-discursive." The reality of U.S. Latino/a "pluriconfessionalism" is, by now, almost a commonplace (what Stringer calls above "multi-discursive competence"); for Latinos/as, boundaries are often perceived as much more porous, precisely because of the subordination of those boundaries to multivalent religious practices and symbols as fundamental markers of religious identity (influenced, as noted above, by the diverse, practice-based medieval and Baroque religiosity to which Latino/a popular religion traces its roots). Many Latinos and Latinas live on the border between official liturgy and local devotions, the little stories and the Big Story dominant and demotic discourses. They also live on the border between confessions.

As I have suggested above, this is hardly a new reality in the history of Christianity but rather has defined the Christian community from the very beginning. This fact has important implications not only for Catholic ecclesiology and liturgical theology but also for ecumenism, particularly among Latino/a Christians. How might Catholic-Pentecostal dialogue and mutual respect be fostered, for example, if we can recognize in the earliest Christian religious practices the common roots of eucharistic worship, personalized lay religious practices, and Spirit-filled worship? Post-Tridentine ecclesiologies and liturgical theologies have tended to separate and compartmentalize those elements that have, for most of Christian history, existed in mutual interrelation:

The two traditions of meal and Spirit, while both being reinvigorated during the twentieth century, have yet to come together in any meaningful way. If or when they do, . . . we will see something very significant within the church and the possibility of a new round of renewal and growth of faith and practice.[68]

If Latinos/as can continue to appreciate (or, perhaps, learn to appreciate) the richness of our diverse religious history rather than fall prey to reductionist ecclesiologies that seek to erect barriers where historically there have been porous borders, we will have much to offer all the Christian churches of our adopted land.

Drawing on the wisdom of our lived faith, Latinos/as can begin to articulate how our own "little stories," in the words of Alejandro García-Rivera, make possible—and have always made possible—the Big Story of Christianity. As *ekklesia*, as a gathered communion, the church will remain a vital, credible sacrament of the reign of God to the extent that the church identifies itself with those women, children, and men who are the privileged witnesses to the crucified and risen Christ. There can be no authentic communion absent such an identification. The legacy of the borderland as a privileged ecclesial location, a privileged place for *being* church, is one that Latinos and Latinas have a responsibility to bequeath not only to our adopted country but, especially, to our church, a church born on the border.

NOTES

[1] See, for example, Gary Riebe-Estrella, "*Pueblo* and Church," in *From the Heart of Our People: Latino/a Explorations in Catholic Systematic Theology*, ed. Orlando O. Espín and Miguel H. Díaz (Maryknoll, NY: Orbis Books, 1999), 172.

[2] Dennis M. Doyle, *Communion Ecclesiology: Vision and Versions* (Maryknoll, NY: Orbis Books, 2000), 12.

[3] Riebe-Estrella, "*Pueblo* and Church," 173.

[4] Ibid.

[5] For a discussion of the ambiguities of communion as an ecclesiological metaphor, see José Comblin, *People of God* (Maryknoll, NY: Orbis Books, 2004), 58–64.

[6] Riebe-Estrella, "*Pueblo* and Church," 178.

[7] Ibid.

[8] Comblin, *People of God,* 41, 45.

[9] Riebe-Estrella, "*Pueblo* and Church," 175.

[10] James Empereur and Eduardo Fernández, *La Vida Sacra: Contemporary Hispanic Sacramental Theology* (Lanham, MD: Rowman and Littlefield, 2006), 68 (referring to the work of Miguel de la Torre and Edwin Aponte).

[11] See, for example, Ada María Isasi-Díaz, *Mujerista Theology: A Theology for the Twenty-First Century* (Maryknoll, NY: Orbis Books, 1996), 137–145; Nancy Pineda-Madrid, "Notes Toward a Chicana Feminist Epistemology (and Why It Is Important for Latina Feminist Theologies)," in *A Reader in Latina Feminist Theology*, ed. María

Pilar Aquino, Daisy L. Machado, and Jeanette Rodríguez, 241–266 (Austin: University of Texas Press, 2002).

[12] Riebe-Estrella, "*Pueblo* and Church," 181.

[13] See Jon Sobrino, *Jesus the Liberator: A Historical-Theological View* (Maryknoll, NY: Orbis Books, 1993), 67–192.

[14] Riebe-Estrella, "*Pueblo* and Church," 182.

[15] Ibid., 182–183.

[16] Ibid., 185.

[17] Jon Sobrino, *The True Church and the Poor* (Maryknoll, NY: Orbis Books, 1984), 92; see also Comblin, *People of God,* 44–45.

[18] Jürgen Moltmann, *The Church in the Power of the Spirit: A Contribution to Messianic Ecclesiology* (New York: Harper and Row, 1977), 351.

[19] Sobrino, *The True Church and the Poor,* 93.

[20] Ibid., 96.

[21] Douglas John Hall, *The Cross in Our Context: Jesus and the Suffering World* (Minneapolis: Fortress Press, 2003), 140.

[22] M. Shawn Copeland, "The Church Is Marked by Suffering," in *The Many Marks of the Church*, ed. William Madges and Michael J. Daley (New London, CT: Twenty-Third Publications, 2006), 214.

[23] Gustavo Gutiérrez, *A Theology of Liberation* (Maryknoll, NY: Orbis Books, 1988), xxvi.

[24] Copeland, "The Church Is Marked by Suffering," 216.

[25] Henri de Lubac, *Corpus Mysticum: l'euchariste et l'Église au moyen âge. Étude historique* (Paris: Aubier, 1949).

[26] Joseph Ratzinger, *The Spirit of the Liturgy* (San Francisco: Ignatius Press, 2000), 88.

[27] Gustavo Gutiérrez, *We Drink from Our Own Wells: The Spiritual Journey of a People* (Maryknoll, NY: Orbis Books, 1984), 69.

[28] Kevin F. Burke, "Christian Salvation and the Disposition of Transcendence: Ignacio Ellacuría's Historical Soteriology," in *Love That Produces Hope: The Thought of Ignacio Ellacuría*, ed. Kevin F. Burke and Robert Lassalle-Klein (Collegeville, MN: Liturgical Press, 2006), 179–180.

[29] Feminist theologians, especially, have underscored the methodological and theological significance of corporeality, as well as its significance for Christology and theological anthropology. See, for example, María Clara Bingemer, "Women in the Future of the Theology of Liberation," in *Feminist Theology from the Third World,* ed. Ursula King (London: SPCK, 1994); Elisabeth Moltmann-Wendel, *I Am My Body: A Theology of Embodiment* (New York: Continuum, 1995); Sallie McFague, *The Body of God: An Ecological Theology* (Minneapolis: Fortress Press, 1993). M. Shawn Copeland has written extensively on this issue; see, for example, "Wading through Many Sorrows": Toward a Theology of Suffering in Womanist Perspective," in *A Troubling in My Soul: Womanist Perspectives on Evil and Suffering,* ed. Emilie Townes, 109–129 (Maryknoll, NY: Orbis Books, 1993). I am grateful to Nancy Pineda-Madrid for her insights on this issue.

[30] Burke, "Christian Salvation and the Disposition of Transcendence," 178.

[31] Gutiérrez, *We Drink from Our Own Wells*, 102–103.

[32] Virgilio Elizondo, *Galilean Journey: The Mexican-American Promise* (Maryknoll, NY: Orbis Books, 1983), 49.

[33] Virgilio Elizondo, "Elements for a Mexican American Mestizo Christology," *Voices from the Third World* 11 (December 1988): 105.

[34] Douglas Edwards, "The Socio-Economic and Cultural Ethos of the Lower Galilee in the First Century: Implications for the Nascent Jesus Movement," in *The Galilee in Late Antiquity*, ed. L. Levine (Cambridge: Harvard University Press, 1992), 54.

[35] Richard A. Horsley, *Galilee: History, Politics, People* (Valley Forge, PA: Trinity Press International, 1995), 241.

[36] Richard A. Horsley, *Archaeology, History, and Society in Galilee: The Social Context of Jesus and the Rabbis* (Valley Forge, PA: Trinity Press International, 1996), 55.

[37] Ibid., 122.

[38] Elizondo, "Elements for a Mexican American Mestizo Christology," 105.

[39] Ibid., 106.

[40] Horsley, *Archaeology, History, and Society in Galilee*, 63.

[41] Ibid., 122.

[42] Jonathan Draper, "Jesus and the Renewal of Local Community in Galilee: Challenge to a Communitarian Christology," *Journal of Theology for Southern Africa* 87 (June 1994): 35–36.

[43] Horsley, *Archaeology, History, and Society in Galilee*, 173.

[44] Alejandro García-Rivera, *St. Martín de Porres: The "Little Stories" and the Semiotics of Culture* (Maryknoll, NY: Orbis Books, 1995), 1–3.

[45] Martin D. Stringer, *A Sociological History of Christian Worship* (Cambridge: Cambridge University Press, 2005), 150ff.

[46] William A. Christian, Jr., "Spain in Latino Religiosity," in *El Cuerpo de Cristo: The Hispanic Presence in the U.S. Catholic Church*, ed. Peter Casarella and Raúl Gómez (New York: Crossroad, 1998), 326–327.

[47] Ibid., 327.

[48] Gary Macy, "Demythologizing 'the Church' in the Middle Ages," *Journal of Hispanic/Latino Theology* 3:1 (August 1995): 27.

[49] Orlando Espín, *The Faith of the People: Theological Reflections on Popular Catholicism* (Maryknoll, NY: Orbis, 1997), 117–119.

[50] Orlando Espín, "Pentecostalism and Popular Catholicism: The Poor and *Traditio*," *Journal of Hispanic/Latino Theology* 3, no. 2 (November 1995): 19.

[51] María Rosa Menocal, *La joya del mundo: musulmanes, judíos y cristianos, y la cultura de la tolerancia en al-Andalus* (Barcelona: Plaza y Janés, 2004), 24.

[52] Espín, "Pentecostalism and Popular Catholicism," 19.

[53] Avery Dulles, *Models of the Church* (Garden City, NY: Doubleday and Co., 1987), 36.

[54] Macy, "Demythologizing 'the Church' in the Middle Ages," 27.

[55] Ibid., 27–32.

[56] Ibid., 31–32, 38.

[57] Ibid., 35.

[58] Ibid.

[59] Mark Francis, "Popular Piety and Liturgical Reform in a Hispanic Context," in *Dialogue Rejoined: Theology and Ministry in the United States Hispanic Reality*, ed. Ana María Pineda and Robert Schreiter (Collegeville, MN: Liturgical Press, 1995), 166.

[60] John W. O'Malley, *Trent and All That: Renaming Catholicism in the Early Modern Era* (Cambridge, MA: Harvard University Press, 2000).

[61] Macy, "Demythologizing 'the Church' in the Middle Ages," 35–37.

[62] Ibid., 40.
[63] Stringer, *A Sociological History of Christian Worship*, 48.
[64] Ibid., 150.
[65] Ibid., 36.
[66] Ibid., 48.
[67] Ibid., 164–165.
[68] Ibid., 235.

8

What Happens to Church When We Move *Latinamente* beyond Inherited Ecclesiologies?

Juan Francisco Martínez

INTRODUCTION

Latinas/os need to create space for Catholic-Protestant dialogue, places where we can go beyond the restatement of our inherited differences and think about what we have in common, what we bring to an ecumenical conversation as Latinos/as, not only as Protestant or Catholic Christians. Focusing on the lived-out faith of concrete communities is a good place to develop, or least point toward, a *mestizo/a* or *mulata/o* ecclesiology.

As a "representative" of Latino/a Protestants (talk about an impossible task) I recognize that most Protestants have not taken time to reflect on the issue at hand, though many have lived it out in the *cotidianidad* of church life. Several Catholic colleagues, including Orlando Espín and Roberto Goizueta, are asking these types of questions and provide a potential framework for conversation and praxis.

Nonetheless, I realize that the ecumenical aspect of this task is made more difficult by the chosen starting point: ecclesiology. I constantly appeal to ecclesial life and practice in this essay but realize that ecclesiology as doctrine will always be in the background complicating any conversation.[1] Yet it is in ecclesial practice where we can gain glimpses of what churches look like when they move *latinamente*.

From the Protestant side of the conversation popular Pentecostalism and similar Free Church and Believers' Church[2] movements provide a useful place to begin looking at what Latino ecclesiology might look like when it is not bound by our inherited ecclesiologies. I want to frame my "Protestant answer" to the question in the title by first defining what I see as the "space for movement" within our existing realities, then recognizing that the type of movement proposed by the question in the title of this presentation almost inevitably will happen (and already happens) on the margins and in the cracks of the formal church structures, and lastly by describing real living Latino/a churches that are pushing the theological edges and taking us in the direction of a *mestizo/a* or *mulata/o* ecclesiology.[3]

DEFINING THE SPACE FOR MOVING "BEYOND"

We cannot begin this conversation without recognizing a certain *quijotesco* quality to the assigned task. We are a part of our ecclesial traditions and would likely strongly defend them, particularly if we felt they were being "attacked" by the "other." We also need to acknowledge that we are always in the midst of our traditions and that they have formed and informed us as Latinas/os. Our church communities are clearly important to us, and they were formed at the intersection of our inherited ecclesiologies and our experiences with God.[4] It is highly unlikely that most of us would be willing to let go of our inherited ecclesiologies, even as we recognize how they have limited or even perverted Latino/a expressions of faith. We cannot easily move beyond inherited ecclesiologies because there is no "beyond" where we can go to have this conversation. We are the children of our inherited ecclesiologies and they have formed our social imaginaries.

We are also living in the midst of a globalized world where our perspectives are being shaped, reshaped, and even misshaped, by interaction with people from beyond our ecclesiologies and our ethnicity. Even as we seek to develop our internal conversation we recognize the importance and need of many other conversations that invite us to move beyond inherited ecclesiologies, including Latino/a inherited ecclesiologies.

It is in the midst of these various conversations that I bring my own ecclesial experience to the table. I am a fifth generation *evangélico*,[5] whose ancestors settled in what is now south Texas during the Spanish colonial period. I am a part of the Free Church tradition, formed by some of its most radical manifestations, the Anabaptist movement of the sixteenth century. That tradition is mediated through the experience of being a *protestante,* a member of a religious minority that has not always been well received within the ethnic minority community of which I am a part.[6] As a pastor and an educator involved in pastoral formation my concerns have been much more focused on ecclesial life and its praxis than on the doctrinal definitions of church. I am a part of the *misión integral* conversation among *evangélicos* and the "missional church" conversation in the United States, though it is not always clear how the two fit together among U.S. Latinos. All this means that my principal concern is with churches as missional communities of faith, with how ecclesiology gets lived out in concrete congregations and the broader context in which these churches live and minister. In my personal church experience Latino Protestants have always lived out their ecclesiology on the margins of the larger "church," so I find it easy address the issue from that perspective.

Yet, in spite of our clear differences, we recognize ourselves in one an-other, and we affirm the term *Latino/a* as one that defines our commonality. We stand together, and apart, in the midst of conversations about the com-plexity of our identity/ies. We recognize that part of our commonality is the complexity of experiences that define what it means to be Latina/o. Many of us use the concept of *mestizaje* as a way of describing the continual process-ing and reprocessing of our identity and the multiple sources that are part of our background. Others have wondered whether *mulatez* is a similar term, or whether it describes a different type of experience and brings up more difficult questions about aspects of our Latino/a identity development. And we are having this conversation in the midst of the Borderlands, where mi-gration and encounter are creating new hybridities beyond the Latina/o com-munity even as we seek to come to terms with our Latino/a experience. I also wish I could say that we are in the midst of a post (internal) colonial conversation, but I am not yet fully convinced that we can add the prefix *post* to the internal colonial experience of many within the Latino/a commu-nity.[7]

Yet this is *our* space, the place where we seek to be faithful our traditions, faithful to our encounters with God through Jesus Christ, and faithful to God's gift of our ethnic identities and experiences. So it is on the margins of the Borderlands, on the margins of our ecclesial traditions, and even (sadly) within the marginalizations with which we struggle within the Latino/a community, where we seek to be those churches that invite us to take our identities seriously as we seek to be the church/es of Jesus Christ. It is here where we accept the challenge to develop church/es that are ours "without ceasing to be universal."[8]

BEING AND DOING CHURCH
ON THE MARGINS AND IN THE CRACKS

Most Latino Protestants, and Latino Pentecostals in particular, have al-ways done church on the margins. Historically, those who are part of North American denominations have found themselves marginalized by the lead-ership of their denominations because they are Latinos and by the Latino community because they are Protestants. They have expressed and devel-oped their faith communities on the edge of their denominations, often mis-understood and misrepresented, but reinterpreting what their traditions have given them in light of their Latino/a identity. If they have been given "space" to express their faith it is often because they are out of the limelight or they are given this freedom because they are "different" or assumed to be "un-able" to develop churches that look like the (normative) center.

Other Latino Protestants have chosen to try to work within denomina-tional systems, near the center. They have sought to be faithful to the inher-ited tradition, looking for "cracks" within the system where their unique

Latino contributions might fit. Their church communities often look like their majority culture counterparts, yet there is usually some Latino flavoring added.

Many Pentecostals, and others like them, have rejected both of these possibilities and have decided to start their own churches and/or denominations, making a virtue out of necessity. These congregations and denominations often find themselves on the edges or even outside of traditional Protestantism, with those at the center sometimes questioning whether they are even "really" Protestant.[9] Because these groups are not defined by the center, they have had the most freedom to develop most *latinamente*, though they are also the ones most likely to be considered heretical by those at or near the center.

Yet it has been at those margins, in those cracks, and on those edges where Latino Protestants have lived out their faith. On the one hand, many Latino/a Protestant faith expressions have developed in relationship to the center. The center has often defined the normative, something Latinos should aim for but seldom seem to obtain fully. Those that have made it to the center have often either felt alienated from their Latino/a identity or as if their ecclesial expressions seemed translated, never seeming to express fully their particularly Latina/o experiences with God.

Those on the edges have often openly rejected the center and have developed their Christian commitment over against the center. Yet even as the center is rejected, it has often become a part of the process, if only as a negative model of what the church community seeks to live out. But as many of these faith communities develop, there is often a growing desire of someday being accepted by the center.

It is to those margins, cracks, and edges, with all of their complexities, where we need to go to see how Latino-oriented Protestant/Pentecostal ecclesial life has developed, and some directions it could take in the future. Most of these communities have not taken the time to reflect consciously on their experience, but they are living out their faith in light of their Latino/a identity. What can be learned will come by participating and reflecting with them in the midst of their experience. We will look into the cracks,[10] but mostly focus on the margins and the edges, in order to describe lived-out Christian faith, both good and bad, and what those experiences might offer the conversation on *mestiza/o* ecclesiology.[11]

LIVING CHURCHES PUSHING THE THEOLOGICAL EDGES OF OUR ECCLESIOLOGIES[12]

When one travels to the edges and margins to participate in Latino Protestant and particularly Pentecostal congregations, the first thing one often notices is the seeming tentativeness of these communities. Many, if not most, of these congregations do not own a building but rent storefronts, warehouses, or other church buildings during "off" hours. They are often nomadic, moving as landlords increase the rent or the churches that previously rented to them change their priorities. Their existence often seems as tentative as that of the members who make up the congregations. These churches seem to put as much energy into merely surviving as do the individual church members that keep them going.

Yet it quickly becomes clear that these churches are meeting profound needs in their members. People are ready to make major sacrifices to keep these congregations alive, because this is where they have encountered God, have found new life, have an extended family, and are able to experience God's presence in their daily existence. It is where God answers prayers through miracles, but also through brothers and sisters who are ready and willing to provide time, energy, and money to meet the concrete needs of those within the community (and beyond).

Because they start from a Believers' Church ecclesiology, these congregations are communities of people who have made adult commitments of faith and have been baptized (usually by immersion) as a testimony to that commitment.[13] This means that membership and participation in these congregations is a voluntary commitment made by people old enough to take personal responsibility for their decisions and for their participation in these churches.

Mission and witness are an integral part of these churches, and all members are expected to be involved in evangelism. Evangelism is understood as the task of calling people to a personal, adult, commitment to Jesus Christ and to baptism as a sign of that commitment. That call is also an invitation to conversion, to experience God's transforming power in specific lifestyle changes. This aspect of the evangelistic call often has very practical implications, particularly for people in destructive lifestyles. It tends to have the greatest impact among Latinos/as (often nominal Catholics) who have not found a vibrant spiritual life in their current religious tradition and who are searching for meaning and power to address the frustrations and addictions with which they are struggling.[14]

Their conversion experiences are often very dramatic and life changing. People often leave addictive lifestyles and experience emotional, psychological, physical, and spiritual healings of various types.[15] The conversions often also have practical implications, such as better relationships in the family and an improving financial situation.[16] But, historically, these conversions have also created tensions. Some Latina/o converts become estranged from their extended families, particularly from those with a strong Roman Catholic commitment. This is usually interpreted as the price to be paid for following Jesus Christ.[17]

The local church community plays a very crucial role in the lives of most Latino/a Protestants. The church services are where people experience God. Particularly in Pentecostal churches, going to church is an opportunity to experience God's touch through the singing, prayers, and spiritual ecstatic experiences, such as speaking in tongues. God is experienced as real, personal, and involved in the life of the people.

The community of believers also validates the experience of the convert and reaffirms the sense of having a new life in Jesus Christ. Many Latino Protestants have powerful *testimonios* about the presence of God in their lives, and most churches make time for members to share them during their worship services. These, in turn, become part of the evangelistic strategy to draw new people. Many of the songs and hymns written by Latino/a Protestants and sung during church services also reaffirm these experiences.[18]

In most Latino Protestant churches the preaching of the Bible is also very important. Historically, most of the revivals that have given birth to Believers' Church movements and denominations have been based on the preaching and/or reading of the word and have been defined as attempts to return to a biblical model. Practically this means that most Latino Protestants see themselves as people of the word. A common sign that a Latino/a has truly been converted is when he or she begins to carry a Bible to church (or even to work).[19] Regular Bible studies are a part of church life, and worship services often include long sermons. These activities are crucial to a sense of seeking God's will through the word.

Another important component in Latino church life is prayer. Congregations often have several prayer services during the week, including home Bible studies and prayer meetings. Prayer times become opportunities to share personal and concrete needs with the church community. There is a strong sense that God hears and answer prayers. But sharing prayer requests often also becomes an opportunity for members of the community to respond concretely to one another's economic, physical, or emotional needs by becoming "God's means" to address the stated need.

For the most part, the liturgy in these churches tends to be very informal, with significant congregational participation, particularly in the smaller churches. Church services can run for more than two hours and might include multiple types of participation from church members. In the smaller churches there is often a sense that all church members can participate, even those who have little or no training in leading worship.

Most Latino Protestant churches are relatively small, usually with fewer than one hundred regular participants, including children and non-members. But these congregations provide believers with concrete support systems and a network that responds like an extended family. The church is a place of affirmation, where people can develop and grow. Though these congregations often have a marginal role in the larger society, they often play a crucial part in the lives of their members and in their local communities. And because so many Latino/a Protestants are converts, they tend to have strong ties and commitments to their churches.[20]

LATINO/A LEADERSHIP ON THE EDGES

There are different models and understandings of pastoral leadership among these Latino churches. But there are also some common characteristics. Leadership is usually seen as a charismatic gift. Churches often have Latino—and a small, though growing, number of Latina—pastors who began as lay leaders in their congregations and who later developed into pastors. It is not uncommon for people with dynamic conversion experiences to eventually become pastors. In many of the smaller churches, pastors are bivocational, usually living and working in the same community as their church members. Many Latino/a pastors do not have much formal education, and in many denominations or independent churches formal ministerial training is not a requirement for ordination. Some would go so far as seeing too much formal training for ministry as suspect.[21]

A key component in these churches is that the large majority of the pastors are Latinos/as. Those pastors who are not Latino usually have extensive experience and service in the community and are strongly committed to it. This makes Latino Protestant churches one of the few places where Latinos/as are in charge of their own religious communities. Because of their Believers' Church ecclesiology, it has been easier for Latino-led churches and denominations to develop and thrive in the United States. The growing number of Latino-focused denominations and networks of churches also provides Latinos and Latinas with leadership roles they seldom hold in Catholic or mainline Protestant denominations.

Because of the Protestant understanding of the "priesthood of all believers" and the relatively small size of most Latino churches, most church members have a role and a responsibility in their congregation. Many Latino church members may be seen as marginal in the larger society because they are undocumented, have little formal education, and/or work in menial jobs. But in Latino Protestant churches they have the opportunity to find a space to serve, contribute, develop skills, and take leadership responsibilities.

MARGINAL CHURCHES AND LATINO/A IDENTITY

Historically Latino Protestant churches have played an ambivalent role in Latina/o identity issues. On the one hand, they have played an important part in cultural identity maintenance. During the nineteenth century and throughout the twentieth century, Latino Protestant churches were often among the few places where formal Spanish was used and a new generation of Latinos learned to read and write in Spanish.[22] And because the churches were in the hands of Latino leaders, worship styles and services are (usually) free to reflect the linguistic, cultural, national background complexities of the community. In these congregations there is the freedom to have services in Spanish, English, Spanglish, or in various bilingual formats.

Spanish-language Bible institutes have also played a role in this process. Students have often studied in Spanish and have strengthened their denominational and Latino/a identities while studying in these programs. They have also often met (and married) other Latinos/as who shared a common sense of a Latino/a Protestant identity. Many of these graduates are now pastors and leaders in Latino churches like the ones in which they grew up.[23]

But Latino Protestant churches have also struggled to find their place in larger society. To be or to become a Latino Protestant means to be a part of a minority within a minority in the United States. It has not always been easy to maintain a Latino Protestant identity because of the pressure to acculturate and the role of religion in that process. For many Latinos/as, one sign of cultural identity is popular Catholicism. For those people, Latino Protestants do not seem to be fully Latino. Yet Latino Protestants have not always had a clear place within the Protestant community in the United States. Historically, Protestant missionaries have often seen their evangelizing task as including making Latinos good Protestants and good Americans. This tendency continues today among some churches that encourage Latinos to cut their ethnic and cultural ties to fit into their new community of believers.[24] It is also not uncommon to see younger acculturating Latino Protestants become part of larger churches where Latinos have few or no leadership roles.[25]

Another tension related to identity maintenance is the denominational and/or social structures. A Believers' Church ecclesiology provides the space for Latinos/as to develop and lead their congregations. But these churches are often on the margins and under pressure to acculturate. This means that while Latino churches support a Latino Protestant identity, this identity is often undermined, or at least circumscribed, by the mere fact of being a Protestant *in the United States*.

MOVING *LATINAMENTE* BEYOND INHERITED ECCLESIOLOGIES FROM THE EDGES AND MARGINS

The lived-out faith of these ecclesial communities provides many interesting possibilities as we search for answers to the question at hand. The first, for me, is one that should seem obvious. It is impossible to move "beyond" if Latinos and Latinas are not in charge of the institutions where we seek the types of changes we think need to occur. The most significant value of the congregations I just described is that Latinas/os are the agents of their own future. We will only be able to answer our question effectively if we have spaces where we lead, are responsible for the implications of our leadership, and have the spaces to experiment with new ecclesial styles. Latino churches on the edges and margins provide us with a model, though not the only one, of how to do that.

This space is crucial not only for theological reflection, but also as the place for the marginalized in our communities to find their voices. More leaders need to develop among the current generation of people in our community. But they are also crucial for a new generation of leaders. We will only develop new leaders committed to the community in spaces where the new generation can see Latinos/as in leadership and can respect and learn from those leaders whom our larger society often considers disposable.

This space can also empower all the members of the church community because they all have a role to play, even those who are often marginalized because they do not have a formal education, work at menial tasks, or are undocumented. All members are needed, and it is assumed that all members are gifted by God to participate in the community and to serve others.

The edges and margins are also where Latino congregations practice being church as a mutually committed community. The church as a community of believers committed to helping one another and to responding missionally to their local context, and beyond, is a crucial contribution to a Latino/a understanding of ecclesiology. Latino churches that have moved "toward the center" have tended to lose sight of their role and responsibility toward those in the community who remain marginalized and oppressed.[26]

These churches also remind us that the task at hand is worth doing because we believe that God is at work in our world and in our lives. The people in these congregations *adoran desde lo profundo*, because they have experienced God in their lives in conversion, in miraculous interventions, in worship experiences, and in the mutual support of the community.[27] It is out on these fringes that people have learned to use Latino styles of music to worship God and to tell others about how God is real in their lives. Moving beyond inherited ecclesiologies is important to the extent that it provides more spaces for God to be made manifest in the lives of real people.[28]

Most Latino Protestant congregations are located where the people are, in the urban spaces, in the midst of life as it is lived by our people. We cannot do ecclesiology, or any other theological reflection, if we are not where the majority of our people call home. Our *locus theologicus* must be where Latinos/as live and struggle.[29] The academy gives us spaces to stop and reflect but can never provide the proper location to answer our question. We will be able to move beyond *latinamente* to the extent that we can walk alongside our sisters and brothers in the midst of our mutual experience of God and Christian community.

It is on the edges of power where the theological concepts of marginality, poverty, exile, *mestizaje,* and solidarity make sense as frameworks for a *teología pastoral* that understands that the church is truly fulfilling its mission when it is in those places where Latinos/as live and seek after God.[30] Though most churches do not have a "theological" vocabulary to describe their mission, their preaching, service, and mutual support show us that moving *latinamente* means understanding churches as local communities of people committed to God and to one another.

The aforementioned concepts are also crucial for reading *la Biblia en español.*[31] In these churches the Bible is experienced as God's word for us here and now. This rereading constantly calls us back (Believers' Church primitivism), reminding us that we are God's people, part of a long tradition, and leads us and points us to the future. It is in the midst of this dynamic interaction with scripture that our academic biblicists can provide the community with language to understand that, in fact, many Latino Pentecostals on the edge are involved in post-colonial readings of scripture.

These churches have developed on the margins and edges, but that space is an important theological frame of reference. Whether implicitly or explicitly, these churches do theology and live out their faith in exile. Latino theologians have pointed out the importance of experienced exile in understanding Latino faith experiences. It is a crucial referent in "reading the Bible" for those who have experienced literal exile or those of us who live "in exile" even though we are in the country of our birth.

Exile is a place of pain and dislocation. There is often an implicit sense that we want to move beyond exile or at least hope that the next generation of Latinos/as in the United States will move beyond exile. But exile is an important theological concept and a crucial location for theological reflection. Much of the Hebrew scriptures was written in exile. A Latina/o focused ecclesiology will be strengthened by drawing from the exile experience of so many of us, and also by focusing on exile as a way of understanding the church in its mission in the world.[32]

It is in their exile experience that people in these churches experience Jesus Christ both as the one who suffers for us, and like us, but also as the one who wins the victory, *desde abajo,* the victory of the cross, of weakness not of strength. These churches show us that we need to move forward, not by seeking the positions of power that have been denied to us, but by recognizing the role of the weak, the victory that comes from weakness.

It is from this location that we can be truly prophetic. We can speak to power because we are not starting from positions of power and are not seeking to impose our position over others. We can empower *los pequeños* because we use the power of weakness, of solidarity, and of pain. By working *desde abajo* we also empower people by making them agents of their own future, finding a voice at church that they have nowhere else. It is also a place with a great deal of potential to *conscientizar* people as they realize that God cares about the whole of their lives.[33]

Most Latino Pentecostal churches also demonstrate our *mestizo* adaptability in their transnationality. They live the reality of being church in a globalized world where people move north and south, and also east and west. Like the Christian slaves of the first century, Latino Protestant migrants are taking their faith with them and confessing the reality of a global church, not through formal structures and declarations, but through the lived-out experiences of expressing and sharing their faith experiences with other people that are migrating around the world. They are also maintaining ties to their churches in their countries of origin, changing the traditional understanding of mission as the work of rich people toward the poor. These are poor people "here" supporting the mission of poor people "over there." And because they are connecting with others in the midst of this post-internal colonial (?), hybrid Borderlands context, they are showing us a model of what the church can look like in a globalized, post-Christendom world.

Because these churches do not speak from power, there is little possibility that they can impose their ideas and perspectives on others. But because they speak from the bottom, they can not only provide ideas to help us answer our question, they can also speak to the global church. Our role in developing ecclesiologies that move "beyond," seen from this perspective, is to use our Latino/a experience to enrich the ecclesiological conversation from below.

CONCERNS RAISED FOR ECCLESIOLOGICAL REFLECTION

In a Believers' Church perspective the church is most clearly manifested as a local visible community of believers, what we call a local church. Theologically we confess that there is a universal church. We also have a sense that there can be unity among Christians, even if there are denominational differences. But the universality[34] of the church is most often manifested in concrete relations between local congregations, particularly with those from the same denomination. Many Latino churches have relations with churches outside their local setting, particularly with congregations in Latin America. But Protestant church structures always end at national borders, with no transnational structures that oversee churches from several countries. There might be international fraternal organizations, but these have no real authority over their member churches.

It is often also difficult for Latino Protestant churches to work together, even if they are from the same denominational perspective. Many times one senses a spirit of competition between churches. Many pastors assume that those who call for churches to work together across denominational lines have other agendas in mind, such as drawing people from other churches into their own congregations.

This becomes more complicated as Latino Protestant churches look beyond their own cultural and theological framework. Linguistic and cultural differences often limit relations with non-Latino churches, but they often also seem to serve as a buffer to avoid relating with churches that are not Latino. But, more important, a Believers' Church framework, as practiced in the Latino community, does not provide clear tools for developing ties with churches, even Latino ones, from other theological traditions. And our Protestant heritage has taught us to question any attempt to define the "universal church" structurally.[35] This leaves unanswered the question of how Latino Protestants can gain a sense of being part of, and relating to, a worldwide church. In other words, where is the sense of a universal (catholic) church, and how does it manifest itself in practice? How can we add our experience to an ecumenical dialogue that is attempting to go beyond our inherited ecclesiologies?

COMING FULL CIRCLE—MOVING BEYOND EVEN AS WE RETURN TO OUR INHERITED ECCLESIOLOGIES

As we look toward the future, it is clear that our inherited ecclesiologies will have less pull on us and our churches, forcing us to look beyond at many different levels. The pace of changes in our globalized world means that we need to rethink what church looks like, particularly as we move beyond a Christendom model of church. It is also clear that the *sensus fidelium* of the Latino believers needs to play an important role in helping us rethink our ecclesiology. Latino Christians have been ignored and/or marginalized in both of our traditions. By questioning our inherited traditions, we are providing a voice that will enrich our own communities and the church beyond our specific cultural framework.

Yet it is in the midst of our need to move beyond our current structures and to think about the church in new ways that our inherited ecclesiologies may yet have an important role to play. The Latino Believers' Church tradition constantly reminds us to return to our biblical and theological roots. Without radical *(radix)* ecclesiologies, we will be tempted to lose sight of the New Testament framing of our Christian faith. But the Roman Catholic tradition will constantly remind us that we cannot ignore twenty centuries of history as we look to new possibilities. That tradition needs to remind us *evangélicos* that in moving beyond we are also seeking to develop holy, apostolic, and catholic churches. So maybe the ecumenical conversation among Latinos/as can go forward as we both move beyond our inherited traditions and continue drawing on what our traditions have taught us.

CONCLUSION

There is a great deal of joy in being *quijotesco*, in being able to be a part of a group of sisters and brothers who believe it is possible to live out the gospel as a community of Latina/o believers. I am excited by the opportunity to move forward with the God who continues to walk with our people.

NOTES

[1] It is difficult to use ecclesiology as a starting point because Catholics and Free Church Protestants (the vast majority of Latino Protestants) have such different views

of the church that each fundamentally questions, formally or informally, whether the other is even "church." Catholic doctrine does not recognize as "church" any structure that is not framed around apostolic succession, thereby eliminating most Latino Protestant congregations from being considered churches in a formal theological sense. Many Free Church Latino Protestants would question whether the Roman Catholic Church is a "Christian church," given our "primitivist" understandings of what constitutes a faithful church. This plays out in ecumenical settings where our current ecclesiologies make it impossible to take communion together. For example, the only time in my life that I have been offered communion by a Catholic priest was in Guatemala by a Spaniard.

[2] There are different ways to define a Believers' Church ecclesiology. It was born as a response to the concept of a state church. It rejects the idea that the church should be linked to any state. Its basic understanding is that the church is a voluntary body, made up of people who make a conscious commitment to be a part. Therefore, only people who have been baptized as adults (usually including adolescents) can be members of the church. It is important to note that a Believers' Church perspective implies a common understanding of what the church is and how it functions and not a historical or denominational link among the various movements that practice this ecclesiology. For more information, see Donald F. Durnbaugh, *The Believers' Church* (New York: Macmillan, 1968); or Paul Basden and David S. Dockery, eds., *The People of God: Essays on the Believers' Church* (Nashville, TN: Broadman Press, 1991).

[3] I will immediately confess my Free Church Protestantism by using the term *churches* referring to living local communities where ecclesiology is lived out and seldom, if ever, using the term *church*. I ask my Catholic colleagues to "translate" my usages into *Catholic* as necessary and appropriate.

[4] Nancy Ammerman provides an excellent perspective on the interaction between the public religious institutions and personal experience in "Religious Identities and Religious Institutions," in *Handbook of the Sociology of Religion*, ed. Michele Dillon (Cambridge: Cambridge University Press, 2003), 207–244.

[5] Historically, *evangélico* has been a broader term in Latin America and the Spanish-speaking United States than *evangelical*. I describe myself as an *evangélico*, because of that broader connotation. I am not always sure if I am an evangelical, but I know that I am an *evangélico*.

[6] Though I was born and raised in the United States I grew up in Latino majority communities in south Texas and central California. As a child I often faced ridicule from the Catholic majority for being an *aleluya* or *protestante*.

[7] Alfredo Mirandé's description of the Chicano experience as "internal-colonialism" continues to be an apt description of the experiences of many Latinas/os in the United States today. For many Latinos there is not yet a "post" that can define their "internal colonial" experience as being a part of the past (see alfredo Mirande, *The Chicano Experience: An Alternative Perspective* [Notre Dame, IN: University of Notre Dame Press, 1985]).

[8] This quotation is from Justo González and Pablo Jiménez, *Púlpito: An Introduction to Hispanic Preaching* (Nashville, TN: Abingdon Press, 2005), 21. González is referring to Latino/a theology and its role in preaching, but later he talks of the importance of the church in this process. I play on his words because of the way he posits the specific Latina/o experience with the reality of a universal church.

[9] Jean-Pierre Bastián questions whether popular Pentecostal movements in Latin America are really a continuation of traditional Protestantism (see Jean-Pierre Bastián,

Protestantismos y modernidad latinoamericana: Historia de unas minorías religiosas activas en América Latina [Mexico City: Fondo de Cultura Económica, 1994]).

[10] Many good books have been written on Latinos/as in mainline Protestant denominations. These include Paul Barton, *Hispanic Methodists, Presbyterians, and Baptists in Texas* (Austin: University of Texas Press, 2006); R. Douglas Brackenridge and Francisco García-Treto, *Iglesia Presbiteriana: A History of Presbyterians and Mexican Americans in the Southwest* (San Antonio, TX: Trinity University Press, 1974); Justo González, ed., *En nuestra propia lengua: Una historia del metodismo unido hispano* (Nashville, TN: Abingdon Press, 1991); Daisy Machado, *Of Borders and Margins: Hispanic Disciples in Texas, 1888–1945* (New York: Oxford University Press, 2003); and David Maldonado, ed., *Protestantes/Protestants: Hispanic Christianity within Mainline Traditions* (Nashville, TN: Abingdon Press, 1999).

[11] I am particularly indebted to the work done by the following: Eldín Villafañe, *El Espíritu Libertador: Hacia una ética social pentecostal hispanoamericana* [San Juan, Puerto Rico: Nueva Creación, 1996]); Arlene Sánchez-Walsh, *Latino Pentecostal Identity: Evangelical Faith, Self, and Identity* (New York: Columbia University Press, 2003); Luis León, *La Llorona's Children: Religion, Life, and Death in the U.S.-Mexican Borderlands* (Berkeley and Los Angeles: University of California Press, 2004); and the various contibutors to *Iglesias peregrinas en busca de identidad Cuadros del protestantismo latino en los Estados Unidos*, ed. Juan Martínez and Luis Scott (Barcelona: Editorial Kairós, 2004). I may not often refer to specific issues raised by these authors, but they are always in the background of my descriptions of the Latino Protestant, and particularly Pentecostal, communities.

[12] I originally developed parts of the following section in "Church: A Latino/a Protestant Perspective," in *Handbook of Latina/o Theologies*, ed. Edwin Aponte and Miguel de la Torre, 550–557 (Atlanta, GA: Chalice Press, 2006).

[13] Though many Protestant churches practice infant baptism, this is not common among most Latino/a Protestants and nonexistent among Pentecostals and the other churches in the Believers' Church tradition.

[14] Edwin Hernández describes the attractiveness of this type of church to Latinas/os by stating: "Sectarian groups, therefore, are more likely to attract followers who are powerless and who have experienced a severe crisis in their lives, such as immigration. The benefits and rewards of belonging to such a religious group arise from the social experience of a living, vibrant, energizing, creative, empathizing, affirming and hoping community" (Edwin Hernández, "Moving from the Cathedral to Storefront Churches," in *Protestantes/Protestants Hispanic Christianity within Mainline Traditions*, ed. David Maldonado (Nashville, TN: Abingdon Press, 1999), 235.

[15] For a description of this phenomenon within Victory Outreach/Alcance Victoria, see Luis León, "Born Again in East L.A., and Beyond," in *La Llorona's Children*, 201–240.

[16] The phenomenon, referred to as "redemption and lift" by evangelical missiologists, occurs when a person leaves a destructive lifestyle. A person who previously had difficulties holding down a steady job or who spent a significant amount of his or her budget for cigarettes or alcohol, now has more income to spend on the family and a desire to see the family situation improve. For a detailed explanation of the concept, see Donald A. McGavran, *Understanding Church Growth* (Grand Rapids, MI: Eerdmans, 1970), 295–313.

[17] A Latino Protestant traditional hymn still sung in many churches, *Hay una senda*, is a description of the costs of becoming a Protestant convert. It includes a

stanza that states that friends and relatives despised the convert when they turned to Christ. (Written by Tomás Estrada, © 1960 R. C. Savage)

[18] Daniel Ramírez describes how hymnology developed in his own denomination, the Apostolic Assembly of the Faith in Jesus Christ, in "Alabaré a mi Señor: Cultura e ideología en la himnología protestante latina," in Martínez and Scott, *Iglesias peregrinas en busca de identidad*, 193–205.

[19] Since the Bible is usually carried under one's arm, someone has jokingly said that the Bible is the Latino Protestant "deodorant."

[20] This means that, as a whole, Latina/o Protestants tend to be more active participants in the lives of their ecclesial communities than their Catholic counterparts.

[21] Some Latino Protestant congregations have become suspicious of seminary education after sending leaders to seminary and seeing them educated out of the community or when those with a seminary education seem to have lost their "fervor" for ministry.

[22] As a U.S.-born Latino, my first regular exposure to Spanish outside the home was in church. Like many other Latino Protestants, I was expected to read the Bible in Spanish and regularly wrote in Spanish for various church activities.

[23] For a description of the role Bible Institutes play in Latino/a Pentecostal identity development and maintenance, see Sánchez-Walsh, *Latino Pentecostal Identity*.

[24] Sánchez-Walsh describes this tendency in several Pentecostal denominations (see *Latino Pentecostal Identity*). Juan Francisco Martínez describes the historical roots of this tendency among majority culture Protestant churches in the United States (see Juan Francisco Martínez, *Sea la Luz: The Making of Mexican Protestantism in the American Southwest, 1829–1900* [Denton: University of North Texas Press, 2007]).

[25] Because missionaries from majority culture churches evangelized many Latino Protestants, it is not uncommon for some Latino Protestants to assume that "Anglos" by definition practice Protestantism better. This sense, mixed with acculturation pressures, sometimes creates situations where some Latino Protestants prefer to worship where there is no Latino leadership. This tendency can be seen among Latino Protestants of most denominational traditions, even those who do not have a Believers' Church ecclesiology.

[26] Eldín Villafañe calls on Latino Pentecostals to move beyond a communitarian ethic to a broader social ethic so that they will not be drawn into a model of church that is individualistically focused, such as that practiced by many majority culture churches in the United States (Villafañe, *El Espíritu Liberatador*, esp. 138–139).

[27] Luis León argues that Pentecostal models of worship link this group of Latinos to their pre-Columbian roots. According to León: "*Los evangélicos* continue practical, spiritual, religious, and ecstatic modes of being and becoming that existed in Mesoamerica prior to Spanish colonization and that have been articulated so completely with(in) Christianity, Catholicism, and now evangelicalism that it is difficult to distinguish precise origins" ("Born Again in East L.A.," 204).

[28] The Anabaptist missiologist Juan Driver argues that it is on the periphery where the people of God are most open to the new things God wants to do in and through the church (see Juan Driver, *La fe en la periferia de la historia: Una historia del pueblo cristiano desde la perspectiva de los movimientos de restauración y reforma radical* [Madrid: Ediciones SEMILLA, 1997]).

[29] Roberto Goizueta, *Caminemos con Jesús: Toward a Hispanic/Latino Theology of Accompaniment* (Maryknoll, NY: Orbis Books, 1995), 173–211.

[30] For an excellent model of what that looks like from within the Roman Catholic tradition, see Casiano Floristán, *Teología práctica: Teoría y praxis de la acción pastoral* (Salamanca: Ediciones Sígueme, 1991). This is the primary text for the core pastoral theology course at Fuller Theological Seminary in the Hispanic Church Studies program.

[31] Justo González, *Santa Biblia: The Bible through Hispanic Eyes* (Nashville, TN: Abingdon Press, 1996).

[32] John Howard Yoder provides a helpful analysis of the role of exile as a tool for understanding the church and its mission in "Retirada y diáspora: Los dos rostros de la liberación," in *Discipulado y liberación La teología de liberación en perspective anabautista*, ed. Daniel Schipani, 90–99 (Madrid: Ediciones SEMILLA, 1993).

[33] It is here where the *misión integral* movement from Latin America is providing Latinos/as tools from within our own theological tradition to address the complex social issues we face as a community. One text that is being used in our churches and that has now been translated into English is C. René Padilla and Tetsunao Yamamori, eds., *La iglesia local como agente de transformación: Una eclesiología para la misión integral* (Ediciones Kairós, 2003). This influence has played out in the growing participation of Latino Pentecostal pastors in the work toward comprehensive immigration reform.

[34] Many Latino Protestants feel uncomfortable with the word *catholic* because of its potential identification with the Roman Catholic Church.

[35] Some in the Believers' Church tradition would go so far as to question any attempt to bring structural unity to the church around the world, such as the World Council of Churches or formal ecumenical efforts of any sort.

PART V

TOWARD THE NEXT STEP

9

Convivencias: What Have We Learned?

Toward a Latino/a Ecumenical Theology

Neomi De Anda and Néstor Medina

Latino/a theology has reached a new level of maturity. Latino/a theologians have moved from asserting their ground as legitimate theological subjects, and articulating experiences of faith of Latino/a communities, to engaging in self-critical theological processes of constructing an ecumenical theology. Within an environment of profound respect, academic rigor, and well-intentioned camaraderie, Protestant and Catholic Latino/a theologians pursued this task at Mount St. Mary's College in Los Angeles on June 3–6, 2007. During the days that we met, the many challenges entailed by such a project became evident. It was pleasantly surprising, however, that in constructing a Latino/a *ecumenical* theology the results could be so rich and encouraging.

These theologians went beyond just knowing one another's traditions, working diligently to foster the theological ecumenical conversation. With a larger number of Catholics than Protestants from different traditions present, the results proved thought provoking and inspiring. The contributions of this initial formal intra-Latino/a ecumenical conversation display a wide range of issues that can prove most helpful to other theological debates on ecumenism. Latino/a theologians used unique methods and approaches that went far beyond other ecumenical conversations organized around key principles.

We have chosen to write this enlace (wrap-up) as a unified piece and an example of *teología de y en conjunto* The other essays in this volume have practiced *teología en y de conjunto* through a commitment to patient oral and written dialogue and discourse-producing pieces written by individuals. We affirm a multiplicity of understandings of processes and outcomes in *teología en y de conjunto*. We firmly believe that theology done in these manners comes from the community *(en conjunto)* and belongs to the community *(de conjunto)*.

In the history of ACHTUS, enlaces have traditionally been the main responsibility of one or two persons. Because of the large number of participants at the symposium, we changed the procedure of the enlace from giving one or two voices the final tasks to being summative and constructive to providing an environment for working groups within the final session.

Our contribution in this essay should not be read as a summary of the different presentations made during the days we met. It is rather an appreciative report and outline of some of the insights we gained and which confirmed key aspects of the Latino/a theological methodology and approach. We have tried to include components of the conversation that happened throughout the week both formally and informally, around the large table in the sessions and around smaller tables at meals, over drinks, and during late-night sharing of reception leftovers, amid the simplicities and complexities of *lo cotidiano*. Some of the insights we gained also contribute to shaping the future course of what can be appropriately identified as an ecumenical Latino/a theology. We have organized this article in three sections. In the first two sections we highlight the points of agreement and divergence that emerged during these debates. In the third section we note some of the central challenges that Latino/a theologians must face as they engage the theological task in general, and specifically as they embark in the Latino/a ecumenical theological project. These three sections show, in no uncertain terms, that as U.S. Latino/a theology comes of age, it sets up new theological directions and trajectories that offer new contributions for other theological communities.

CONVERGENCIAS:
TEOLOGÍA EN CONJUNTO
ACROSS DENOMINATIONAL ALLEGIANCES

As Latino/a theologians engaged the particular issues assigned to them, they made clear that their reflections emerged from a particular historical location and history. This is consistent with the Latino/a theological methodology as it seeks to articulate the experience of faith of the Latino/a communities. These theologians did not intend to construct abstract theological conceptual edifices. Rather, they sought to engage key questions as they relate to the unique and concrete historical reality of the U.S. Latino/a communities, Protestant and Catholics alike, of which they are part. As Goizueta's presentation reiterated, an ecumenical Latino/a theology had to be grounded on the praxis of the people.

Since the point of departure of these reflections is the reality of the people, it became evident that Latino/a people are, irrespective of their religious tradition, heirs to a history of colonization. Lurking in the background of this theological encounter were the five centuries of racialized despoliation, marginalization, and exploitation of peoples that produce many detrimental effects among the Latino/a peoples and communities even today. We realized we all have felt the impact of the imperial forces that, at different times and in different ways, have imposed upon the Latino/a peoples foreign ideas, intellectual frameworks and categories, and ways of understanding and interacting with the world. These, we learned, must be deconstructed and interrogated so as not to reinscribe the colonial impetus of all types of negative discrimination and hierarchical racialization of peoples.

The retrieval of our collective memory requires that Latino/a people engage in the painful process of acknowledging the violence enacted by multiple colonizers, many through attempts to preach their versions of Christianity (Western European and North Atlantic), while at the same time declaring the people's cultures and religious practices anathema. Here it would have been great to acknowledge the diverse religious presences, particularly the indigenous and African ancestors and living communities that so color the Latino/a historical and cultural landscape, but that always remain in the background of our reflections, with little explicit articulation.

The exercise of retrieving our collective memory is one that hinges upon our celebration of community as the locus of God's salvation. In (re)locating salvation in the survival of our communities, Miguel Díaz invited us to reformulate our understanding of ecumenicity. Indeed, Roberto Goizueta challenged us to retake the concept of the people of God as an appropriate gateway for reclaiming the preferential option for the poor. But the discussion broadened his proposal. The question was who fits under the category of children or people of God? The challenge, which will require much careful reflection, is the recognition of an existence among Latino/a communities of a matrix of many peoples who belong to different traditions within Christianity (Jehovah Witnesses, Mormons) and outside Christianity (Buddhists, Hare Krishnas, Jews, Muslims, and others), and who cannot be excluded from a broader understanding of the people of God.

In this light, said Díaz, questions of individual salvation are intimately linked to the community and not to the denomination, which then makes relevant concerns for justice. As he emphasized, the struggle for justice and survival must be seen as a human struggle, not limited to Catholics and Protestants. The implication of this assertion is the broadening of the understanding of the *oikoumene* (the household of God). In his Rahnerian way to conceive grace as always open, Díaz reminded us that if we are not for Asians, African Americans, and so on, we are not for ourselves. Here the ecumenical insight may be for Christian Latino/a theologians to come to terms with the reality that Asians, Africans Americans, Muslims, and Jews already exist within Latino/a communities.

Along the lines of historical remembering, we uncovered the revelatory character of our memories. This is not just a repackaging of the biblical call to the people of Israel constantly to remember what God has done for them. It is the recognition that in the midst of invasion, colonialism, oppression, and marginalization, God is found at work among the Latino/a peoples. In this way, remembering contains an important theological revelatory import. And the disclosure of the divine can be found concretely in the people's stories, experiences, narratives, testimonies, and oral traditions, which contain kernels of revelatory truths and are sources of divine revelation. This is, asserted Díaz, our *memoria rota,* the gracious divine act of self-disclosure through the brokenness, discontinuities, and fissures of our historical past and present.

Latino/a peoples, Catholics and Protestants, received a particular tradition outside of which we cannot function, affirmed Juan Martínez. Although, according to Jean-Pierre Ruíz, the issue remains that our communities do church, celebrate the reality of God, and interact with the biblical text differently. While questions of criteria for reading the text evaded these conversations on ecumenism, it remained clear that for Latino/a communities the biblical text remains authoritative. People re-create their traditions by infusing them with their ethnocultural unique practices; this results in newer and fresher expressions of Christianity *a lo Latino/a.*

Ruíz challenged us, stating that the Latino/a people relate to the biblical text by way of reinterpreting the text and finding themselves in the story of the text in ways that demand a systematic formulation of our understanding of revelation. Ruíz invited us to recover the biblical text in order to read our stories in its narrative. This is not a blind literalism of the Bible, he insists, but a reading of the text that in turn engages and critiques the text, and discerns the divine at work in our present context.

Leticia Guardiola-Sáenz added that this engagement with the text is a complex process of cross-fertilization whereby the people at once interact with the text and their social reality in ways that (re)establish the authority of the text but that at the same time break down the boundaries between the people's experience of faith and the biblical narrative. This, she claimed, is being changed dramatically with the people's interaction with the Internet and technology, as new frontiers of interaction with the Bible are drawn. In this way, she, like Ruíz, invited us to interrogate our common assumptions about the manner in which people interact with the text and what they bring with them in reading the text. Most particularly, Ruíz warned us to be careful not to pursue any theologies of correspondence. It is important that as people engage the text they keep in mind that they are not the people in the biblical text. In this way, Latino theologians and scholars challenged contemporary approaches to reading the text separated from the concrete context of people.

It is at this point that both concepts of *lo cotidiano* and popular religion were affirmed as inseparable by these discussions on ecumenicity. Popular religion reminds us of the praxis of faith of the people, and *lo cotidiano* of the way in which they make their faith concrete and historical. Goizueta emphasized the importance on grounding our theological affirmation in history. These Latino/a theologians (re)affirmed that this only happens in the context of *lo cotidiano,* as the space where people face the complex and messy reality of suffering, shame, brokenness, and struggle toward transformation of their world and reality.

In this way the religious expressions of the people become prophetic spaces of divine grace, as they envision a more inclusive and just world. Along this line we played with the concept of waste and manure as illustrating life; at the same time that manure is actual waste, it is also actual fertilizer for the possibilities of life to continue. In this same way, as people engage the reality of God and express their faith in God in the middle of their reality of pain, suffering, and exclusion (manure as waste), their faith prophetically announces a future world as they struggle to transform their present reality (manure as fertilizer). In other words, in *lo cotidiano,* Latino/a peoples and communities envision the possibilities of coming alongside with God in the building of the kindom of God.

We do not wish to propose a romanticized version of life or of Latino/a communities. It is the sobering realization that life does not come neat and organized, removed from suffering and pain. It is also the realization of the human condition of brokenness. But it is also the celebration of the divine act of grace manifest amid and in spite of such limitations. Thus, concepts such as popular religion and *lo cotidiano* served us as guiding posts whereby our theological reflections would remain grounded on the reality of our peoples and communities.

None of the presenters illustrated this better than José David Rodríguez. His poignant recovery of popular literature emerging from the Latino/a communities refocused the interdisciplinary character of Latino/a theology. Most important, he invited us to access literature as theological resources in the creative process of fostering the Latino/a spiritual imagination. For him, this type of literature reveals aspects often left untouched by theologians. Literature, he insisted, reveals the complex web of issues in the Latino/a social reality that elucidate the ways people encounter and interact with God, as well as express their faith. "Lower case" literature, he told us, makes us privy to many aspects of the Latino/a reality that can enrich our understanding of their experience of faith in God.

In order to move the conversation further, there was a general consensus that we needed to go *beyond* each other's denominational allegiances and differences. We agreed that part of the cost of ecumenism was being dislocated from our comfort zone. Ecumenical conversations require a sense of displacement and dislocation, but that was not perceived as necessarily bad. At the same time, denominational and cultural boundaries were not perceived as hermetically sealed, but rather fluid and porous as open new spaces are created where the *rostros distintos de Dios* (Elsa Tamez) can all coexist.

The perceived problem was the nature of this proposed "beyond." What would it look like? Who would be included? What would be the tenor and content of the discussions? All these key questions were reflected upon. In part, the apprehension expressed by one of the working groups was that one of the common models readily available is the nondenominational mega-churches. Such models are limited because they run counter to the very efforts of justice and recognition of different religious traditions. They present a generic version of church that collapses ethnic and cultural differences, converting them in one undifferentiated whole, without challenging the social and cultural prejudices that privilege one ethnic and culture group over another. This group stated that the model of the mega-church may look comfortable, but such models represent a "serious loss of integrity and diversity." In proposing a universal *ekklesia*, they historicize an assimilationist version of the church by removing ethnic and cultural differences, which are perceived as divisive.

By contrast, the members of another group noted one another's denominations are the point of departure in this conversation. There is no point of neutrality or neutral space from which to depart. But this group also affirmed that such moves toward ecumenism must be characterized by small steps safeguarding the integrity of the traditions each of the participants represent.

One of the toughest challenges in the conversation was the discussion of the central symbol of Mary, which for so many Protestants is an obstacle in ecumenical conversations. The task fell upon Cármen Nanko-Fernández, who offered us an alternative way for interpreting the person of Mary as portrayed in the biblical text. Her interpretation may prove helpful in bringing Protestants and Catholics closer by way of retrieving the biblical Mary as the one filled with the Spirit. Focusing primarily on the relational character of Mary, Nanko-Fernández affirmed that when understood from this position, Mary stops being an obstacle in ecumenical discussions, because she becomes the role model to follow and imitate in what it means to follow Christ. Her proposal is ground-breaking and welcome in opening a new space for peoples in the Latino/a communities to recover the biblical view of Mary for both Catholics and Protestants.

An important aspect of these ecumenical discussions was the reframing of our understanding of and language about God. According to Mayra Rivera, language about God must be refined and rearticulated. For her, ideas of the radical separation of God and creation simplify the complex web of issues operating in our understanding of God. She correctly pointed out that, drawing a wedge between God and creation, or between the sacred and the mundane, ultimately reduces these realities to constructed categories with no social grounding. Rivera's intuition is central for our understanding of God among the Latino/a communities. The assertion of the transcendent God exiles God from being present in creation. For this reason, opined Rivera, old concepts of God are inappropriate in describing reality as it really is. In reconfiguring our language about God, Díaz also noted, a trinitarian discussion is more helpful in acknowledging difference and otherness even in the reality of Godself, as opposed to a Christocentric emphasis.

Another important subject that received much attention was our understanding and redefining of church as people of God and community. In general, Latino/a theologians reflected on the role of the people as agents of grace and divine disclosure, and their relation to the world. Their concern was how to articulate the notion of the household of God in ways that there is room for all. In order to confront this daunting task, *teología en y de conjunto* became the format and platform for theological reflection. This theological approach, unique to the Latino/a communities, is both a celebration of the different intersections among Latino/a people and an attitude of risking contact with one another. It is a coming together of different people from different traditions.

As an exercise in the participation of the members of the collective, *teología en y de conjunto* is the bold affirmation that one person alone does not have all the answers. This is an intentional rejection of the classical "ivory tower approach," replaced by a space of conversation and interaction; theological insights are examined, challenged, and refined within the context of the community, drawing from the wisdom of the different gifts of each participant. In other words, *teología en y de conjunto* is an intrinsic ingredient of this and any ecumenical conversation, and the assertion of the participatory nature of Latino/a theology.

DIVERGENCIES:
JUNTOS PERO NO REVUELTOS,
THERE IS NO CATHOLICITY

For much of the discussion during this initial ecumenical colloquium, it almost appeared as if there were no clear differences between Catholics and Protestants, and as if all Protestants, including Pentecostals, agreed on everything. But the truth is quite different. Juan Martínez reminded us that an ecumenical conversation also has to include a different type of historical retrieval. His experience as a Protestant from the Free Church forced us to remember the discriminatory acts done to Protestants by the Catholic Church. And although it was not made explicit, it is also important to uncover the animosity that some Protestant churches—specifically fundamentalist—express against Catholic believers. These are clear obstacles to working toward an ecumenical theology.

Here it is important to acknowledge the undercurrents of imperial motifs in this discussion that go as far as back as the time of the Reformation. We have a history of imperial motivations and tensions packaged in the form of religious rhetoric. The conflicts of Spain versus England and later the United States, and the imperialist attitude of the United States toward Latin America and U.S. Latino/a peoples, are also of religious character. So our differences are profound and rooted in strong historical realities that we ought to deconstruct and rearticulate.

The degree of our differences is yet to be determined. Not only are Catholics from different traditions, but also Protestants are quite diverse. So it is very difficult to arrive at a consensus that reflects the voice of all of the traditions. As to whether that is even possible is still a matter of debate. The issue is that different traditions express their religious faith differently, and often have different nonnegotiables, which change over time: Mary, the Bible, specific language, views of ecclesial authority, and so on. Appropriately, one of the groups suggested that only in conversation can we find out what is really a nonnegotiable. At the same time, we must not be naive in thinking that by willing ecumenicity we can do away with the historical conflicts and tensions between traditions, particularly when they are the space from which we enter these ecumenical conversations. In any case, conversation remains the venue through which we can build upon ecumenism.

The same group also pointed out that Catholic and Protestant Latino/a scholars have had so many experiences together that the differences are not so markedly manifest as they would be if there were Mormons and Jehovah Witnesses in the conversations. This is at once positive and negative. Positively, it is a reflection of the ecumenical character of Latino/a theology since its inception. Negatively, it raises a flag about what it is we identify as ecumenicity. Who is invited to the table and how they are invited to the table need much reflection. Two important implications began to emerge in the discussion of this first colloquium: one, the emphasis between unity and multiplicity, and two, the question of the relation between interreligious debates and ecumenism.

On the one hand, it became evident that there were certain unsettling feelings when multiplicity and differences were emphasized; that an emphasis on differences had to be immediately juxtaposed with an emphasis on unity. This suggested that we are uncomfortable—or at least that there is a residual fear that any suggestion of differences may point to division. Here we need to be suspicious of any facile move toward unity, for it can easily turn into homogeneity and uniformity. Perhaps we ought to think more along the lines of discerning unity *with* differences. Similarly, as one of the groups noted, the emphasis on unity poses the challenge of asking what is the minimum of agreement needed if we are to be able to live with the differences. This group suggested that a both/and approach can easily slip into the stronger swallowing up the weaker or smaller. And perhaps we need to reconsider recovering the value of *either/or*. This is crucial, as we ask whether ecumenicity means that *all are in*, or whether there are criteria that warrant the exclusion of some groups or points of view.

On the other hand, it appears that we should not easily separate or distinguish "ecumenical" from "interreligious" debates. One of the operating assumptions behind such a separation is that there is such a thing as a "pure" version of Christianity. Latino/a religious faith expressions are syncretistic, which means that when we are talking about different Christian traditions we are also talking about different non-Christian traditions. It is important to keep in mind that for many people among the Latino/a communities, the interreligious question is not just between Christianity and other so-called world religions like Islam and Judaism. It is also between Christianity and

African and indigenous religious roots surviving within the very texture of Christianity. So these debates must be simultaneously interreligious and ecumenical.

Admittedly, we find it easier to accept some conversations than others. The recognition of the various religious influences in our versions of Christianity demands that we enter into conversation with those religious traditions. The question that one of the groups posed was whether we are ready to engage in such an enterprise. And the challenge of this same group was that dialogue with other traditions is easy when compared to the question of concrete Christian service.

FUTURE CHALLENGES:
DIME CON QUIEN ANDAS Y TE DIRÉ QUIEN ERES

As the conversations and panels took place, we came to realize that engaging in the daunting task of constructing a Latino/a ecumenical theology confronts a number of significant challenges. These challenges, we consider, are in the form of cautionary elements to be handled with care, because they can potentially subvert the constructive process itself. The realization that Latino/a communities are heirs to a colonial past has profound detrimental effects even in the way we understand and define our identity as people. Our ideas, language, and even our theological frameworks are tainted with the notions of the empire, and at times it is necessary to take a self-critical stance in the way we consider and reflect upon the reality of our communities.

This is particularly true in the way we use the adjective or category *Latino/a*. There is much lack of clarity as to what it is we mean when we use this term, and yet we use it quite easily, and often uncritically. What is it we mean when we say that we move or theologize or imagine *a lo Latino/a*? This may very well be shorthand pointing to some *assumed set of distinguishing ethnic and cultural characteristics that make us different from other ethnocultural groups*; as to what these characteristics are, the jury is still out. We have used this label also because of its political expediency, representing the diverse Latino/a communities as a united front, and as such it has worked for many years. But our changing reality dictates that we begin to recognize the polyphonic, multivalent, and multidimensional character of our communities. In other words, the complex, dynamic, and organic realities of these communities and peoples are not reducible to one set of categories, as Rivera reminded us.

We must always be creating new language and reformulating old terms in order to reflect more appropriately the rich ethnic, cultural, and religious diversity and plurality of the Latino/a peoples. Different scholars have already attempted to deal with some of the issues surrounding this discussion, such as Gracia, Mignolo, and Segovia. And they have discussed different aspects of the imperial ghost behind the use of the terms *Hispanic* and *Latinas/os*. The results are mixed! Their lack of agreement points to the slippery character of these terms, and the suggestion that we ought to handle them with care. Whatever we understand as Latino/a identity or identities must be deconstructed to make room for the internal diversity of the Latino/a peoples.

Similar criticisms are applicable to the use of the category of *mestizaje*. Edwin Aponte and Miguel de la Torre have told us that too often we tend to identify the oppressive structures of the dominant Eurocentric culture but fail to see the repression present within our own communities. This is particularly true of the way Latino/a scholars have used *mestizaje*. Rivera correctly acknowledged the contributions of Latino/a theologians in adopting *mestizaje* as a theological category. She appropriately recognized the contested character of the term when it comes to identity discussion of otherness. For her, Latino/a theologies "limited" the potential of *mestizaje* by "reducing *mestizaje* to another identity label." And she clearly stated that privileging communality and unity in using *mestizaje* can "reproduce exclusivist paradigms."

But her analysis, as well as the critiques of *mestizaje* by other Latino/a scholars such as Benjamín Valentín and Rubén Rosario Rodríguez, remains superficial. There is an inherent fallacy in the use of *mestizaje* as synonymous and exchangeable with, and reducible to, *hybridity*. The affirmation of hybridity being already present among the Spaniards or Anglos misplaces the focus of the debates replacing *mestizaje* with miscegenation, masking the unique character of *mestizaje* as it took place in Latin America. It does not directly connect with the actual reality and context of Latin America and the U.S. Latino/a peoples. In other words, the *mestizaje* that took place in Latin America is not merely the continuation of the intermixture or hybridity that had already taken place among the Europeans. Even the analysis of Robert J. C. Young's *Colonial Desire* is relevant only by way of elucidating the manner in which miscegenation was racialized and articulated in Europe and from there exported to the rest of the world in the works of Spencer, Gobineau, Agassiz, and even Hitler—and, I would add, in the positivist school and ideologies that reigned supreme in Latin America during the nineteenth century. Focused on Europe, his work tells us very little of the intricate and complex internal dynamics in which *mestizaje* as a construction of a particular kind of society in Latin America was imposed and became the sociocultural and ethnic imaginary of those in power. It is in this way that *mestizaje* became a mechanism for "whitening" the population since the times of the colony, to the wars of independence, to today's emergence of those indigenous and African voices. Latino/a theologians must first come to grips with this reality and not pretend that the term can be easily divorced from its historical baggage.

This is not just a matter of excluding African and indigenous peoples, although it is that. It a matter of interrogating the impetus behind this wrongly assumed "coming together" of different peoples and cultures, without taking seriously the power structures that feed into a *dangerous telos* of absorbing and erasing differences by way of "mesticizing" them. This is what Klor de Alva explains when he identifies *mestizaje* as a cipherspace, functioning "as a register (e.g., a myth) through which a new people can be brought into existence, or as an elucidating metaphor that helps to make sense of the masking that goes on when fusion fails to take place as different peoples meet under asymmetrical conditions."

During our conversations *mestizaje* was often used uncritically under the operating assumption that there is *one generally agreed upon meaning and version of mestizaje*, and that we all know what that is. Some of the participants spoke of *mestizaje* as if it is one thing that we can define, that it can be contained, and as if it points to *one* experience shared by all Latinas/os. In reclaiming our historical baggage, we must also acknowledge the historical violence, assimilation, xenophobia, and systematic genocide, in different places and at different times, perpetrated by those self-identified as *mestizos/as*. This is a plea to grounding our concepts and categories in history, and to allowing history and those most affected by it to interrogate those terms that have meant so much violence to their communities. For many peoples among the Latino/a communities and in Latin America, the questions of the violence of *mestizaje* is not a matter of the past but of the present, as can be seen in Guatemala, Mexico, Colombia, Peru, and Bolivia.

Let us realize and accept that there are entire communities that do not fit, or wish to fit, into our categories because they recall a violent past and present. We ought to make space for their voices to be heard and interrogate our formulations. Let us not reduce all the Latino/a peoples to *mestizos/as*, and in doing so continue the colonial ethos of erasing people's *otherness*. Let us be careful not to reconcile differences prematurely by using categories that are designed to mask internal differences as unity because reality will quickly spill out of our categories.

Admittedly, the initial reaction may be to assume that in removing or limiting the use of commonly accepted language we are left with no language to speak. Some may even feel paralyzed, unable to speak. In reality, it is a sign of the maturity reached by Latino/a theology in re-creating itself. This is the auspicious moment to rethink the Latino/a theological project and invent new language in order to map out new possible future directions for U.S. Latino/a theology.

This raises a serious question of the particular project of constructing an ecumenical theology that is distinctively Latino/a. It was quite logical that as theologians, trained in a discipline that depends heavily on old categories and concepts, we resort to the use of those categories that are in many ways foreign to "Latino/a" intellectual ethos. As illustrated by some of the presentations, it is becoming increasingly problematic to assume language such as soteriology, ecclesiology, or notions of God as omnipotent, and so on. With his intercultural proposal Raúl Fornet-Betancourt inspires us to draw from our own ethnic and cultural reservoir in the creation of new categories that reflect more adequately the way we process information, express our faith in God, and understand reality. These categories, he claims, do not have to be European. We must carefully use such classical and Germanic languages to speak theologically, but use them with flexibility and adaptability. In a way we must begin to see ourselves as Calibán, as the slave that learned the language of the master to curse them, as Fernández Retamar would say.

The same thing applies to the use of kyriarchical language (Elisabeth Schüssler Fiorenza). To be consistent with our liberative efforts demands that we exercise discrimination in the language we use when speaking theologically. It is necessary that we remain conscious of the inherently patriarchal, masculine, and heterosexist character of theological language, particularly as we shift among languages: kingdom of God, Father, Son, Spirit, Lord. It is true that to keep older labels expedites the conversations, and at times to speak in inclusive ways is awkward, but for the sake of our sisters and brothers present and those not yet sitting at the ecumenical table we cannot neglect doing this. As people of habits, we need to reeducate ourselves so that it becomes second nature to use a more inclusive language in any language we use to communicate our reflections.

ENFOCADOS HACIA EL FUTURO: CONTINUANDO LAS CONVIVENCIAS

We have diligently tried to offer our perspectives of these dialogues, discussions, and discourses. Since we have been so intentional about the collective, participatory nature of our ways of doing theology as an intrinsic ingredient of this ecumenical conversation, then we ask: Are *en conjunto*, *community*, and *relationality* synonymous? If not, what are some distinguishing features? What are some similarities? Do challenges exist that need to be addressed urgently? If so, what are these challenges?

We look to the future *empapados* (saturated/soaked) with hope in an ability to continue as we acknowledge and understand that our particularities and the fluidity of those particularities form a richer picture. We continue to hold important the building upon places of convergence among Christian traditions from Latino/a perspectives. We also strongly recognize the need for Christian traditions to continue to identify and define themselves as different from one another as a means of recognizing and rejoicing in the polyphonic, multivalent, and multidimensional character of our communities where no group dominates or holds power over another. As Latino/a theology continues its process and growth toward contributions within Christian traditions, Latino/a Christian theologians continue the processes of self-critical evaluation, not as a way of competing with one another, but in order to continue to build through *teología de y en conjunto* a kindom of God.

Index

Abbey of Gethsemani, 13
Abelard, Peter, 117
Academy of Catholic Hispanic Theologians of the United States (ACHTUS), 2007 colloquium, 1–2, 8–9, 185–96
adoration, distinguishing, from veneration, 16
African Americans and the Bible (Wimbush), 50–51
aliens, status as, affecting biblical interpretation, 81–83
Althaus-Reid, Marcella, 41
Alva, Klor de, 195
American Academy of Religion, 52
Anabaptists, concern over transformation of Christ's lordship, 119
annunciation, artistic representation of, 22
Anselm, 116, 117–18
anthropological reductionism, Rahner's desire to avoid, 94
Aponte, Edwin, 194
Aquino, Jorge, 43n25
Asian Christology, 122
atonement, theories of, 115–17
Aulén, Gustav, 117

Barth, Karl, 121
Befriending the Beloved Disciple: A Jewish Reading of the Gospel of John (Reinhartz), 49
Believers' Church movement, 167, 171, 173, 174, 177, 179n2, 182n35
Bhabha, Homi, 34
Bible: authoritative for Latino/a communities, 188; bearing diverse witness to ancient and modern exilic experience, 82; community reading of, 77–80; importance of, 3; Latino/a Pentecostal

readings of, engendering focus on justice and community, 75; place of, in life of Latinos/as, 53–54; preaching and reading of, importance to Latino/a Protestant churches, 172, 176; reader's economic status affecting interpretation of, 81; various effects of, on its readers, 55–56
biblical studies, decolonizing of, 70
biblical tradition: de-centering, 60–61; minority readers' harmonizing otherness with, 60
black liberation theology, 122
bodily wisdom, embrace of, 32
body, Western preoccupation with, as abstract ideal, 151
body of Christ: applied to community of the faithful, 150–51; present incarnation of, 156; seeing it as it is, 152
Boff, Leonardo, 98, 121
Bonhoeffer, Dietrich, 121
Booth, Wayne, 49
borderland ecclesiology, 152–56, 169
Boyarin, Daniel, 67n52
Braaten, Carl E., 137n70
Brunner, Emil, 121
Burke, Kevin, 150

Cajetan, Thomas, 156
Calvin, John, 118
Carrasco, Teok, 110n55
Carrión, Juan de, 22
Catechism of the Catholic Church, 15
Catholicism: Cuban exile, 110n54; Iberian, response to Protestant reforms, 156; Latino/a, viewed with suspicion, 160–61; Latino/a popular, 157–58; northern European, 156–57; popular, differences between Latin American

197